OH WHAT A
FEELING

A VITAL HISTORY OF CANADIAN MUSIC

THE CANADIAN ACADEMY OF RECORDING ARTS AND SCIENCES
is pleased to donate a copy of this book to all
elementary and secondary schools in Canada.

THE CANADIAN ACADEMY OF RECORDING ARTS AND SCIENCES
gratefully acknowledges the support of

TRIED,
TESTED
& TRUE.
CHEVROLET

You'll be hearing from me baby, long after I'm gone
I'll be speaking to you sweetly from my window,
in the tower of song

— Leonard Cohen

OH WHAT A FEELING

FEELING

A VITAL HISTORY OF
CANADIAN MUSIC

BY MARTIN MELHUISH

QUARRY PRESS

Foreword

Oh What A Feeling

On the occasion of the 25th anniversary of the Juno Awards, it seems particularly fitting that the celebrations include a book that salutes Canadian recording artists and commemorates the history of Canadian music. The song "Oh What a Feeling" by Crowbar strikes me as a most appropriate title for a book that embraces the spirit and traces the evolution of the Canadian music industry, a spirit that has been expansive and an evolution that has been rapid during the past quarter of a century. From that dark age when Canadian musicians and their music were treated as second class, even in their own country, until today when many Canadian artists are international superstars, proudly embraced by their fellow citizens, the Juno Awards have been there documenting and celebrating their successes each step of the way.

For many of those years, the unofficial mandate of the Juno Awards was to build a star system in support of the artists and their music. To support a strong and established star system might be a more appropriate way of stating that mandate today. The musical talent has always been present in Canada, as Martin Melhuish makes clear in this book for the first time; it is our industry's ability to market that talent that has taken time to mature. If you need further proof of that maturity beyond this book, I recommend that you seek out its musical companion, namely a four CD box set also entitled *Oh What A Feeling,* featuring over 70 of the greatest Canadian songs recorded in the last 30 years.

The most gratifying aspect of compiling this history of Canadian music and the Juno Awards comes from acknowledging the rich and varied repertoire that is Canadian music. Canadian music is alive and well — and living in Canada. Our artists have never been more creative and our music has never sounded better. Enjoy this historical salute that allows us to reflect on our cultural heritage while moving forward with confidence through the next phase of our country's musical evolution.

— **Lee Silversides**
President
Canadian Academy of
Recording Arts & Sciences

Contents

Stand Tall

Introduction

What do Bryan Adams, Alias, Paul Anka, April Wine, Dan Aykroyd, Bachman-Turner Overdrive, The Band, Barenaked Ladies, The Bells, Blue Rodeo, Liona Boyd, Oscar Brand, Lenny Breau, Buffalo Springfield, Gary Buck, The Canadian Brass, Wilf Carter, Jane Child, Chilliwack, Tommy Chong, David Clayton-Thomas, Tom Cochrane, Leonard Cohen, Bruce Cockburn, Holly Cole Trio, Dorothy Collins, Patricia Conroy, Gene Cornish, Cowboy Junkies, Crash Test Dummies, The Crew Cuts, Burton Cummings, Bobby Curtola, The DeFranco Family, The Diamonds, Celine Dion, Denny Doherty, Dream Warriors, Edward Bear, Percy Faith, Robert Farnon, Maureen Forrester, David Foster, The Four Lads, George Fox, Full Tilt Boogie Band, Gale Garnett, Nick Gilder, Glass Tiger, Glenn Gould, Robert Goulet, The Guess Who, Ofra Harnoy, Ronnie Hawkins, The Jeff Healey Band, Dan Hill, Ian & Sylvia, The Irish Rovers, Terry Jacks, Colin James, Sass Jordan, John Kay, Andy Kim, Corky Laing, k.d. lang, Daniel Lanois, Gordon Lightfoot, Lighthouse, Guy Lombardo, Louis Lortie, Loverboy, Gisele MacKenzie, Sarah McLachlan, Murray McLauchlan, Rita MacNeil, Mahogany Rush, Mashmakhan, Rob McConnell and the Boss Brass, Galt MacDermot, Loreena McKennitt, Men Without Hats, Don Messer, Frank Mills, Joni Mitchell, Kim Mitchell, Alanis Morissette, Motherlode, Anne Murray, Alannah Myles, Bob Nolan, The Nylons, Ocean, Orford String Quartet, Walter Ostanek, Oscar Peterson, Raffi, Rhinoceros, Robbie Robertson, The Rover Boys, Rush, Brenda Russell, Buffy Sainte-Marie, Jack Scott, Paul Shaffer, Sharon Lois & Bram, Sheriff, Skylark, Floyd Sneed, Snow, Hank Snow, Alexander "Skip" Spence, The Stampeders, Lucille Starr, Steppenwolf, Teresa Stratas, Tafelmusik, R. Dean Taylor, The Tragically Hip, Triumph, Domenic Troiano, Shania Twain, Valdy, Gino Vannelli, Denny Vaughan, Roch Voisine, Michelle Wright, Priscilla Wright, Neil Young, Zal Yanovsky have in common?

All are remarkable Canadian recording
artists whose names are well-known
beyond our borders, though few
Canadians are acquainted with the full
impact these artists have had on our own
musical heritage and on music around
the world. To speak the names of these
artists is to chart a course through the
history of Canadian music.

Oh What A Feeling is the first attempt
to chronicle the history of Canadian
music and to celebrate the musical
genius of our artists on the occasion of
the 25th anniversary of the Juno Awards,
founded in 1971 to recognize annually the
achievements of the industry and to
commemorate the special contributions
of individuals inducted into the Canadian
Music Hall of Fame. One way to introduce
Canada's music heritage and this book is
to walk through the Hall of Fame,
stopping along the way to meet briefly
twenty-five artists who have helped
shape our culture. As *Oh What A Feeling* unfolds page by page, year
by year, artist by artist, achievement by achievement, you will find
many reasons to celebrate not only these Hall of Fame artists and
their fellow musicians, but also the inventors, executives,
producers, technicians, and others who make the recording arts
and sciences in Canada one of the most innovative and highly
respected cultural enterprises in the world today. To borrow a line
from Burton Cummings, Canadians have good reason to "stand tall"
when we consider our musical heritage.

Although many Canadian songwriters gained international renown before 1920, a good starting place for documenting Canada's musical heritage is with Hall of Fame member Guy Lombardo and his band of Royal Canadians, who had became well-known internationally in the late 1920s. Though Lombardo became legendary and his name synonymous with New Year's Eve celebrations, it was Percy Faith, a former staff conductor with the Canadian Broadcasting Company, who was one of the first Canadians to have chart success at home and abroad with a string of big band and orchestral hits such as *Theme From "A Summer Place"* in the 1950s and early 1960s.

While Lombardo and Faith were defining the big band sound of Canada,

Hank Snow and Wilf Carter (a.k.a. Montana Slim), two singers from the Maritimes and both Hall of Fame members, made enormous contributions to the world of country music. A fellow Maritimer, Bob Nolan, working with Roy Rogers and the Sons of the Pioneers, defined the music of cowboy culture with his songs like *Tumbling Tumbleweeds* and *Cool Water.*

Three Canadian "doo-wop" groups — The Four Lads, The Crew Cuts, and The Diamonds — also made a significant impact on the international charts in the early to mid-1950s, and are joined in the Canadian Music Hall of Fame by a young singer/songwriter from Ottawa by the name of Paul Anka, Canada's first international teen idol. By the late 1950s, Paul Anka wasn't the only major Canadian singer making an impact on pop culture internationally. Jack Scafone, Jr., better known as Jack Scott, had a string of hits, and Robert Goulet, who grew up in Edmonton, made his mark on the CBC as a singer and actor before moving to America to star as Lancelot in the hit musical *Camelot.*

While these Canadians were giving a Canadian sound to pop music, contralto Maureen Forrester and pianist Glenn Gould were performing on the classical music concert stage to international acclaim. Forrester has been the voice of Canada for almost five decades as she has performed in places as far flung as the former Soviet Union, Australia, Israel, India, Japan, China, and most European countries, while Gould, as conductor Herbert von Karajan once commented, "created a style which led to the future" as he made brilliant modern variations on classical compositions. Another significant Canadian contribution to the world of opera was the work of Wilfrid

Guy Lombardo

Pelletier as musical conductor of the Metropolitan Opera in New York from 1929 to 1950.

In 1958, a singer destined to develop some of Canada's top rock musicians crossed the border into Canada to play a few dates with his band. He was so impressed with the quality of Canada's musical talent and lifestyle that he ended up putting down roots just outside of Toronto. Arkansas-born rockabilly star Ronnie Hawkins, who claims former Arkansas governor and current U.S. president Bill Clinton as a personal friend, put together a new band of Canadian musicians and called them the Hawks. They played the Canadian bar circuit for five years before deciding to chart a new course south, where they met Bob Dylan and became his backing group as he made the transition from acoustic to electric folk. When Dylan's motorcycle accident forced him to take a lengthy break from touring and recording, the Hawks headed out on their own, changing their name to The Band and recording the classic rock album MUSIC FROM BIG PINK in Woodstock, New York. The Band went on to become one of the great originals in the history of rock music — and worthy members of the Canadian Music Hall of Fame.

Before Canadian rock and pop stars made their mark internationally, a number of jazz players, notably Moe Koffman, Maynard Ferguson, and Hall of Fame inductee Oscar Peterson had become widely respected in jazz and contemporary music circles around the world. In 1948, woodwind player Koffman won a jazz poll in *Metronome* magazine, subsequently signed a record deal in the U.S., and had an international hit with his composition *Blues à la Canadiana* later retitled *Swingin' Shepherd Blues* in 1958. Maynard

Hank Snow

Wilf Carter

The Four Lads

The Crew Cuts

Ferguson made a name for himself playing in bands led by such legends as Jimmy Dorsey, Charlie Barnet, and Stan Kenton. Oscar Peterson, a bona fide Canadian musical genius, has since the early 1950s been one of the most widely recorded jazz musicians in history,.

David Clayton-Thomas, the lead singer for Blood, Sweat & Tears, had a long-time obsession with the idea of jazz/rock fusion that stretched back to his mid-1960s group The Bossmen featuring pianist and child prodigy Tony Collacott who had backed Sarah Vaughan when just a teenager. As frontman and one of the main songwriters for Blood, Sweat & Tears in the late 1960s, Clayton-Thomas had a significant influence on the future of jazz and rock music, a contribution recognized by his induction in 1996 into the Hall of Fame. Another late 1960s musical experiment was the result of the meeting of two unlikely musical partners, jazz/classical musician Paul Hoffert and rock drummer Skip Prokop, who had been in the Toronto group The Paupers. Prokop wanted to put together a group that at its core was a rock band but also had an "orchestra" of jazz and classical musicians. The result was the 13-piece group Lighthouse. When the band debuted in Toronto, even Duke Ellington dropped by to see what was shakin'.

Over the years, there were a number of personnel changes in the group but none that came as opportunely as Howard Shore's departure. He was one of the group's original sax players and a friend of CBC-TV producer Lorne Michaels who would later be responsible for putting *Saturday Night Live* on the air at NBC. Shore became the show's music director and, in putting together the Saturday Night Live show band, called up an old friend, keyboardist Paul Shaffer, who went on to become David Letterman's band leader and sidekick on the highly-rated *Late Night* show. Shore is currently much in-demand as composer of movie scores.

Lorne Michaels used many Canadian comedic artists on *Saturday Night Live* over the years, and certainly one of the most successful was Dan Aykroyd, who, among other things, will be remembered as one half of the Blues Brothers with his sidekick, the late John Belushi. On SNL, on the subsequent best-selling records, and in the box-office blockbuster films about the trials of Jake and Elwood Blues, Aykroyd's musical roots in Canadian R&B music of the 1960s was reflected. The Mandala, an R&B group fronted by George Olliver ("The Blue-Eyed Prince of Soul") and powered by the guitar of Hall of Fame member Domenic Troiano, defined this scene with their ongoing "Soul Crusade." After the break-up of The Mandala,

Troiano formed the group Bush and then went on to play with The James Gang in the United States before returning to Canada to join The Guess Who.

Another *Saturday Night Live* alumnus, Mike Myers, was responsible for a glimpse of Toronto pop culture of the 1970s in the box-office smash movie *Wayne's World*. One of the film's settings is Stan Mikita's Donuts, which Meyers has said is modeled after a Tim Horton's Donuts he and his friends would visit late at night after seeing local rock acts like Max Webster, Goddo, Triumph, and Hall of Fame members Rush at clubs like the Gasworks on Yonge Street. The international following for Rush among rock music fans has only grown in number as the years pass.

Hall of Fame members The Guess Who from Winnipeg became the first

The Diamonds

Paul Anka

Canadian rock band to place a number one single on the influential Billboard chart in 1970 with *American Woman,* while fellow Hall of Famer John Kay, lead singer for Steppenwolf, belted out *Born To Be Wild*, a song written by Canadian Dennis Edmonton (a.k.a. Mars Bonfire), not only on the airwaves but also in the classic 1960s era movie, *Easy Rider,* starring Peter Fonda, Dennis Hopper, and Jack Nicholson.

Other Canadian artists had a significant impact on 1960s culture in Canada and the United States. Andy Kim and R. Dean Taylor left Canada to make their way in the U.S., joining a group of remarkably talented expatriots, including Gene Cornish of The Rascals, Corky Laing of Mountain, Alexander "Skip" Spence of Jefferson Airplane, Floyd Sneed of Three Dog Night, and Janis Joplin's The Full Tilt Boogie Band.

None were more influential than one-time fellow members of the folk group The Mugwumps and now members of the Hall of Fame, Denny Doherty, who formed The Mamas and The Papas with Cass Elliott and John and Michelle Phillips, and Zal Yanovsky, who formed The Lovin' Spoonful with John Sebastian.

Through the 1960s and early 1970s, the hub of Canada's folk music scene was Yorkville Village in Toronto, a scene not much different from San Francisco's Haight-Ashbury or New York's Greenwich Village. You could sit in bistros and small coffee houses, discuss the world's ills, and listen to exciting new performers at places like The Purple Onion or The Riverboat, which was not only a popular venue for some of the top international folk acts, but also a launching pad for most of the Canadian folk artists who eventually appeared in the international spotlight. It was as highly regarded in North American music circles as The Troubadour in Los Angeles, the Bitter End in New York, or the Boarding House in San Francisco. Canadian Music Hall of Fame members Ian & Sylvia, Gordon Lightfoot, Neil Young, and Joni Mitchell all paid their dues in Yorkville.

Gordon Lightfoot frequented the Yorkville clubs and developed his distinctive Canadian folk sound there before taking it to New York. Ian & Sylvia played a big part in funneling his music into a particular style and giving it exposure by recording some of his material themselves. When all is said and done, it is perhaps the singer/song-writers of Canada who best reflect the Canadian experience in their work. Recent Hall of Fame member Buffy Sainte-Marie has pointed out that "Native" Canadian folksingers have been making indigenous music for over 10,000 years.

Neil Young came to Yorkville from Winnipeg and spent time playing with various local bands, including the Mynah Birds, which also included funk star Rick James. When he began to feel stifled, Young packed up and moved to Los Angeles, where he was reunited with Stephen Stills, whom he had met briefly in Thunder Bay while passing through to Toronto in his infamous black hearse. They formed Buffalo Springfield, which evolved into Crosby, Stills, Nash & Young, before Young embarked on a solo career that has seen him defy all attempts to categorize his music — country, folk, rock, metal, grunge, traditional, avant-garde, and more.

Joni Mitchell came to Yorkville from her hometown of Saskatoon,

Maureen Forrester

Glenn Gould

The Band

following a stint at the folk clubs in Calgary. She washed dishes in a local Yorkville club while she practiced piano and literally got her act together before departing for Detroit, New York, and Los Angeles for a long and distinguished musical career. Along with Joan Baez, she is one of the first ladies of folk music, whose lyrics are poetic treasures.

Poet, singer, and songwriter Leonard Cohen also passed through Yorkville on his way to international literary and musical fame. Although his albums may outsell his books, he remains Canada's most popular poet whose recitation of *The Tower of Song* at the Juno Awards in 1991 when he was inducted into the Hall of Fame gave the Canadian music industry a metaphor to define itself.

Hall of Fame member Anne Murray's emergence into the international spotlight in the early 1970s with a string of chart-topping cross-over pop and country songs led music critics to herald her as the greatest popular singer in the world, rivaled only by Barbara Streisand. Nothing she has done in the intervening years has done anything to change this opinion. She quite simply is Canada's most popular female artist.

And the achievements continue into the next generation. Five Canadian artists — Bryan Adams, Corey Hart, Alannah Myles, Celine Dion, and Tom Cochrane — have hit the million mark in sales. Adams has been certified diamond twice for his albums *Reckless* (1985) and *Waking Up The Neighbours* (1992). Shania Twain stormed the country music charts in 1995, and Alanis Morissette did the same to the pop charts with her single and album *Jagged Little Pill*. Bands like The Tragically Hip and Crash Test Dummies are on the verge of international stardom. Many other Canadian artists and groups are only a break away from such recognition. The Canadian Music Hall of Fame awaits the arrival of a new generation of talented rock, folk, jazz, country, and classical artists.

However talented Canadian recording artists may be, they would not be so successful without the contributions of recording engineers, technicians, producers, executives, and even bureaucrats like Pierre Juneau, for whom the Juno Awards are named. This contribution is enormous.

To trace Canada's place in the history of the music, recording, and broadcasting industries you have to go back to a time well before the turn of the century as the first devices for recording and playback were being invented. In 1880, Canadian Alexander Graham Bell, known primarily for his work with the telephone, his cousin Chichester Bell, and English inventor Charles Tainter developed a wax cylinder player called the Graphophone which was ultimately bought and manufactured by the Columbia Graphophone Co. (now Sony Music).

In 1897, Emile Berliner, who had established the United States Gramophone Co. (later to become the Victor Talking Machine Co.) and was in the process of setting up the Gramophone Co. in England (now EMI) through his emissary William Barry Owen, moved to Montreal and set up his operation there with his son Herbert. In 1898, his brother Joseph

Oscar Peterson

David Clayton-Thomas

Rush

Domenic Troiano

traveled to Germany and founded the Deutsche Grammophon company in Hanover (now Deutsche Grammophon and PolyGram). Around this time, Emile Berliner discovered a piece of art that was destined to become one of the most recognizable trademarks in history. During a visit to London, Berliner chanced upon a painting William Owen had bought which was gathering dust in a storage room. Titled *His Master's Voice* and painted by Francis Burraud, the painting portrayed the artist's dog Nipper looking down the horn of a phonograph. Berliner immediately went to Burraud and bought the rights to the painting and registered it as a trademark by an act of Canadian parliament on May 28, 1900. The image would be used by the Victor Talking Machine Co. two years later and by the British Gramophone Co. in 1909. The painting ultimately inspired the name of His Master's Voice records and subsequently the HMV retail store chain.

By 1918, Emile's son Herbert had founded the Compo Company in Lachine, a suburb of Montreal, as well as recording studios in his hometown and in New York. As Victor moved to obtain controlling interest of the Berliner organization in the 1920s and thereby dominate the Canadian record industry, Herbert set up an alternate network of record distribution across the country and thereby became the first "rack jobber." In 1925, Compo issued the first electronically recorded discs on its Apex label using a process initially developed by two Canadian former Royal Air Force officers, Lionel Guest and Horace Owen Merriman who had recorded the ceremony of the burial of the Unknown Warrior in Westminster Abbey five years previously. In 1950, Decca Records purchased Compo from Berliner. It would later evolve into the current day MCA Records.

A major hardware staple of the early recording industry was the jukebox, and it was a Canadian, David Rockola of Virden, Manitoba, who was instrumental in its development as he introduced his Rock-Ola Multi-Selector phonograph in the mid-1930s.

As the major advances in recording were being made early in the century, a number of milestones were being established in broadcasting as well. Canada's enormous land mass and the need for efficient communication over that great expanse has always kept Canada in the forefront of broadcast technology. On December 12, 1901, Marconi received the first "wireless" transmission from Cornwall, England at Signal Hill, Newfoundland, and on Christmas Eve of that same year, Canadian Reginald Aubrey Fessenden demonstrated AM radio as he made the first "wireless" broadcast to ships at sea from Brant Rock, near Boston.

On May 20, 1920, Marconi's Montreal station XWA (later CFCF and now country station CIQC) became the first radio station on the air (in a non-experimental mode) as it broadcast a music show from Montreal to a meeting of the Royal Society of Canada in Ottawa. On Dominion Day, July 1, 1927, the first North American coast-to-coast radio network broadcast was conducted in the form of speeches by Prime Minister Mackenzie King and music from the Diamond Jubilee of Canadian Confederation celebrations in Ottawa.

Canadian Edward (Ted) Samuel Rogers invented the 110 volt vacuum tube in 1926, making it possible to operate radios without batteries, and the technological advances in both recording and broadcasting have subsequently been staggering. FM radio, the 33 1/3 LP and the 45 RPM single, and the transistor arrived in the 1930s and 1940s, while the 1950s and 1960s brought television, videotape recording, stereo recording and broadcast, 8-track cartridges, quadraphonic sound, and cassette tapes. During this era, the Canadian government through the offices of the CRBC, the CBC, and eventually the CRTC governed the industry and promoted Canadian artists, never so successfully as in the introduction of Canadian content regulations for AM radio broadcasts in January 1971, one

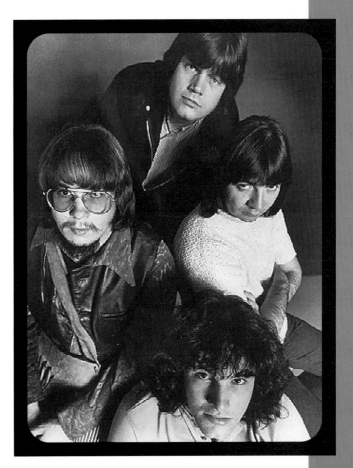

The Guess Who

John Kay

Denny Doherty

month before the celebration of the first annual Juno Awards, created to recognize the achievements of the Canadian recording arts and sciences.

The Juno Awards had their humble beginnings as a poll conducted by the Canadian trade magazine *RPM Weekly* on December 7, 1964. There was very little fanfare at the time as the editor and publisher of *RPM* Walt Grealis remembers, just a simple ballot inviting readers to choose "year-end notable Canadian artists and industry figures." The poll drew a surprisingly high 150 replies, and on December 28, 1964, the winners were listed on the front page of the year-end edition.

This balloting process continued annually until 1970 when the RPM Gold Leaf Awards, as they were then known, were presented for the first time in a ceremony at St. Lawrence Hall in Toronto on February 23rd. Country singer Diane Leigh, voted Top Female Country Vocalist, was the first recipient of a Canadian music trophy. Stan Klees, an old school friend of Walt Grealis, produced this show and designed the RPM Gold Leaf Award, an 18-inch high elongated metronome made of solid walnut. In 1971, the Gold Leaf Awards were renamed the Juno Awards in tribute to Pierre Juneau, first Chairman of the Canadian Radio-Television Commission (CRTC) who spearheaded the introduction of the so-called "CanCon" policy for governing Canadian AM radio content.

By 1974, there was a growing feeling that the awards should be voted on by the whole music industry rather than by the subscribers to any one magazine. The idea of the Maple Music Awards, with an accompanying one-hour telecast on the CTV network, was

Zal Yanovsky

put forth but abandoned. Soon after, a committee called the Canadian Music Awards Association was formed and negotiations began with the CBC that resulted in the Juno Awards being broadcast for the first time on March 24, 1975 from the Queen Elizabeth Theatre, hosted by Paul Anka. Stan Klees redesigned the award as a 23-inch acrylic trophy for the occasion.

The same year, the Canadian Academy of Recording Arts and Sciences (CARAS), with Mel Shaw as its first president, was formed to oversee the annual Juno Awards ceremony. Shaw has aligned the three aims of the founders of CARAS with the three sides of the Juno statue itself. "First was the actual creation of the awards by Walt Grealis and Stan Klees to recognize the

Ian & Sylvia

Gordon Lightfoot

Buffy Sainte-Marie

dreamers, music creators, and artists who were striving for validity in Canada. They worked through the silent years, before the sound of applause for Canadian recording artists echoed across Canada. Second came the growth and maturing of the Canadian music community in combining all the participants into one unifying organization from all facets of the recording industry. The Academy has grown to encompass thousands of the nation's music industry professionals. Third was the necessary involvement of the public, the countless individuals whose love of music creates the enthusiastic audience we have today for Canadian artists."

Membership in CARAS was open to everyone involved in the recording industry, thus broadening the voting base for the Junos. Walt Grealis and Capitol Records-EMI of Canada president Arnold Gosewich were later presented with founders plaques for their efforts in making CARAS a reality.

In 1977, CARAS came to an agreement with awards founders Grealis and Klees to take over control of the Junos. The Walt Grealis Special Achievement Award, inaugurated in 1984 and presented each year at the Juno Awards, honors a member of the Canadian music community deemed to have been instrumental in furthering the interests and prestige of the recording industry in Canada. Significantly, in 1995 the Juno Awards ceremonies moved from the relatively small confines of a Toronto convention hall or theatre to Copps Coliseum in Hamilton, Ontario, where 10,000 enthusiastic fans joined the festivities. The aims of the founders of CARAS have been realized.

The year 1996 marks the 25th anniversary of the Juno Awards

founded in 1971, a pivotal year in the history of Canadian music. That year the coveted RPM Gold Leaf Awards were renamed the Juno Awards in tribute to Pierre Juneau, and the legislation that committed Canadian AM radio stations to devote at least 30 percent of their broadcast day to Canadian artists and their music was introduced. The notion at the time was that if something were not done to stem the domination of Canadian radio airwaves by a foreign repertoire, the domestic recording industry would shrivel up and die from lack of exposure.

It is no surprise, then, that for the Canadian recording industry Pierre Juneau should be held in high esteem and forever associated with music excellence. At those first Juno Awards

Neil Young

Joni Mitchell

Leonard Cohen

in 1971, Juneau was honored as Music Industry Man of the Year. In 1989, with the benefit of retrospect and tangible evidence of a booming Canadian recording industry, Juneau was presented with the first Lifetime Achievement Award at the awards show by Peter Steinmetz, then President of the Canadian Academy of Recording Arts & Sciences (CARAS). "When countries are young and their structure is still unformed, one person can, and often does, have an astounding influence over matters of public policy," Steinmetz told the gathering in Toronto. "In Canada, we always believe that one of the most important of those public

pursuits is our culture, the music, words and images we give each other. There is without a doubt no Canadian who has had as pervasive an influence on how we see ourselves as Pierre Juneau. As the first chairman of the CRTC, Juneau was on hand for a media revolution. Over the previous decade, Canada had been forced to move quickly into the new information age. Canada had opened up, and Juneau was faced with the task of preserving a Canadian identity in a world whose borders were disappearing. He left his mark on policy almost immediately. Canadian radio and television stations are 80 percent owned by Canadians because Juneau's CRTC made it that way. And when the CRTC decided in 1970 that 30 percent of recorded music on radio must be Canadian, a Canadian recording industry was born almost overnight. The fact that tonight's awards are named after him is recognition of that one bold controversial decision."

The first Canadian single to be released under the auspices of Juneau's CanCon policy was an appropriately rousing song by Crowbar, "Oh What A Feeling." That a book celebrating Canada's music heritage and a companion four CD box set of vital Canadian music should adopt this title is only fitting.

— **Martin Melhuish**

Anne Murray

As The Years Go By

The Maple Leaf Forever
1866–1920

The Maple Leaf Forever
1866–1920

1866: George Johnson, a Toronto school teacher, writes the hit song, *When You And I Were Young Maggie*, for his girlfriend Maggie Clark. The farm in Stoney Creek, Ontario where Maggie lived now has a plaque commemorating the song, thanks to the late radio show host Ray Sonin of Toronto's CFRB and his program *Down Memory Lane*.

1867: Alexander Muir composes the patriotic song *The Maple Leaf Forever*.

1877: Emile Berliner, a German immigrant living in Washington, D.C. who moved to Canada in 1897, invents the microphone, and Thomas Alva Edison, scion of a Canadian family, makes the first ever sound recording (*Mary Had A Little Lamb*) which he plays back on the first phonograph (cylinder and tin foil) in the New York offices of *Scientific American*.

1878: Canada's Governor General, **Lord Dufferin**, receives a demonstration unit of Edison's phonograph or "talking machine," and to amuse guests at his Rideau Hall residence in Ottawa, he makes a number of recordings, the first ever in Canada.

1880: Alexander Graham Bell develops a wax cylinder player which is subsequently patented in 1889 as a "Graphophone" by Chichester Bell and Charles Sumner Tainter and manufactured as the first record player by the Columbia Graphophone Co.

1886: First gramophone, or disc player, is patented by **Emile Berliner**.

1888: Whaley, Royce and Co. Ltd., the music publishers and manufacturer of musical instruments who once referred to themselves as "Canada's Greatest Music House," is founded in Toronto by **Eri Whaley** and **George Royce**.

1894: Music trade magazine *Billboard* begins publication in the U.S.A.

1894: Massey Hall opens in Toronto on June 14th with a performance of Handel's *Messiah*.

1895: The Toronto **Mendelssohn Choir**, formed in 1894 by Augustus Stephen Voght at the Jarvis Street Baptist Church, debuts in concert at Massey Hall.

1897: The Vancouver Symphony Orchestra first performs.

1897: Emile Berliner, who had established the Gramophone Co. in the United States (later known as the Victor Talking Machine Co.) and in

England (the forerunner to EMI) moves to Montreal and sets up his operation with his son Herbert, while his brother Joseph travels to Germany and founds the Deutsche Grammophon Company.

1899: The first jukebox is installed at the Palais Royal Hotel in San Francisco by the Pacific Phonograph Company.

1900: Canadian **Reginald A. Fessenden**, who forms the Wireless Telegraph Co. of Canada and comes to be known as the father of radio, transmits the sound of a voice over a distance of 50 miles using the principle of "continuous-wave" transmission.

1900: By an act of Canadian parliament, **Emile Berliner** registers one of the most recognizable trademarks in history, a painting titled *His Master's Voice* by artist Francis Burraud of his dog, a fox terrier by the name of Nipper, looking down the horn of a phonograph. The image is later used by the Victor Talking Machine Co. and by the British Gramophone Co. for their Black Label recordings, ultimately inspiring the name of His Master's Voice records and the HMV retail record store chain.

1901: The Victor Talking Machine Co. is founded in Camden, New Jersey, and the company's recordings are pressed and distributed in Canada by the **Berliner Gramophone Co**. of Montreal.

1901: Marconi makes the first trans-Atlantic "interrupted code" transmission from St. John's, Newfoundland, and the Canadian government subsequently gives him, rather than native son Reginald Fessenden, the exclusive rights to build the first transmitting station in Canada at Glace Bay, Nova Scotia.

1902: The **Belleville Kilties Band** become the first Canadian group or ensemble to record.

1902: Gaetano Alberto Lombardo (Guy Lombardo) is born on June 19th in London, Ontario.

1902: The **Quebec Symphony Orchestra/Orchestre symphonique de Quebec** debuts on June 24th at Laval university on the occasion of the school's golden jubilee.

1904: Wilf Carter is born on December 18th in Port Hilford, Nova Scotia.

1904: The Columbia Graphophone Co. establishes a Toronto branch under the name Columbia Phonograph.

1906: The Toronto Symphony is first formed as the Toronto Conservatory Symphony Orchestra.

1906: The Victor Talking Machine Co. of New Jersey markets the first Victrola, a gramophone with a speaker in the cabinet, for $200.

1906: Reginald Fessenden makes a "continuous-wave" transmission from Boston to Scotland from a 420 ft. tall mast on Brant Rock, Massachusetts owned by the National Electric Signalling Co. This first advertised radio broadcast includes Handel's *Largo*.

1908: Percy Faith is born on April 7th in Toronto, Ontario.

1908: Canada's national anthem, *O Canada*, with English lyrics by **Robert Stanley Weir**, is published for the first time by Montreal-based Delmar Music Co.

1908: The Regina Symphony Orchestra, founded by Frank Laubach, gives its inaugural concert on December 3rd.

1910: The Brown Brothers Saxophone Quintet (later the Six Brown Brothers) from Lindsay, Ontario take their show on the road on the North American vaudeville circuit and establish the saxophone as a popular instrument for contemporary music.

1910: Written by Canadian songwriter **Shelton Brooks** (who also wrote *Darktown Strutters' Ball*), Sophie Tucker introduces *Some Of These Days*, the song with which she will always be identified.

1913: The Canadian Vitaphone Company, Canadian manufacturers and distributors of the Vitaphone and importer of records on the Columbia label in the U.S., is established in Toronto.

1913: The song *Peg O' My Heart*, co-written by Brantford, Ontario lyricist **Alfred Bryan** and American composer Fred Fisher, is published and inspires a movie of the same name, first filmed in 1923 and then remade in 1933 with actress Marion Davies. The Harmonicats have a million-seller with the song in 1947. Bryan also co-wrote a number of other early hit songs, including *Come Josephine In My Flying Machine*, again with Fred Fisher (1910), and *I Didn't Raise My Boy To Be A Soldier* with Al Piantadosi (1915).

1914: Toronto born singer/comedienne **Beatrice Lillie** makes her stage debut at the Chatham Music Hall in England.

1914: Clarence Eugene Snow (Hank Snow) is born on May 9th in Liverpool, Nova Scotia.

1917: The Starr Co. of Canada (formerly the Canadian Phonograph Supply Co.) is established in London, Ontario as an importer of records from its parent company, The Starr Piano Company, and the Gennett label.

1917: A recording of *Darktown Strutter's Ball*, written by Amherstburg, Ontario native **Shelton Brooks** and performed by the Original Dixieland Jazz Band, is one of the first, if not the first, commercially-made jazz records.

1918: *Til' We Meet Again*, the wartime hit song written by Windsor, Ontario born lyricist **Raymond Egan** and American writing partner Richard Whiting, is published (Remick). A few years later in 1921, he collaborates with Whiting and Gus Kahn on the song *Ain't We Got Fun*.

Compo Company Ltd. Pressing Plant

1918: *K-K-K-Katy (The Stammering Song)*, a tune written by **Geoffrey O'Hara** in Kingston, Ontario, is published on March 16th and sells over one million copies in sheet music form. Jack Oakie revives the song in the movie musical *Tin Pan Alley* (1940). Another song of the World War I era, *Mademoiselle From Armentieres,* is written by **Captain Gitz Rice** of Montreal.

1918: The Compo Company Ltd., the first Canadian independent pressing plant, is established in Lachine, Quebec by **Herbert S. Berliner**.

1918: The Authors and Composers Association of Canada is founded by Gordon V. Thompson.

1919: *The World Is Waiting For The Sunrise*, written by London, Ontario born actor/lyricist **Eugene Lockhart** and concert pianist/faculty member of the Toronto Conservatory of Music **Ernest J. Seitz** (a.k.a. Raymond Roberts), is first heard. Though over a hundred versions of the song have been recorded, a 1949 recording for Capitol Records by Les Paul and Mary Ford sells over a million copies.

1920: The Canadian Marconi Co. station **XWA Montreal** (later CFCF and now CIQC) makes the first scheduled broadcast in North America on May 20th.

*T*umbling Tumbleweeds
1920–1940

TUMBLEWEED TRAILS
The Sons Of The Pioneers

Tumbling Tumbleweeds
1920–1940

1920: The Edmonton Symphony Orchestra debuts at Pantages Theatre on November 15th.

1921: The Canadian Copyright Act establishes performing rights of musical works as a constituent part of copyright.

1921: Herbert S. Berliner resigns as vice-president of the Berliner Gramophone Co. and moves to the Compo Company Ltd. which opens the affiliated Sun record label, later renamed Apex.

1922: Montreal daily newspaper La Presse launches **CKAC**, the first French-language radio station in Canada.

1923: Pianist **Percy Faith**, who is working as a silent-film accompanist in Toronto movies houses, gives his first piano recital at the Toronto Conservatory of Music and makes his Massey Hall debut at age 15.

1923: Formed initially as The Lombardo Brother's Orchestra and Concert Company in London, Ontario and featuring brothers Guy, Carmen, and Lebert Lombardo, the group goes through a name change to **Guy Lombardo and His Royal Canadians** during a two year residency at the Claremont Tent nightclub in Cleveland.

1924: Beatrice Lillie makes her New York debut in the Andre Charlot Revue of 1924.

1924: Trumpeter **Alfie Noakes** travels to England with the New Princes' Toronto Band and thereafter becomes one of Britain's top dance-band musicians.

1924: Guy Lombardo and His Royal Canadians make their first recording on March 10th in Richmond, Indiana for the Gennett label.

1924: Victor purchases the Berliner Gramophone Co. and forms the **Victor Talking Machine Co. of Canada** with Edgar Berliner as president.

1924: Canadian National Railways, at the instigation of president Sir Henry Thornton, installs radio receivers on their transcontinental trains and builds their first transmitting studio in Ottawa with the call letters CNRO.

1925: The Canadian Performing Rights Society (CPRS), a subsidiary of the U.K.'s Performing Rights Society (PRS) and the forerunner to the Composers, Authors, and Publishers Association of Canada Limited (CAPAC) and ultimately SOCAN, is created to administer the royalties of composers, lyricists, and music publishers whose works are performed in Canada.

1925: Compo Company Ltd. issues the first electronically-recorded discs on its Apex label using a process initially developed by

two former Canadian Royal Air Force officers, **Lionel Guest** and **Horace Owen Merriman** who had recorded the ceremony of the burial of the Unknown Warrior in Westminster Abbey five years previously.

1925: Oscar Peterson is born on August 15th in Montreal, Quebec.

1926: Clarence Eugene Snow, later known as Hank, runs away to sea at the age of 12 to work as a cabin boy on the freighter *Grace Boehner* out of Lunenburg, Nova Scotia.

1926: Batteryless radio is introduced as **Edward (Ted) Samuels Rogers** of Toronto invents the 110 volt AC vacuum tube and one year later founds Toronto radio station CFRB (Canada's First Rogers Batteryless).

1927: To commemorate the Diamond Jubilee of Canada's Confederation, the festivities from Parliament Hill in Ottawa involving an orchestra, various music ensembles, a 1000-voice choir, the inauguration of the Peace

Tower carillon, and speeches from **Prime Minister W. L. Mackenzie King** are successfully broadcast across Canada.

1927: The **Saskatoon Symphony Orchestra** is founded.

1928: Newfoundlander **Arthur Scammell** at age 15 writes *Squid-jiggin' Ground*, the song that will forever be associated with this region.

1928: During their residency at Chicago's Granada Cafe, Ashton Stevens of the Chicago Tribune refers to the musical sound of **Guy Lombardo and His Royal Canadians** as "the sweetest music this side of Heaven," a description that stays with the band over their long career.

1929: Guy Lombardo and His Royal Canadians begin a 33-year residency at The Roosevelt Grill in New York. It is here, and later from The Waldorf Astoria, that CBS begins broadcasting the band's annual New Year's Eve performance that for many becomes an indispensable part of the yearly transition from the old year to the new.

1929: Don Messer begins his radio career on CFBO, Saint John, New Brunswick.

1929: Wilfrid Pelletier becomes the conductor of the Metropolitan Opera in New York, a position he holds until 1950.

1929: Victor is purchased by the Radio Corporation of America (RCA) and RCA Victor Co., Ltd. is formed.

1929: The Royal Commission on Broadcasting, also known as the **Aird Commission**, recommends the

establishment of a publicly-owned broadcast system.

1930: A. Hugh Joseph replaces Edgar Berliner as president of RCA Victor Co., Ltd. and begins to record Canadian country artists Hank Snow and Wilf Carter.

1930: Wilf Carter conducts his first live radio broadcast on CFCN, Calgary, Alberta.

1930: Hank Snow returns home to Lunenburg, Nova Scotia where his mother and stepfather are living. His mother, who had already instilled a love of traditional music in the young Hank, had bought a copy of Jimmie Rodgers' *Moonlight and Skies*. It was a defining moment in Snow's life as he became a devotee of Rodgers' music and is inspired to follow in "The Blue Yodeler's" footsteps.

1930: Maureen Forrester is born on July 25th in Montreal, Quebec.

1931: Bert Niosi, later known as Canada's King of Swing, forms a nine-piece band to play at the Embassy Club in Toronto.

1932: Glenn Gould is born on September 25th in Toronto, Ontario.

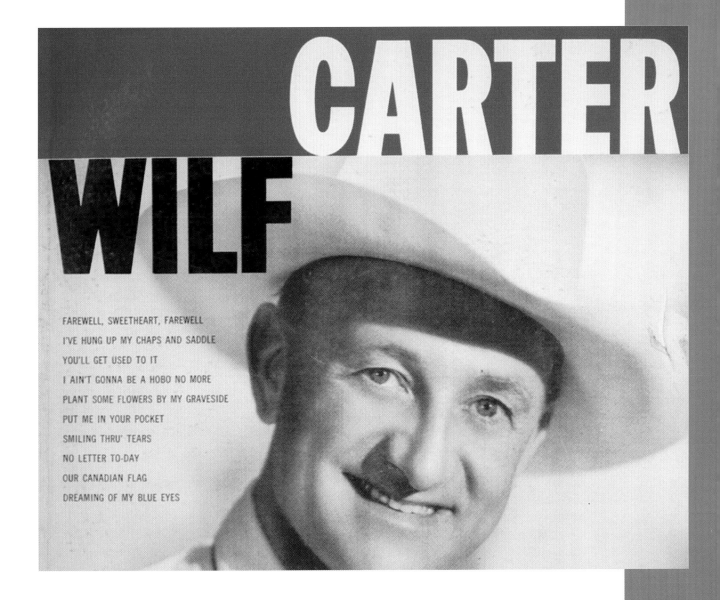

WILF CARTER

FAREWELL, SWEETHEART, FAREWELL

I'VE HUNG UP MY CHAPS AND SADDLE

YOU'LL GET USED TO IT

I AIN'T GONNA BE A HOBO NO MORE

PLANT SOME FLOWERS BY MY GRAVESIDE

PUT ME IN YOUR POCKET

SMILING THRU' TEARS

NO LETTER TO-DAY

OUR CANADIAN FLAG

DREAMING OF MY BLUE EYES

1932: The **Wilf Carter** single *My Swiss Moonlight Lullabye*, recorded for the Canadian Victor label by A. Hugh Joseph, becomes the first Canadian hit recorded domestically.

1932: Brunswick Records is signed to the Compo Co. for manufacturing and sales in Canada.

1932: The Canadian Radio Broadcasting Commission (CRBC) is created as the public broadcasting system for the nation, later to be renamed the Canadian Broadcasting Corporation (CBC).

1933: Canadian Music and Radio Trades, formerly the *Canadian Music Trades Journal*, publishes its last issue after a 33-year run.

1933: The Sons Of the Pioneers form in Los Angeles around Roy

Rogers, New Brunswick-native **Bob Nolan**, and Tim Spencer.

1933: Ian Tyson is born on September 25th in Victoria, British Columbia.

1934: Leonard Cohen is born on September 21st in Montreal, Quebec.

1934: In Bridgewater, Nova Scotia, **Hank Snow** makes his first public appearance at a minstrel show. He is subsequently offered his own radio show on CHNS in Halifax, where he is billed as "Clarence Snow and His Guitar."

1934: Guy Lombardo and His Royal Canadians appear in the first of a number of movies as they are seen in the Burns & Allen musical comedy *Many Happy Returns*. Though they appear on screen during Larry Adler's harmonica number, it is actually Duke Ellington who provides the music. Lombardo makes cameo appearances in a number of World War II era films, including *Stage Door Canteen* (1943) and *No Leave, No Love* (1946).

1934: Don Messer's band, the New Brunswick Lumberjacks, featuring vocalist Charlie Chamberlain, begin broadcasting from CHSJ Saint John, New Brunswick.

1935: New Brunswick native **Bob Nolan** of The Sons of the Pioneers has his song *Tumbling Tumbleweeds* introduced to a wider audience by Gene Autry in the movie of the same name. Autry reprises the song in the film *Don't Fence Me In* in 1945. Sons Of the Pioneers member Roy Rogers performs it in the film *Silver*

Spurs (1943) and the group performs what has become their signature tune in the movie Hollywood *Canteen* (1944). Bing Crosby tops the charts with the song in 1940.

1935: The Montreal Symphony Orchestra/ L'orchestre symphonique de Montreal, then known as the Societe des concerts de Montreal, play their first concert on January 14th at Plateau Hall. Wilfrid Pelletier becomes the orchestra's first artistic director on April 11th.

1935: Music publisher **Boosey & Hawkes** (Canada) Ltd. opens in Toronto.

1935: Compo Company Ltd. becomes the Canadian licensee for the Decca Records label.

1935: *Your Lucky Strike Hit Parade*, the first record chart of any kind, debuts on radio in the U.S.

1935: Canadian **David Rockola** of Virden, Manitoba is instrumental in the development of the jukebox as he introduces his Rock- Ola Multi-Selector phonograph.

1936: Singer **Phyllis Marshall** debuts on radio station CRCT and later on CBC Radio with Percy Faith.

1936: Kindersley, Saskatchewan natives **The Harmony Kids** (initially Hahn and His Kids), featuring siblings Robert, Lloyd, Kay and Joyce Hahn, head from Saskatchewan to the bright lights of

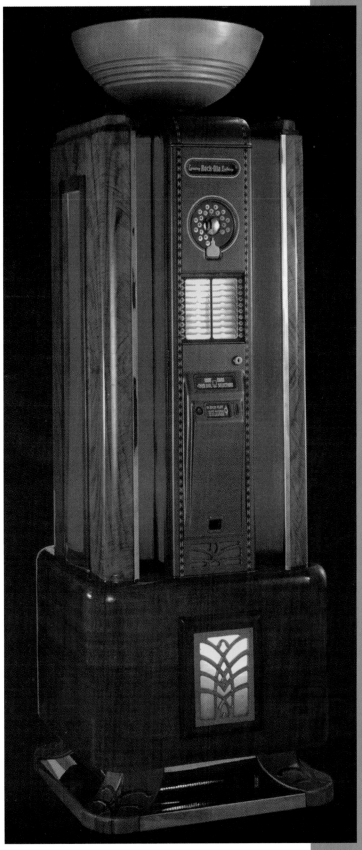

Broadway during the Great Depression. **Joyce Hahn** becomes one of Canada's first television stars in the early 1950s.

1936: Hank Snow successfully auditions for A. Hugh Joseph at RCA Victor in Montreal on October 29th — he records his own compositions *Lonesome Blue Yodel* and *The Prisoned Cowboy* — and is signed to the label initially as Hank, The Yodeling Ranger. For the next twelve years, his records are released exclusively in Canada on the RCA Bluebird label.

1937: Canada's **Happy Gang**, a troupe of musical entertainers, debut their popular radio show on June 14th at Toronto CBC affiliate CRCT. The show runs for 22 years. One of the broadcast executives responsible for bringing the show to the air is William D. Byles, whose daughter is rock singer Alannah Myles.

1937: Garth Hudson (The Band) is born on August 2nd in London, Ontario.

1937: Over four days in early November, **Hank Snow** records eight songs for RCA Victor in Montreal, including *The Blue Velvet Band*, one of his biggest hits, before making his first cross-Canada tour.

1937: Renowned record retailer **Sam "The Record Man" Sniderman** first enters the world of records while working in the family business, then

Don Messer and His Islanders

known as Sniderman Radio Sales and Service, on College Street in Toronto.

1938: While working at the CRBC, **Percy Faith** introduces his own show, *Music By Faith*, which is also heard in the U.S. on the Mutual Broadcasting System (MBS).

1938: Dorothy Collins from Windsor, Ontario gets her first taste of show biz as she enters a hometown talent contest, wins a wristwatch and a chance to sing on a children's radio program in Detroit.

1938: Gordon Lightfoot is born on November 17th in Orillia, Ontario.

1939: Don Messer and His Islanders first perform on radio station CFCY in Charlottetown, Prince Edward Island.

1939: Sparton Records becomes the exclusive licensee in Canada of the CBS-owned Columbia Records.

1940: Performing rights society **BMI Canada Ltd.** is established.

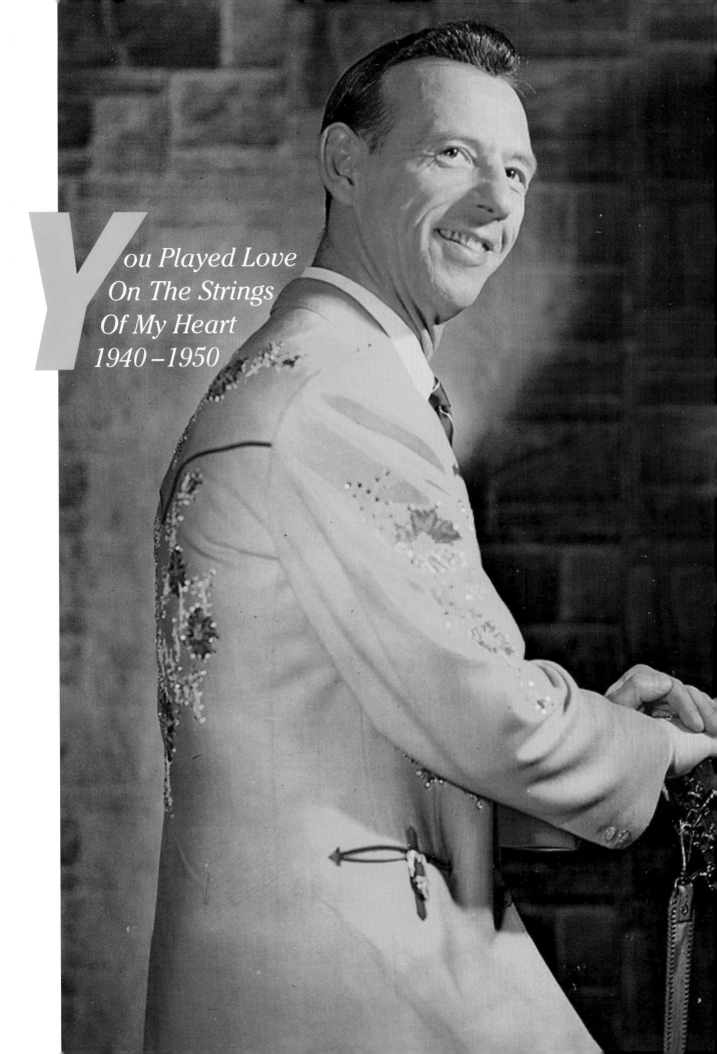

*Y*ou Played Love
On The Strings
Of My Heart
1940 – 1950

You Played Love On The Strings Of My Heart
1940–1950

1940: CBC staff conductor **Percy Faith** lands a job in Chicago as music director of *The Carnation Contented Hour* on NBC Radio. In 1946, he takes on the musical directorship of Coca Cola's *The Pause That Refreshes*.

1940: An automobile accident causes **Wilf Carter** to retire from the music business for nine years.

1940: *I'll Never Smile Again*, written by **Ruth Lowe** of Toronto and performed by the Tommy Dorsey Orchestra with Frank Sinatra on vocals, tops the first-ever *Billboard* magazine singles chart. The song was also recorded by Glenn Miller, but Dorsey's version defines forever this kind of big band vocal styling. Sinatra later commissioned Lowe to compose his closing theme, *Put Your Dreams Away For Another Day*.

1940: Sylvia Fricker (Sylvia Tyson) is born on September 19th in Chatham, Ontario.

1940: Denny Doherty (The Mamas and the Papas) is born on November 20th in Halifax, Nova Scotia.

1941: Buffy Sainte-Marie is born on February 20th in Craven, Saskatchewan.

1941: Paul Anka is born on July 30th in Ottawa, Ontario.

1941: David Thomsett (David Clayton-Thomas) is born on September 13th in Surrey, England.

1941: The Victoria Symphony Orchestra is founded by conductor Melvin Knudson.

1942: Dorothy Collins is introduced to band leader Raymond Scott, whose quintet she subsequently joins.

1942: The Canadian Army Show, a weekly music revue featuring artists like comedy team **Wayne & Shuster**, trumpeter and director **Robert Farnon**, and singers **Roger Doucet** and **Denny Vaughan**, debuts at Toronto's Victoria Theatre and then sets out across Canada in April 1943.

1943: Richard Manuel (The Band) is born on April 3rd in Stratford, Ontario.

1943: Randy Bachman (The Guess Who and Bachman-Turner Overdrive) is born on September 27th in Winnipeg, Manitoba.

1943: Roberta Joan Anderson (Joni Mitchell) is born on November 7th in Lethbridge, Alberta.

1943: The Canadian Army Show (now **The Army Show**), which has been split into five units to entertain the troops overseas, arrives in England in late December. Two members of the troupe, **Robert Farnon** and **Denny Vaughan**, remain in England and become major stars. Recording under his own name and working with artists like Vera Lynn and Ted Heath's band as well as international singing stars like Tony Bennett, Frank Sinatra, Lena Horne, and Sarah Vaughan, Robert Farnon becomes one of the world's most renowned composers, arrangers, and conductors. Denny Vaughan, once dubbed "the English Sinatra," moves to New York in 1951, where he works as an arranger for

The Army Show

singers like Kate Smith, Eddie Fisher, and Ezio Pinza.

1943: Lorne Greene founds the Academy of Radio Arts, a broadcasting school which counts among its students **Leslie Nielsen** and **James Doohan** (later Engineer Montgomery Scott of the Star Trek starship Enterprise).

1944: Music publisher **Peer-Southern Organization** (Canada) opens in Toronto.

1944: Hank Snow makes his first U.S. appearance in Philadelphia, where he sings on local radio stations WCAU and WIP.

1944: Joachim Kruledat (John Kay) is born on April 12th in Tilsit, East Prussia.

The Rhythm Pals

1944: Robbie Robertson (The Band) is born on July 5th in Toronto, Ontario.

1944: Zal Yanovsky (Lovin' Spoonful) is born on December 19th in Toronto, Ontario.

1944: At a recording session for RCA Victor in Montreal, **Hank Snow** records, among others, *You Played Love On the Strings Of My Heart*, one of his biggest sellers in Canada.

1945: Glenn Gould makes his first concert appearance on the organ at the Toronto Conservatory of Music on February 16th.

1945: Anne Murray is born on June 20th in Springhill, Nova Scotia.

1945: Neil Young is born on November 12th in Toronto, Ontario.

1945: The Canadian Performing Rights Society (CPRS) becomes the **Composers, Authors, and Publishers Association of Canada Limited/ Association des compositeurs, auteurs et éditeurs du Canada Ltée.**

1945: CBC International Service (CBC IS), known as "the voice of Canada abroad," produces its first music recordings — five 78 RPM discs known as *Canadian Album No. 1* — and later evolves into the CBC-SM and CBC-LM labels in 1966, which, in 1982, come under the auspices of CBC Enterprises, formed to market CBC-produced discs.

1945: CHUM Toronto begins to broadcast on October 1st.

1946: Musicana Records begins manufacturing and distributing records in Canada for newly-formed Capitol Records U.S.A. which establishes Capitol Records of Canada, Ltd. in 1947 in London, Ontario.

1946: After the war, **Hank Snow** begins spending more time in the United States appearing on radio stations like WWVA, Wheeling, West Virginia. Snow becomes a self-contained touring unit with his own grandstand tent and a top-of-the-line Buick automobile for towing a house trailer for his family and a van for his horse Shawnee, now an integral part of his stage show.

1946: Country trio **The Rhythm Pals** form in New Westminster, B.C. They are destined to take the honors for longevity of any group in Canadian music history.

1946: Glenn Gould debuts on May 8th as a pianist with the Toronto Conservatory Symphony Orchestra at Toronto's Massey Hall.

Glenn Gould

1947: Winchester, Ontario born bass/baritone **George Beverly Shea** becomes a soloist with Billy Graham's evangelical crusade, a position he holds for more than 40 years. He has been called "the most widely recognized voice in Christian music."

1947: The Four Lads, originally The Four Dukes, form in Toronto around Jimmy Arnold, Bernie Toorish, Frank Busseri, and Connie Codarini, all former members of St. Michael's Cathedral Choir School.

1947: Vocalist **Marg Osborne** joins Don Messer and His Islanders.

1947: Vocalist **Phyllis Marshall** tours the U.S. with the Cab Calloway Orchestra.

1947: Glenn Gould plays Beethoven's *Concerto No. 4* with the Toronto Symphony Orchestra on January 14th and later in the year on October 20th

gives his recital debut as a pianist at the Eaton Auditorium in Toronto.

1947: Burton Cummings (The Guess Who) is born on December 31st in Winnipeg, Manitoba.

1948: Toronto jazz musician **Moe Koffman** wins a poll as best flute player in *Metronome* magazine, which leads to his signing to New York-based Mainstream Records.

1948: *What A Fool I Was*, written and recorded by Saskatchewan-native **Stu Davis**, a pioneer of Canadian country radio and television, becomes a major hit when re-recorded by country artist Eddy Arnold.

1948: Gordon Lightfoot at age 10 is singled out in the junior choir as a soloist. Lightfoot later points to choir master Ray Williams as a major influence on his early career.

1948: The Rhythm Pals become one of the first Canadian groups to appear on television in the United States.

1948: Earl Heywood, known as "Canada's Number One Cowboy Singer," signs to RCA Victor and records a number of hits, including *Alberta Waltz* and *Tears Of St. Anne*.

1948: Moe Koffman first records for the Mainstream label in Buffalo, New York.

1948: Singer/pianist **Billy O'Connor** begins his career on CBC Radio and becomes a regular headliner over the next decade on shows like *The Late Show*, *Club O'Connor*, and *Saturday Date*, which were early boosters of home-grown talent like **Peter Appleyard**, **Juliette**, **Vonda King**, **Rhonda Silver**, and the **Two Tones**, featuring **Gordon Lightfoot**.

1948: The London Gramophone Corp. of Canada opens in Montreal.

Earl Heywood

1948: Columbia Records announces mass production of 33 1/3 RPM records.

1949: The Canadian Music Publisher's Association (CMPA)/Association canadienne des éditeurs de musique is formed.

1949: Capitol Records of Canada, Ltd. is purchased by W. Lockwood Miller.

1949: Rodeo Records Ltd. is founded in Montreal by Don Johnson and George Taylor.

1949: RCA Records issues the world's first 45 RPM single.

1949: Wilf Carter returns to the North American circuit and tours Canada with the Canadian Plowboy, Orval Prophet.

1949: Joan Anderson (Joni Mitchell) moves with her parents to North Battleford, Saskatchewan.

INTRODUCING
the record that plays up to 45 minutes!

the sensational new — — — — — — — ->

COLUMBIA (Lp)
LONG PLAYING
MICROGROOVE
RECORD

...finer tone quality
...more music for your money
...saves storage space
...nonbreakable Vinylite

NOW—A COMPLETE ALBUM OF MUSIC ON ONE RECORD!

1949: The Four Lads debut on Elwood Glover's *Canadian Cavalacade* show on the CBC, tour Canada, and subsequently get a regular paying gig at New York's Ruban Bleu, where they are booked for close to eight months.

1949: Oscar Peterson, having turned down offers to join the Count Basie and the Jimmie Lunceford bands, catches on with impresario Norman Granz, who plants Peterson in the audience at Carnegie Hall during one of his *Jazz At The Philharmonic Presentations* and invites him on stage as a surprise guest. Peterson brings the house down and launches his career internationally.

1949: Hank Snow and family relocate to New Westminster, B.C., where he sings with the staff band at radio station CKNW. **The Rhythm Pals** are also regulars on the station. U.S. country star Ernest Tubb, who had previously met Hank Snow in Fort Worth, Texas where they had shared a concert bill, records Snow's *My Filipino Rose,* which Tubb takes into the Top 10 of the U.S. country charts in September. Snow has his first U.S. Top 10 country hit in December with *Marriage Vow* and becomes "Hank Snow, The Singing Ranger."

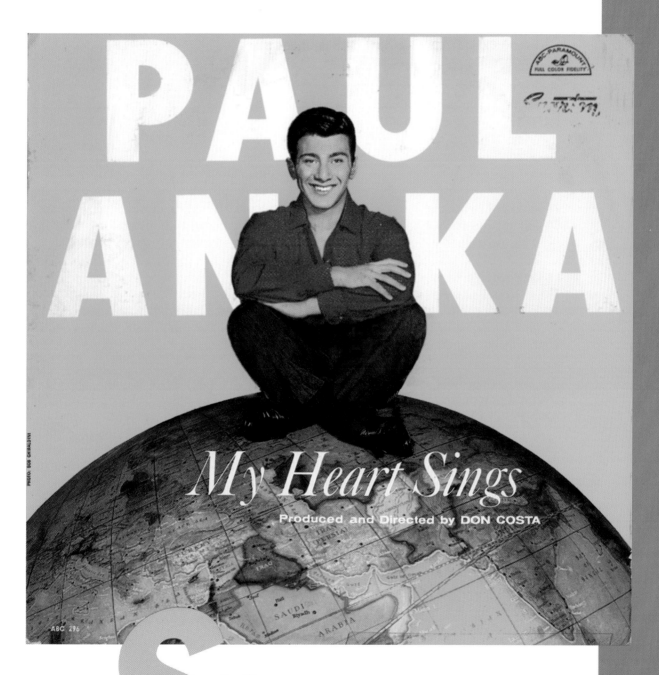

Sh-Boom
1950–1960

Sh-Boom
1950–1960

1950: Hank Snow makes his first appearance at the Grand Ole Opry in Nashville on January 7th, and on August 19th his single *I'm Movin' On* tops the *Billboard* country chart, a position it holds for 21 weeks, a run topped only twice before or since.

1950: Wilf Carter plays to close to 70,000 fans during a one-week stint at the CNE Bandshell in Toronto.

1950: Percy Faith is hired by Mitch Miller to become director of popular music for Columbia Records.

1950: During his stint with Stan Kenton's band, **Maynard Ferguson** wins the *Down Beat* Readers' Poll for best trumpet player three consecutive years from 1950 to 1952.

1950: Winnipeg-born singer **Gisele MacKenzie** moves to New York, where she hooks up with fellow Canadian Percy Faith and his orchestra on CBS Radio.

1950: Dorothy Collins becomes a featured singer on the popular American TV show *Your Hit Parade* as it begins its first season.

1950: Glenn Gould makes his CBC network broadcast debut on December 24th.

1950: Canadian Music Sales, distributor of Columbia Records in Canada during the 1930s, establishes the Dominion record label which over the years records country and folk performers like **Isidore Soucy**, **Stompin' Tom Connors**, and **Earl Heywood**.

1950: Quality Records Ltd. is founded in Toronto.

1951: Decca Records purchases the Compo Company Ltd.

1951: The Four Lads back up Johnny Ray on his hit song *Cry*. Group member Bernard Toorish would later arrange their background vocals for Ray's *Little White Cloud That Cried* as well as Frankie Laine's 1954 single *Rain, Rain, Rain*.

1951: *Meet Gisele*, a National Film Board documentary on **Gisele MacKenzie's** life, is released.

1951: Leonard Cohen plays country with The Buckskin Boys while attending Montreal's McGill University.

1951: Contralto **Maureen Forrester** makes her professional debut with the Montreal Elgar Choir in **Elgar's** *The Music Makers* at the Salvation Army Citadel.

1952: Percy Faith has his first major pop hit with *Delicado*.

1952: The Four Lads own recording career begins with the single *Mocking Bird*.

1952: Country singer **Ronnie Prophet** makes his debut in Ottawa at the age of 15 on radio station CFRA's country show, *The Happy Wanderers*.

1952: Bert Niosi and his band begin an 18-year residency at Toronto's Palais Royale dance hall.

THE FABULOUS "45"

LET'S LOOK AT THE RECORD...

1952: Rudi Maugeri and **John Perkins**, former students at St. Michael's Cathedral Choir School in Toronto, quit the group The Jordonaires and put together The Four Tones, the group that would evolve into The Canadaires and then **The Crew Cuts**.

1952: The first CBC Television broadcast season includes Canada's first country music TV show, *Holiday Ranch.*

1952: Neil Peart (Rush) is born on September 12th in Hamilton, Ontario.

1953: Percy Faith records the theme from the motion picture *The Song From Moulin Rouge (Where Is Your Heart?)* which becomes the top-selling single of the year.

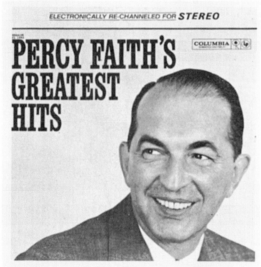

PERCY FAITH'S GREATEST HITS   CS 8637
The Theme From "A Summer Place"; Non Dimenticar; Till; All My Love; Jamaican Rhumba; Delicado; The Song From Moulin Rouge; Tropical Merengue; They Can't Take That Away From Me; The Rain in Spain; The Syncopated Clock; Swedish Rhapsody

1953: After appearing on CBC-TV's *The Big Revue*, vocalist **Shirley Harmer** works in the U.S. over the next five years on Dave Garroway's NBC-TV show, *Paul Whiteman's Orchestra* on ABC Radio, and NBC-TV's *The George Gobel Show.*

1953: Gisele MacKenzie begins a long association with comedian Jack Benny and becomes a regular on the NBC-TV show *Your Hit Parade. Hard To Get*, a song first heard on an episode of NBC-TV's *Justice*, reaches number four on the *Billboard* chart.

1953: Toronto-born trombonist **Murray McEachern**, working as a Hollywood studio musician, handles the trombone solos heard in the movies *The Glenn Miller Story* (1953), *The Benny Goodman Story* (1955), and *Paris Blues* (1961).

1953: After coming second on the influential *Arthur Godfrey Talent Hunt* TV show in New York, **The Crew Cuts** return to Toronto to appear in concert with **Gisele MacKenzie**.

1953: Maureen Forrester makes her recital debut on March 29th at the Montreal YMCA with **John Newmark,** who will become her regular accompanist and collaborator over the years.

1953: Folk group **The Travellers** form in Toronto around **Jerry Gray**, **Sid Dolgay**, **Helen Gray**, **Jerry Goodis,** and **Oscar Ross**.

1953: Gisele MacKenzie begins a 29 week non-consecutive run on the British chart with the single *Seven Lonely Days.*

1953: Gary Lee Weinrib (Geddy Lee) of Rush is born on July 29th in Toronto, Ontario.

1953: Alex Zivojinovich (Alex Lifeson) of Rush is born on August 29th in Fernie, British Columbia.

Percy Faith

1953: Joan Anderson (Joni Mitchell) contracts polio and spends several months away from school. She later credits her seventh grade English teacher, Mr Kratzman, for piquing her interest in writing and dedicates her first album to him.

1953: The Crew Cuts, then known as the Canadairs, appear on the *Gene Carrol* TV Show in Cleveland where they also meet deejay Bill Randle who is not only responsible for the change of their name to The Crew Cuts (after the hairstyles they were all sporting at the time), but he also arranges for an audition for them at Mercury Records in Chicago. They were signed shortly after and in April 1954 had their first hit with the Rudi Maugeri / Pat Barrett composition *Crazy 'Bout You Baby.*

1953: Maureen Forrester makes her Montreal Symphony Orchestra debut in Beethoven's *Ninth Symphony.*

1954: Hank Snow has his second million-selling single with the **Jack Rollins/Don Robertson** song *I Don't Hurt Anymore,* which tops the *Billboard* country chart for 20 weeks.

1954: Dave Somerville, **Ted Kowalski**, **Phil Levitt,** and **Bill Reed**, collectively known as **The Diamonds**, form at the University of Toronto.

1954: Lucille Starr begins her singing career in Vancouver.

1954: The Travellers make their TV debut on CBC's *Haunted House.*

1954: The **Denny Vaughan** Show debuts on CBC-TV.

1954: Trombonist **Rob McConnell** begins his musical career in Edmonton as a member of saxophonist Don Thompson's band.

1954: The Crew Cuts' cover of The Chords R&B hit *Sh-Boom* hits number one on the *Billboard* music popularity chart, where it remains for seven weeks.

1954: Capitol Records of Canada, Ltd. is replaced by Capitol Record Distributors of Canada, Ltd. with head offices relocated to Toronto from London, Ontario.

1954: Columbia Records of Canada is founded with offices in Toronto.

1955: At age 14, country singer **Myrna Lorrie** has her biggest hit with *Are You Mine?*

1955: Denny Doherty's singing career begins in his hometown of Halifax as vocalist for a dance band led by Peter Power.

1955: Joyce Hahn and **Wally Koster** begin a six-year stint as co-stars on CBC-TV's popular *Cross Canada Hit Parade.*

1955: Toronto doo-wop group **The Diamonds** make their TV debut on the CBC show *Pick The Stars* and the same year play the Alpine Village Club in Cleveland, where local radio personality Bill Randle sees them and arranges a recording contract with Mercury Records.

1955: Hank Snow's management contract with "Colonel" Tom Parker goes into effect.

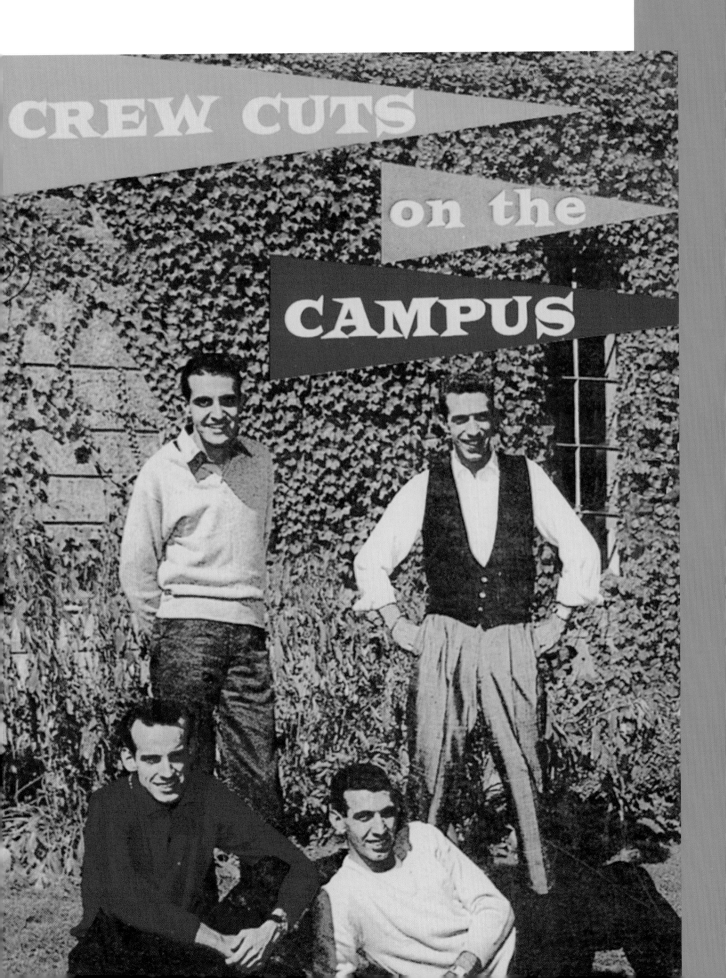

CREW CUTS on the CAMPUS

1955: Glenn Gould makes his U.S. debut on January 2nd at the Phillips Gallery in Washington, D.C.

1955: The Crew Cuts are winners of radio station WNEW New York's annual music popularity poll along with Perry Como, Patti Page, and Ray Anthony. Their cover of The Penguin's 1954 number one R&B hit *Earth Angel* begins a 20-week run on the British charts on April 15th and hits number three in the U.S.A.

1955: Maureen Forrester makes her European debut in Paris at the Salle Gaveau.

1955: Fifteen-year-old **Priscilla Wright** records *Man In A Raincoat* at London, Ontario radio station CFPL, a song arranged by her father Don Wright, a noted Canadian choir conductor/broadcaster/arranger, which becomes a number one hit in Canada and a Top 10

record in the U.S., the U.K., Australia and New Zealand, qualifying it as the first Canadian record by a female to become an international hit. *Cashbox* magazine also names her Most Promising Singer of the Year. She appears on CBS-TV's *The Ed Sullivan Show* and tours with Elvis Presley and Pat Boone.

1955: Glenn Gould first records Bach's *Goldberg Variations* in June at Columbia Studios in New York.

1955: Hank Snow Enterprises-Jamboree Attractions, headed by Snow and his manager Colonel Tom Parker, sign 20-year-old Elvis Presley . . . or so Snow believes. Parker and Snow split later in the year when Snow finds that Elvis had in fact been signed to a personal contract with Parker.

1955: The Four Lads' *Moments To Remember* enters the the Top Five on the U.S. charts on October 29th.

1956: The Diamonds hit number 12 on the U.S. charts with the single *Why Do Fools Fall In Love?*

1956: Toronto vocal group **The Rover Boys** sign with producer Don Costa at ABC/Paramount Records, where they record their biggest hit, *Graduation Day*.

1956: Trumpeter **Johnny Cowell** has his biggest hit with the self-penned single *Walk Hand In Hand*, which hits the top of the sheet music chart in the U.K., where fellow Canadian **Denny Vaughan** records a version for Oriole Records.

1956: Moe Koffman returns to Toronto after six years of touring with a variety of big bands and forms the Moe Koffman Quartette. They record *Blues À La Canadiana* which becomes *Swingin' Shepherd Blues* and a North American hit for Koffman in 1958.

Moe Koffman

1956: Ian Tyson, whose main interest in youth had been the rodeo, attends the Vancouver Art School and sings at the Heidelberg Cafe.

1956: Lucille Starr and **Bob Regan** form the country duo, **The Canadian Sweethearts**, and tour extensively throughout the world for the next two decades.

1956: The popular CBC-TV program *Juliette* debuts and runs for 11 years, usually following *Hockey Night In Canada* on Saturday nights.

1956: Country singer/songwriter **Larry Mercey** begins his career on the CKNX Barn Dance in Wingham, Ontario.

1956: Leonard Cohen's first book, *Let Us Compare Mythologies*, is published.

1956: The Happy Gang make their TV debut on CBC's *Cross-Canada Hit Parade*.

1956: Gisele MacKenzie becomes one of **Dinah Shore's** summer replacements on NBC-TV's *The Chevy Show*.

1956: Doug Cole opens George's Jazz Room in George's Spaghetti House in downtown Toronto, now the longest running jazz club in Canada.

1957: *Music World*, a bi-weekly magazine billed by its publisher and managing editor **Ray Sonin** as "Canada's Only Publication Devoted To Popular Music," is launched.

1957: Harold Jenkins (a.k.a. Conway Twitty) writes his biggest hit, *It's Only Make Believe*, while performing at the Fisher Hotel and the Flamingo Lounge in Hamilton, Ontario.

1957: The Diamonds have their biggest hit with *Little Darlin'* and they prompt a dance craze with their single *The Stroll,* which becomes very popular with the teens on Dick Clark's *American Bandstand* show.

1957: Jack Scott is signed by ABC Paramount Records in New York and has his first hit with *Two Timin' Woman*.

1957: Gordon Lightfoot plays drums in a number of jazz bands before moving from Toronto to Los Angeles for 14 months to take a course in contemporary jazz, orchestration, and harmony at Westlake College.

1957: Buddy Knox becomes the first artist of the rock era to occupy the penthouse of the *Billboard* Top 100 chart with the self-penned song *Party Doll*, co-written with Jimmy Bowen. Like Ronnie Hawkins, Knox began spending an increasing amount of time in Canada in the late 1950s and eventually became a permanent resident.

1957: Paul Anka convinces his parents to send him to New York, where he spends time with **The Diamonds**, whose hotel room bath tub he occupies at the Forest Hotel, and **The Rover Boys**, who recommend him to their record company, ABC Paramount, where he records *Diana* and *Don't Gamble On Me*. On September 9th, *Diana* reaches number one on the *Billboard Top 100* chart, destined to become one of the best-selling singles in music history.

1957: Glenn Gould makes his European debut with the Moscow Philharmonic as he begins a month long tour that also takes him to Leningrad, Berlin, and Vienna.

1957: *The Gisele MacKenzie Show* has its first telecast in September on NBC-TV showcasing MacKenzie's talents as a singer, violinist, dancer, and actress.

**Gisele Mackenzie
with Jimmie Durante**

1957: In December, **Paul Anka** sets out on a tour of Europe, including dates in Britain, where he appears on the TV show *Saturday Night At The Paladium*. Reportedly, Chuck Berry writes *Sweet Little Sixteen* after seeing film footage of Anka performing to a crowd of screaming girls during an Ottawa concert in 1957.

1958: Paul Anka tours Hawaii and Australia with Buddy Holly and Jerry Lee Lewis before making his movie debut in the film *Let's Rock* (also known as *Keep It Cool*).

1958: Following a stint with country group **The Sensational Stripes**, **Ian Tyson** moves to Toronto from Vancouver and joins the local folk scene.

1958: Jackie Rae, who spent the war years in England flying Spitfires, returns to old blighty where he becomes a music variety regular on British TV and records for the Philips/Fontana label. Such is his fame that in 1961 he gives a Royal Command Performance at London's Victoria Palace. He returns to Toronto in 1976.

1958: Oscar Peterson records his *On the Town* album at Toronto's Town Tavern.

1958: John Kay arrives in Toronto from Germany in March and attends Humberside Collegiate.

1958: Mercury Records produces two three-minute films for **The Diamonds** and The Platters performing their current releases and makes them available free to a list of 200 TV personalities with afternoon teenage programs. Film (and later video) as a marketing tool in the music business is born.

1958: Arc Records is founded in Toronto by Phil Anderson and Bill Gilliland.

1958: Board of Broadcast Governors is created to regulate Canadian radio.

1958: RCA Records becomes the first major record company to release stereo recordings.

1959: The first Grammy Awards are presented by the National Academy of Recording Arts and Sciences during a formal dinner banquet in the Grand Ballroom of the Beverly Hilton Hotel in Hollywood.

1959: Country singer **Dick Damron** begins his recording career on his own Holiday Records label.

1959: Gordon Lightfoot heads home from Los Angeles to pursue his music career as a member of the chorus on the CBC-TV show *Country Hoedown* and as a vocalist with the Gino Silvi Singers.

1959: Ian Tyson begins singing with **Sylvia Fricker**, who had recently moved to Toronto from Chatham, Ontario and was performing in Yorkville Village.

1959: The Buddy Holly single *It Doesn't Matter Anymore*, written by **Paul Anka**, is released in January. It is to be the last record from Holly before his untimely death the following month in a plane crash with Ritchie Valens and the Big Bopper, a flight Anka would have taken if not for the advice of his manager Irvin Feld.

1959: Glenn Gould makes his British debut on May 20th with The London Symphony.

1959: The last regular broadcast of *The Happy Gang* is heard on CBC Radio on June 5th.

1959: Paul Anka's *Lonely Boy* reaches number one on the *Billboard* Top 100 singles chart on July 13th, where it remains for four weeks. In August, Anka debuts at the Sahara Hotel in Las Vegas.

1959: The Don Messer Show, soon after renamed *Don Messer's Jubilee*, begins broadcasting on CBC-TV in August and runs for a decade on the CBC and in syndication from CHCH-TV in Hamilton, Ontario until Messer's death in 1973.

Ronnie Hawkins & The Hawks

1959: Ronnie Hawkins & The Hawks perform *Forty Days* and *Mary Lou* on Dick Clark's *American Bandstand* TV show on August 17th and appear on Alan Freed's huge Labor Day show at the Brooklyn Fox. Roulette Records releases his self-titled RONNIE HAWKINS album in mid-September and in late October Hawkins records two songs by Robbie Robertson, *Hey Boba Lou* and *Someone Like You*, as part of his album session for MR. DYNAMO.

1959: Bryan Adams is born on November 5th in Kingston, Ontario.

The Oscar Peterson Trio
Canadiana Suite

Canadiana Suite
1960–1967

Canadiana Suite
1960–1967

1960: The **Tommy Hunter** Show debuts on CBC Radio with **The Rhythm Pals** as regular guests.

1960: Singalong Jubilee debuts locally on CBC-TV Halifax.

1960: Bobby Curtola teams up with songwriters **Dyer** and **Basil Hurdon** in his hometown of Port Arthur (now Thunder Bay), Ontario, and has his first single, *Hand In Hand With You,* released on Tartan Records in February. Curtola soon becomes a teen idol with hits like *Fortune Teller*, *Aladdin*, *Three Rows Over,* and *Hitchhiker*.

1960: Percy Faith's rendition of the **Max Steiner** composition *Theme From A Summer Place* is *Billboard*'s number one single of 1960 and wins a Grammy Award as Record of the Year.

1960: Paul Anka opens at the Copacabana in New York in June, the youngest star ever to appear there, and performs an unprecedented three shows to satisfy the demand for tickets.

1960: Robert Goulet is warmly received in the role of Lancelot starring opposite Richard Burton and Julie Andrews as the Lerner and Lowe musical *Camelot* premieres at the newly-opened O'Keefe Centre for the Performing Arts in Toronto.

1961: Toronto folk singer/songwriter **Bonnie Dobson** writes *(Walk Me Out In the) Morning Dew* in Los Angeles while on tour, a song initially recorded in the mid-1960s by folksingers Fred Neil and Tim Rose which becomes a rock and pop staple recorded by artists like the Jeff Beck Group (with Rod Stewart), the Grateful Dead, Nazareth, Long John Baldry, Devo, Dave Edmunds, the Chieftains and Lulu, whose version hits the pop charts in 1968.

1961: The Two Tones, an act formed by **Gordon Lightfoot** and **Terry Whelan**, begin playing the coffeehouse circuit and record three albums over the next three years.

1961: Ian Tyson and **Sylvia Fricker** form the folk duo **Ian & Sylvia** and subsequently sign to the prestigious Vanguard Records label in the U.S. While working in New York, Ian Tyson writes his folk classic *Four Strong Winds* at the office of his manager Albert Grossman.

1961: Dorothy Collins joins the cast of popular TV show *Candid Camera*.

1961: The first annual Mariposa Folk Festival, held on August 18th at Oval Park in Orillia, Ontario, features **Ian & Sylvia**, **The Travellers**, **Jean Carignan**, **O.J. Abbott**, **Alan Mills**, and **Jacques Labrecque**.

1961: The first *Tonight Show* hosted by Johnny Carson is broadcast on NBC-TV with theme music written by **Paul Anka**.

1961: Garth Hudson joins **Robbie Robertson**, **Levon Helm**, **Rick Danko**, and **Richard Manuel** as members of **Ronnie Hawkins'** group **The Hawks.**

1961: Record retailer **Sam Sniderman** opens the flagship Sam the Record Man store at 347 Yonge Street in the heart of downtown Toronto.

Bobby Curtola

1962: The Canadian Talent Library (CTL) is founded by broadcast executive **J. Lyman Potts** and the Standard Broadcasting Corporation-owned radio stations CFRB Toronto and CJAD Montreal.

1962: Vancouver's **Little Daddy and the Bachelors**, featuring guitarist **Tommy Chong**, release the single *Too Much Monkey Business/Junior's Jerk*. The group is later known as **Four Niggers and a Chink** and then **Bobby Taylor and the Vancouvers**. Chong goes on to become one half of the comedy duo **Cheech & Chong**.

1962: Gordon Lightfoot's first single *Remember Me (I'm the One Who Loves You)*, recorded in Nashville, is released on the Toronto-based Chateau label.

1962: Lucille Starr is heard on the popular TV series *The Beverly Hillbillies* yodeling for the character Cousin Pearl Bodine.

1962: The Travellers live up to their name as they make an excursion to the U.S.S.R. with their show A Musical Tour of Canada.

1962: The **Montreal Symphony Orchestra** embarks on a European tour, the first by a Canadian orchestra.

1962: Prior to a **Glenn Gould** performance of Brahms' *D Minor Concerto* with the New York Philharmonic on April 6th, conductor Leonard Bernstein disassociates himself with the "unothodox performance" of the work that the audience is about to hear.

1963: Country singer/songwriter **Gary Buck** hits the international charts with the song *Happy To Be Unhappy*, and *Cashbox* hails him as Newcomer of the Year.

1963: The Halifax Three, featuring **Denny Doherty** and **Zal Yanovsky**, record an album for Epic Records titled *San Francisco Bay Blues*. After leaving the group, Doherty ends up in New York where he works with a group called **The** Big Three, featuring Cass Elliott and Tim Rose.

1963: Ian & Sylvia appear at the Newport Folk Festival for the first time.

1963: Kate and Anna McGarrigle begin playing Montreal coffeehouses as members of the **Mountain City Four.**

1963: Oscar Peterson's *Canadiana Suite* has its debut.

1963: *Charlena*, recorded by Toronto group **Ritchie Knight & the Mid-Knights**, becomes the first single recorded in Canada to reach number one on the influential chart published by radio station CHUM in Toronto. Bass player **Doug Chappell** later becomes the president of Mercury/Polydor Records in Canada.

1963: Gordon Lightfoot, now married, moves to England and hosts the BBC-TV summer replacement program, *The Country and Western Show.*

Ian & Sylvia

1963: *Let's Sing Out*, a half-hour folk music series, is launched in the fall season on CTV with Winnipeg-native **Oscar Brand** as host.

1963: The Hawks jump ship and set out on their own, first as the **Levon Helm's Sextet** and then as **Levon and the Hawks.**

1963: Singer/songwriter **Les Emmerson** joins **The Staccatos** at a time when the group is a regular fixture at La Chaudière Club in Hull, Québec.

1963: Scopatones are introduced with about a thousand made for jukeboxes in pre-video days.

1963: The Canadian Record Manufacturer's Association (CRMA), the forerunner to the Canadian Recording Industry Association (CRIA), is founded in April by ten participating companies.

1964: Decca Records is purchased by MCA, and an additional pressing plant is subsequently established in Cornwall, Ontario, which closes in the 1970s along with the Lachine, Quebec plant. The Compo and Apex labels are in use until 1971.

1964: Canadian music trade magazine *RPM Weekly* is founded on February 24th in Toronto by editor and publisher Walt Grealis.

1964: Irish/Canadian group **The Carlton Showband** is formed in Toronto and subsequently become the house band for a decade (1967–77) for CTV's *Pig and Whistle* variety show.

1964: Stompin' Tom Connors makes his professional debut in Timmins, Ontario at the Maple Leaf Hotel and on local radio station CKGB.

1964: Anne Murray auditions, unsuccessfully, for *Singalong Jubilee* and meets Brian Ahern, musical director for the show and eventual producer of her first ten albums.

1964: Joan Anderson (**Joni Mitchell**) visits Toronto for the first time to see the Mariposa Folk Festival, which features an appearance by **Buffy Sainte-Marie**. She stays when she finds work at a Yorkville club called The Penny Farthing, where she meets Chuck Mitchell whom she marries soon after in Detroit before heading to New York to perform with him as a duo at the Gaslight Cafe in Greenwich Village.

1964: Will Millar puts **The Irish Rovers** together while singing at tables at Phil's Pancake House in Calgary, Alberta.

1964: Ian & Sylvia become the first act to record a **Gordon Lightfoot** song — his *Early Morning Rain* is the title cut of their third album. They introduce him to agent Albert Grossman who places his songs *For Lovin' Me* and *Early Morning Rain* with **Peter, Paul & Mary**. Lightfoot makes his Mariposa Folk Festival debut.

1964: David Clayton-Thomas and the Shays tour with Dave Clark Five.

1964: Ray Griff, whose songs have already been recorded by a number of major country artists including Jim Reeves and Johnny Horton, moves to Nashville where he becomes a respected member of the songwriting community in Music City U.S.A.

1964: Burl Ives' recording of the **Alan Mills** song *I Know An Old Lady Who Swallowed A Fly* becomes the soundtrack for a National Film Board film of the same name.

1964: Trombonist **Rob McConnell** works in New York with **Maynard Ferguson's** big band.

1964: Vancouver native **Terry Black's** recording career begins with a number

Gordon Lightfoot

of singles recorded for the Toronto-based Yorkville label, including the hit *Unless You Care.*

1964: Denny Doherty, Zal Yanovsky, Cass Elliot, James Hendricks, and later **John Sebastian** form the Mugwumps. The group breaks up shortly after and Yanovsky and Sebastian head for New York where they form the **Lovin' Spoonful.** Doherty becomes Marshall Brickman's replacement in John and Michelle Phillips' group **The New Journeymen**.

1964: Glenn Gould plays his last concert on April 10th in Los Angeles.

1964: With the success of her single *The French Song (Quand le soleil dit bonjours aux montagnes)* **Lucille Starr** becomes the first Canadian female vocalist to have a million seller.

1964: The Riverboat is opened in October at 134 Yorkville Avenue in Toronto by former coffee salesman Bernie Fiedler.

1964: The Stampeders form in Calgary, evolving from the local group **The Rebounds**.

1964: Quality Records releases the single *Shakin' All Over* by a group from Winnipeg previously known as **Chad Allan and the Expressions,** but only a question mark appears on the label inviting listeners to "guess who" the band really is. **The Guess Who** name stuck, and by the early spring of 1965, *Shakin' All Over* had topped the charts in Canada and eventually peaked at number 22 in the U.S. for their American label, Wand/Sceptre.

1964: Lorne Greene, the former CBC newscaster who went on to find TV immortality in the role of Ben

Cartwright on the NBC series *Bonanza,* hits number one on the *Billboard* Top 100 chart on December 5th with the single *Ringo.*

1965: John and Michelle Phillips, **Denny Doherty,** and Cass Elliott form **The Mamas and the Papas** in Los Angeles.

1965: Harmonica player **Lee Oskar,** who played in the Toronto group **Butterfly** with **Arnie Wiskin** in the early 1960s, leaves for the U.S. and later becomes a member of the group War before recording his first solo album in 1976.

1965: Neil Young moves from Winnipeg to Toronto, and before the end of the year he joins the group **The Mynah Birds,** which also features **Rick James, Goldy McJohn,** and **Bruce Palmer**.

1965: *The Tommy Hunter Show,* hosted by "Canada's Country Gentleman," succeeds the weekly *Country Hoedown* show on CBC-TV.

1965: Peter, Paul & Mary have a Top 30 U.S. hit with the **Gordon Lightfoot** song *For Lovin' Me.*

1965: John Kay returns to Toronto from Los Angeles in June, where he meets **The Sparrow** (formerly Jack London and the Sparrows) playing at the Devil's Den club. By September, Kay and former Mynah Birds keyboard player **Goldy McJohn** join band members **Jerry** and **Dennis Edmonton** (a.k.a. Mars Bonfire) and **Nick St. Nicholas**.

1965: Kama Sutra records releases *Do You Believe In Magic* on July 20th, the debut single by **The Lovin' Spoonful,** named after a line in Mississippi John Hurt's *Coffee Blues.*

The Lovin' Spoonful

1965: Mary Martin, an old friend of **The Hawks** from Toronto and now the assistant to Bob Dylan's manager Albert Grossman, arranges for **Robbie Robertson** and **Levon Helm** to back Dylan's electric performances at the Forest Hills tennis stadium and later in August at the Hollywood Bowl. In September Dylan flies to Toronto to rehearse with **Levon and the Hawks** after hours at Friars Tavern in preparation for playing Carnegie Hall on October 1st and Massey Hall on November 14th and 15th.

1965: *You Were On My Mind*, written by **Sylvia Tyson** and recorded by the group **We Five**, peaks at number three on the *Billboard* Hot 100 chart on September 25th.

1965: Buffy Sainte-Marie's *Universal Soldier*, written at Toronto's Purple Onion coffeehouse, becomes an international hit for Donovan.

The Mandala

1965: Burton Cummings is recruited in December to replace the departing **Chad Allan** on vocals for **The Guess Who**.

1965: Johnny Bower, the renowned goaltender for the Toronto Maple Leafs, makes his first and only foray into the music business with the single *Honky the Christmas Goose*.

1965: 8-track tape (Stereo 8) is introduced in Canada.

1965: Gamma Records is founded in Montreal by brothers Jack and Daniel Lazare.

1966: Polydor Ltd. is established in Canada.

1966: While visiting France, **Paul Anka** purchases world rights to the Claude Francois song *Comme D'Habitude* and rewrites the lyrics under the title *My Way* before presenting the song to Frank Sinatra. *My Way* becomes one of the most covered songs in the history of pop music.

1966: The Mandala, formerly **The Rogues** and the house band at Toronto's Club Bluenote, record the single *Opportunity* at the Chess Records Studios in Chicago with vocal group The Dells singing backup.

1966: Calgary pop group **The Stampeders** head east, bringing a little cowboy culture with them.

1966: Murray McLauchlan makes his first major concert appearance at the Mariposa Folk Festival.

1966: The Bossmen, inspired by the piano virtuosity of child prodigy **Tony Collacott** who had played with Sarah Vaughan at the age of 14, become **David Clayton-Thomas**' first experiment in the fusion of jazz and rock three years before his involvement with **Blood, Sweat & Tears**. The group's single

Buffalo Springfield

fusion of jazz and rock three years before his involvement with **Blood, Sweat & Tears**. The group's single *Brainwashed*, a scathing commentary on the Vietnam war which had the word "damn" bleeped out on the recording because of a threatened ban in the U.S., becomes a number one record in Canada.

1966: Leonard Cohen sings a couple of his poems, including *Suzanne* and *Stranger,* during a reading in March at the YMCA in New York and launches his career as a singer/songwriter.

1966: Neil Young and **Bruce Palmer** meet Stephen Stills and Richie Furay in a traffic jam in Los Angeles, and with the addition of **Dewey Martin** from Chesterville, Ontario, form **Buffalo Springfield**.

Anne Murray

1966: Paul Anka hosts the last episode of the TV pop music show *Hullabaloo* on April 11th.

1966: The Mamas and the Papas hit the top of the *Billboard* Top 100 singles chart with *Monday, Monday* on May 7th.

1966: Bob Dylan and **The Hawks'** world tour culminates in a concert at Royal Albert Hall in London with the Rolling Stones, fresh from taping *Paint It Black* for BBC-TV's Top of the Pops program, and members of The Beatles attending.

1966: Buffalo Springfield play a concert at the Hollywood Bowl on July 25th even before they have a record released.

1966: Bob Dylan breaks his neck in a motorcycle accident in Woodstock, New York, where he is soon joined by **Levon and the Hawks** who adopt the name **The Crackers**, then simply **The Band**, and live in a house dubbed Big Pink while Dylan recuperates and they work on their first album, MUSIC FROM BIG PINK.

1966: The Lovin' Spoonful's *Summer In The City* reaches number one on the *Billboard* Hot 100 singles chart on August 13th.

1966: Anne Murray joins the faculty of Athena Regional High School in Summerside, Prince Edward Island as a physical education teacher and becomes a member of the chorus on *Singalong Jubilee*.

Born To Be Wild
1967–1971

Born To Be Wild
1967–1971

1967: Gordon Lightfoot's *Canadian Railroad Trilogy*, commissioned by the CBC for the centennial show *100 Years Young*, is first heard during the airing of the program on January 1st. On March 31st he performs his first annual concert at Massey Hall, a musical tradition that runs until 1984 and every 18 months thereafter.

1967: *CA-NA-DA*, the song written for Canada's centennial by trumpeter **Bobby Gimby** and performed by Gimby and the **Young Canada Singers**, becomes the top single of 1967.

1967: Bruce Cockburn, who had previously played in the Ottawa-based groups **The Esquires** and **The Children**, makes his first appearance at the Mariposa Festival.

1967: Anne Murray begins appearing on the CBC Halifax pop music TV show *Let's Go*, later known as *Frank's Bandstand*.

1967: The Collectors, later known as **Chilliwack**, record their first album and tour with Jefferson Airplane, The Doors, and Procol Harum.

1967: Toronto group **The Paupers** open for Jefferson Airplane at the Cafe Au Go Go in New York to great critical acclaim. Drummer **Skip Prokop** records with Peter, Paul & Mary and is heard on their subsequent hit single, *I Dig Rock And Roll Music*.

1967: Ian & Sylvia appear at Carnegie Hall on April 30th for the first time.

1967: *To Sir With Love*, the title song from the movie co-written by Montrealer **Mark London** and lyricist **Don Black**, becomes a number one single for Lulu on the *Billboard* Hot 100.

1967: In a pop poll held by the *Toronto Telegram*'s "After Four" teen section in December, **Gordon Lightfoot** is named Top Canadian Male Singer, **Susan Taylor** takes the honors as Top Canadian Female Singer, and **The Big Town Boys** are named Top Canadian Group.

1967: Steppenwolf record their debut album, featuring the definitive rock anthem *Born To Be Wild*, written by **Dennis Edmonton** (a.k.a. **Mars Bonfire**). A phrase from the song, "heavy metal thunder," is believed by some to be the source of the rock music term "heavy metal," although the term previously appeared in the cult novel *Naked Lunch* by Beat novelist William Burroughs.

1967: The present day **Warner Music Canada** is first established in Canada as Warner Reprise Canada Ltd.

1967: London Records of Canada (1967) Ltd. evolves from the London Gramophone Co. of Canada.

1967: *Rolling Stone* magazine first publishes on November 9th from San Francisco.

1968: The Canadian Radio-Television Commission (CRTC) is created under a new broadcast legislation.

Bruce Cockburn

1968: The **Sackville** record label is established.

1968: The 16-piece big band **Boss Brass**, led by **Rob McConnell**, is formed.

1968: Joni Mitchell's composition *Both Sides Now* is recorded by Judy Collins and included on Mitchell's album CLOUDS, for which she receives a Grammy Award in the category of Best Folk Performance.

1968: Terry Jacks meets **Susan Pesklevits** on CBC-TV's *Music Hop* show out of Vancouver. The two subsequently marry and form the group **The Poppy Family**.

1968: Celine Dion is born on March 30th in Charlemagne, Quebec.

1968: *Hair*, "The American Tribal Love-Rock Musical," opens on April 28th at New York's Biltmore Theatre, with musical score and direction by Montreal composer **Galt MacDermot**.

1968: When band founder founder Al Kooper and saxophonist Randy Brecker leave Blood, Sweat & Tears after recording the group's first album, CHILD IS FATHER TO THE MAN, **David Clayton-Thomas** is recruited as the group's vocalist and frontman.

1968: Buffalo Springfield play their final concert on May 5th in Long Beach, California.

1968: The Stampeders, now based full-time in Toronto, are reduced from a sextet to a trio as three of the group's members head back to Calgary, leaving Rich Dodson, Ronnie King, and Kim Berly to carry on.

1968: Steppenwolf earn their first gold record in the U.S. on September 19th with the single *Born To Be Wild*, a song later featured along with *The Pusher* and **The Band**'s *The Weight* in the soundtrack of the film *Easy Rider*, starring Dennis Hopper, Peter Fonda, and Jack Nicholson, released in 1969.

1968: The Guess Who enter A&R Studios in New York on September 19th to start recording their debut album, *Wheatfield Soul*.

1968: Skip Prokop of the **The Paupers** flies to San Francisco to be part of a three-day live jam session at Bill Graham's Fillmore Auditorium with Al Kooper, Michael Bloomfield, Elvin Bishop, Carlos Santana, and Steve Miller, among others, recorded for a double-album titled THE LIVE ADVENTURES OF MIKE BLOOMFIELD AND AL KOOPER.

1968: Ian & Sylvia play the Cafe Au Go Go in New York prior to a nationwide tour of college campuses and begin to form their back-up band the Great Speckled Bird (after a Wilf Carter song) with the addition of a pedal steel guitar.

1969: *Singalong Jubilee* goes national on the CBC-TV network giving viewers across the country their first glimpse of a show regular, **Anne Murray**.

1969: Rush, initially comprised of bassist/vocalist **Geddy Lee**, guitarist **Alex Lifeson**, and drummer **John Rutsey**, form at Vanier High in Willowdale, a suburb of Toronto.

1969: Montreal drummer **Corky Laing**, a former member of local groups like **Bartholomew Plus Three** and **Energy**, joins the group Mountain, famous for the song *Mississippi Queen*.

1969: Tom Northcott returns to Canada following a three year period in England, and within a year he appears in concert with the **Vancouver Symphony Orchestra** performing his original composition *And God Created Woman*.

1969: Jackie Rae has his biggest chart success as his *Please Don't Go* becomes an international hit for Eddy Arnold and is named country song of the year by ASCAP, while *Happy Heart*, co-written with German bandleader James Last, is a million seller for Andy Williams, one of the many artists who cover the song.

1969: Hamilton, Ontario native **Harrison Kennedy** joins Detroit-based group Chairmen of the Board, who have their biggest hit, *Give Me Just A Little More Time*, the following year.

1969: Blood, Sweat & Tears' self-titled LP, featuring vocalist **David Clayton-Thomas,** who is also the writer of a couple of the record's biggest songs, notably the hit *Spinning Wheel*, is released on January 18th and hits number one on the *Billboard* chart on March 29th, holding this position non-consecutively for seven weeks.

1969: The Irish Rovers, in the wake of the enormous success of their **Shel Silverstein**-penned single *The Unicorn* which sells over eight million copies worldwide, launch an Australian tour before returning to the U.S. for a full schedule of TV and college engagements.

1969: Neil Young returns to Toronto in February for a week long appearance at the Riverboat Coffee House in Yorkville Village as he resumes his solo career after the break up of Buffalo Springfield.

1969: Joni Mitchell plays Carnegie Hall in New York on February 1st.

1969: Buffy Sainte-Marie and **Ian & Sylvia** play the Fillmore East in New York on March 7th.

1969: The Band perform their first concert as an independent group on April 17th at Winterland in San Francisco, and **Robbie Robertson** is so overwhelmed by the experience that he can only perform while under hypnosis.

1969: Rock orchestra **Lighthouse**, formed by rock dummer **Skip Prokop** and jazz pianist **Paul Hoffert**, debut in Toronto at the Rock Pile on May 14th and plays Carnegie Hall on June 25th in New York for the first time, with radio personality Murray the K awarding a free Lighthouse album, courtesy of RCA, to everyone in the audience.

1969: The Mandala, featuring Domenic Troiano, Roy Kenner, and Whitey Glan, hold their last "soul crusade" on June 1st.

1969: John Lennon and Yoko Ono (Plastic Ono Band) record the single *Give Peace A Chance* on June 2nd during their bed-in at Montreal's Queen Elizabeth Hotel. Joining in are guests Tommy Smothers on guitar, Timothy

Leary, Beatles' press officer Derek Taylor, a Toronto rabbi, and a host of others, including local journalists and a TV camera crew. The song is recorded on an 8-track machine supplied by Montreal studio owner **André Perry**.

1969: Toronto's first major rock festival, the two-day Toronto Pop Festival, is held on June 21st at Varsity Stadium and Varsity Arena, where 50,000 people see performances by **Steppenwolf**, **The Band**, Procol Harum, Chuck Berry, **Blood, Sweat & Tears**, The Byrds, Jose Feliciano, Al Kooper, Tiny Tim, Slim Harpo, **Robert Charlebois**, **Kensington Market,** and **Tobi Lark**. For Steppenwolf, it marks their first ever appearance in their hometown.

1969: Crowbar, Ronnie Hawkins' new backing band and then simply known as **And Many Others**, is formed and subsequently make their U.S. debut with Hawkins in New York at the Fillmore East on the same bill as Joe Cocker, with Bob Dylan in the audience.

1969: Toronto group **Motherlode** has a number one hit in Canada and Top 20 hit in the U.S. with the single *When I Die* from their debut album of the same name.

1969: Neil Young makes his first in-concert appearance with Crosby, Stills and Nash on July 25th at New York's Fillmore East.

1969: The Rock 'N' Roll Revival, held at Toronto's Varsity Stadium on September 13th, features the debut of John Lennon and Yoko Ono's Plastic Ono Band with guitarist Eric Clapton, as well as performances by Chuck Berry, Alice Cooper, Tony Joe White, Little Richard, Bo Diddley, Chicago Transit Authority, Jerry Lee Lewis, Cat Mother and the All-Night News Boys, Doug Kershaw, **Milkwood,** and Screaming Lord Sutch

backed by local bluesmen **Whiskey Howl**. The event produces the PLASTIC ONO BAND — LIVE IN TORONTO album, while John and Yoko's performance is eventually cut from a film made of the concert (*Sweet Toronto*) because the producer fears that the couple appear too spaced out.

1969: The Guess Who perform *Undun* on **Dick Clark's** *American Bandstand* on August 16th and are presented with a gold record for their Top 10 hit single, *These Eyes*.

The Guess Who

1969: The Archies' *Sugar, Sugar*, co-written by Montreal-native **Andy Kim** and Jeff Barry and arguably the definitive "bubble gum" song, hits the number one position on the *Billboard* Hot 100 singles chart on September 20th, where it remains for four weeks.

1969: As her debut album THIS WAY IS MY WAY is released, **Anne Murray** plays her

first major solo concert at Saint Mary's University in Halifax, Nova Scotia, organized by **Leonard Rambeau**, a student placement officer on campus, who will later become Murray's manager, a position he holds for close to 25 years until his death in April 1995.

1969: Bonnie Dobson makes her London, England debut at the Queen Elizabeth Music Hall on November 3rd and soon becomes a regular performer on television, radio, and in concert not only in the U.K., but throughout Europe as well.

1969: John and Yoko spend five days at Ronnie Hawkins' farm near Toronto in December, then meet with Prime Minister Pierre Trudeau in Ottawa on December 22nd as well as Health Minister and John Munro to discuss drug abuse.

1969: True North Records is founded in Toronto by Bernie Finkelstein.

1969: GRT of Canada Ltd., the Canadian subsidiary of General Recorded Tape of California, opens initially in London, Ontario but moves to Toronto later in the year.

1969: Toronto's **Panavista Production** pitches the Canadian record industry on the idea of using its audio-visual service to make VTR recordings on one-inch tape of various recording artists for use in promotion or selling the artists to agents, bookers, and distributors.

1969: Columbia Records in Canada announces its first releases on cassette tape.

1969: A group of 12 key Canadian Top 40

radio stations form the *Maple Leaf System* (MLS) to give exposure to Canadian talent by programming a minimum of three local records each week.

1970: A&M Records of Canada Ltd., the Canadian subsidiary of A&M Records, is established in Canada.

1970: Aquarius Records Ltd. is founded in Montreal by Terry Flood, Donald Tarlton, Bob Lemm, Jack and Dan Lazare.

1970: MCA Records Canada is established in Toronto.

1970: Bruce Cockburn provides the soundtrack for the critically-acclaimed Canadian feature film, *Goin' Down the Road*.

1970: Full Tilt Boogie Band, formed by ex-Pauper **Brad Campbell**, guitarist **John Till**, pianist **Richard Bell**, organist **Ken Pearson**, and drummer Clark Pierson, make their debut in May as Janis Joplin's backing band at a Hell's Angels' benefit in San Rafael, California.

1970: Leonard Cohen tours extensively in America and in Europe with backing group The Army, which includes producer and longtime friend Bob Johnston, and appears at the Isle of Wight Festival in England on the same bill as Jimi Hendrix who is making one of his last concert appearances.

1970: The Band makes the cover of *Time* magazine on January 12th, and **Garth Hudson** is referred to as "beyond question, the most brilliant organist in the rock world."

1970: Ronnie Hawkins and rock journalist **Ritchie Yorke** set out on an around the world trip as peace emissaries for John Lennon, risking their lives at one point to hold up posters in both Chinese and English at the Hong Kong/China border that read: "War Is Over (If You Want It)."

1970: The Five Bells, formed around husband and wife team of **Cliff** and **Anne Edwards**, changes its name to **The Bells** following the departure of **Anne Edwards** and the arrival of her sister **Jackie Ralph**, whose unique vocal style, showcased at its sensual best on the group's biggest hit *Stay Awhile*, written by **Ken Tobias**, eventually defined the group's sound and brought them to the concert stage and television appearances on The Tonight Show and *The Merv Griffin Show*, among others.

1970: The Guess Who hit the top of the *Billboard* Hot 100 chart on May 9th with the single *American Woman/No Sugar Tonight,* where it remains for three weeks, making them the first Canadian group to have a number one record in the U.S.A. and the first to have a Top 10 album (AMERICAN WOMAN). One week later on May 16th soon after an appearance at the White House in Washington, D.C. with Prince Charles and Princess Anne in attendance (where they are politely asked by First Lady Pat Nixon not to perform *American Woman*), founding member **Randy Bachman** decides to leave the group after one last concert at New York's Fillmore East and is replaced by former members of the Winnipeg group **Gettysburg Address**, guitarists **Greg Leskiw** and **Kurt "The Walrus" Winter**.

1970: The Poppy family hit the number two position on *Billboard*'s Hot 100 singles chart with *Which Way You Goin', Billy?*, which sells over 50,000 copies in Canada, as lead singer **Susan Jacks** becomes the first Canadian female singer to have a gold record.

1970: Blood Sweat & Tears embark on a tour of Yugoslavia, Romania, and Poland in June, one of the first tours by a rock band from the west of then East Soviet-bloc countries.

1970: The Festival Express Toronto-Calgary train/concert excursion sets out from Toronto on June 28th with **The Band**, Janis Joplin and the **Full Tilt Boogie Band**, Delaney & Bonnie and Friends, Buddy Guy's Band, **Ian & Sylvia and the Great Speckled Bird**, Eric Andersen, Tom Rush, **James and the Good Brothers**, The New Riders of the Purple Sage, **Robert Charlebois**, **Mashmakhan,** and Bob Weir of the Grateful Dead on board.

1970: *A Ballet High*, a collaboration between **Lighthouse** and the Royal Winnipeg Ballet, opens at Ottawa's National Arts Centre in July before moving on to Toronto's St. Lawrence Centre.

1970: Mashmakhan (formerly The Triangle) make an immediate impact with the single *As The Years Go By* from their self-titled debut album at home and abroad, especially in Japan where the group makes its biggest mark selling close to 800,000 copies of the single there.

1970: The Strawberry Fields Rock Festival, organized to take advantage of the publicity surrounding John Lennon's aborted peace festival which was to have happened in July, is held over three days at the Mosport Race Track in Ontario during August.

1970: Janis Joplin and the **Full Tilt Boogie Band** play their final concert at Havard Stadium, Cambridge, Massachusetts in front of 40,000 fans, and enter the studio in the fall to record her last album, PEARL, before she dies on October 4th.

1970: Ian Tyson and the Great Speckled Bird star in new CTV series, *Nashville North*.

1970: Toronto-born songwriter/ producer/ recording artist **R. Dean Taylor** hits the Top 5 of the *Billboard* Hot 100 singles chart with *Indiana Wants Me*.

1970: Anne Murray makes her first appearance on CBS-TV's *The Glenn Campbell Goodtime Hour*, where, over the next two years, she becomes a regular guest, and receives a gold record on November 10th for *Snowbird* on *The Merv Griffin Show*, the first record by a Canadian female singer to exceed a million sales in the U.S.A.

1970: Joni Mitchell, who has gained international recognition as a songwriter through the Judy Collins rendition of *Both Sides Now* and the Matthews

Blood, Sweat & Tears

Lighthouse

Southern Comfort and Crosby, Stills, Nash & Young versions of *Woodstock*, picks up a gold record in the U.S.A. for her third album, LADIES OF THE CANYON.

1970: Crosby, Stills, Nash & Young's *Déjà Vu* is the year's best-selling album in the U.S.A.

1970: Crowbar appears with Van Morrison at Toronto's Massey Hall on November 22nd shortly before the release of their album BAD MANORS and the single *Oh What A Feeling*, the biggest hit of their career and the first Canadian single released after the inception of the CRTC Canadian Content rulings for AM radio on January 18th, 1971.

1971: The first annual **Juno Awards** celebration is held on February 22nd at the St. Lawrence Hall in Toronto.

Tower of Song

**FIRST
ANNUAL
JUNO
AWARDS**
February 22, 1971
St. Lawrence Hall,
Toronto
Host:
George Wilson,
CFRB Toronto

Snowbird
1971

"Spread your tiny wings and fly away," an unforgettable line from the song *Snowbird*, is perhaps the best way to describe the Canadian music industry during the celebration of the first Juno Awards in 1971, for a fledgling industry came of age with the incredible success of this song.

Snowbird

1971 JUNO AWARD WINNERS

(For the 1970 Voting Year)

TOP FEMALE VOCALIST	**Anne Murray**
TOP MALE VOCALIST	**Gordon Lightfoot**
TOP VOCAL INSTRUMENTAL GROUP	**The Guess Who**
TOP FOLK SINGER (OR GROUP)	**Bruce Cockburn**
TOP COUNTRY SINGER, MALE	**Stompin' Tom Connors**
TOP COUNTRY SINGER, FEMALE	**Myrna Lorrie**
TOP COUNTRY INSTRUMENTAL VOCAL GROUP	**The Mercey Brothers**
SPECIAL AWARD CANADIAN COMPOSER	**Gene MacLellan**
BEST PRODUCED SINGLE	**Brian Ahern** for *Snowbird* by **Anne Murray**
BEST PRODUCED MOR ALBUM	**Brian Ahern** for HONEY, WHEAT & LAUGHTER by **Anne Murray**
TOP CANADIAN CONTENT COMPANY	**Quality Records**
TOP RECORD COMPANY IN PROMOTIONAL ACTIVITIES	**Capitol Records of Canada**
TOP RECORD COMPANY	**Capitol Records of Canada**
BROADCASTER OF THE YEAR	**Standard Broadcasting**
MUSIC JOURNALIST OF THE YEAR	**Dave Bist,** *Montreal Gazette*
MUSIC INDUSTRY MAN OF THE YEAR	**Pierre Juneau**

Myrna Lorrie

Snowbird emerged as the story from these first Junos, responsible for 5 of the 16 trophies presented, including Anne Murray's first ever Juno, which she picks up for Top Female Vocalist, and the Composer of the Year Juno, which is taken home by Gene MacLellan, the song's writer. Anne Murray appeared on stage wearing shoes, not barefoot like on *Singalong Jubilee* and *Frank's Bandstand*, and referred to her management team as the "Maritime Mafia," a name that soon became synonymous with Balmur Ltd.,

her management company. Almost 40 percent of the Junos were presented to industry organizations, and the award presenters were all Canadian music industry executives. Just over a month after the Canadian Content regulations for radio had taken effect, Pierre Juneau, Chairman of the Canadian Radio-Television Commission (CRTC), who had been the person most responsible for their introduction and after whom the awards are named, received an award as Music Industry Man of the Year.

1971: Wilf Carter (a.k.a. **Montana Slim**) is inducted into the Nashville Song-writers Association Hall of Fame.

1971: Leonard Cohen provides the soundtrack for the Warren Beatty film *McCabe and Mrs. Miller*.

1971: The **Ian Tyson** Show (formerly known as *Nashville North*) debuts on the CTV Network.

1971: Ten-year-old **Rene Simard** makes his performance debut at Montreal's Place des Arts and is an instant hit.

1971: Trumpeter **Maynard Ferguson**, having previously moved to the U.K., makes his North American debut with his 17-piece English band.

1971: The Irish Rovers begin a five-year run with their own CBC-TV series out of Vancouver.

The Irish Rovers

1971: Dorothy Collins is given a star-ring role in the Stephen Sondheim musi-cal *Follies*, in which she sings one of the showstoppers, *Losing My Mind*. She receives a Tony nomination for her per-formance.

1971: Blue Rodeo's **Jim Cuddy** and **Greg Keelor** are first down and 110 yards to go with their music career as they play for the North Toronto Collegiate football team.

Gene MacLellan performing with Anne Murray

1971: Sixteen-year-old singer/songwriter **Shirley Eikhard**, who has already appeared on CBC-TV's *Singalong Jubilee* and at the Mariposa Folk Festival, gets her big career break as her song *It Takes Time* is recorded by **Anne Murray**, and subsequently signs with Capitol Records.

1971: Anne Murray moves to Toronto from Springhill, Nova Scotia in January, marking a new era in her career and in the history of Canadian music.

1971: Ocean have a hit on their hands with *Put Your Hand in the Hand*, a song written by Gene MacLellan who also wrote Anne Murray's hit *Snowbird*.

1971: Rita MacNeil moves from Big Pond, Cape Breton, and moves to Toronto, where she takes odd jobs as a cleaner and records her self-titled debut album.

1971: Guitarist **Danny Marks** leaves **Edward Bear** and joins **Rick James' Stone City Band**, while **Edward Bear**, led by drummer/vocalist **Larry Evoy**, hit the top of the charts with the singles *Last Song* (1972) and *Close Your Eyes* (1973).

1971: Canadian Content Regulations for AM radio go into effect on January 18th, requiring that 30 percent of all musical compositions played between 6:00 am and midnight be Canadian.

1971: April Wine, who have become a regular attraction at the Laugh-In club in Montreal, record their first album for Aquarius Records in February.

1971: Janis Joplin, backed by Canadian group **The Full Tilt Boogie Band**, tops the *Billboard* Hot 100 singles chart for two weeks in March with the Kris Kristofferson-penned song *Me and Bobby McGee* from the album PEARL. The album was left unfinished at the time of her death in October 1970.

1971: Gordon Lightfoot is the first non-classical act booked to play New York's Philharmonic Hall at Lincoln Center on May 3rd.

1971: The Crosby, Stills, Nash & Young album FOUR WAY STREET hits the number one position on the *Billboard* albums chart on May 15th, the group's second consecutive number one album following DEJA VU in 1970.

1971: The Band complete their first European tour on June 3rd with a concert at London's celebrated Royal Albert Hall.

1971: Crowbar make their U.S. debut at the Whisky A Go Go in Los Angeles during the summer and return to Massey Hall on September 23rd for a homecoming concert date.

Procol Harum with Ritchie Yorke

1971: The **Edmonton Symphony Orchestra**, with conductor **Lawrence Leonard** and the 24-member **Da Camera Singers**, record a live album with British group Procol Harum for A&M Records during the course of a concert on August 6th at the Jubilee Auditorium in Edmonton, Alberta. This album, PROCOL HARUM WITH THE EDMONTON SYMPHONY ORCHESTRA, becomes the group's most successful LP in the wake of the hit single, *Conquistador*.

1971: The Stampeders' single *Sweet City Woman* follows up a chart-topping summer in Canada by climbing into the Top 10 of *Billboard*'s Hot 100 singles chart on September 11th, peaking on this day at number eight.

1971: Bob Dylan joins **The Band** onstage for their encore at a New Year's concert at the New York Academy of Music. The Band's set is later released as the live album, ROCK OF AGES.

1971: David Clayton-Thomas makes his last appearance (for the moment) with **Blood, Sweat & Tears** at the Anaheim Convention Center on New Year's Eve, which also marks the last gig for **The Poppy Family** who are on the same bill.

Sweet City Woman 1972

2ND ANNUAL JUNO AWARDS
February 28, 1972
Centennial Ballroom, Inn on the Park, Toronto
Host:
George Wilson, CFRB Toronto

THE STAMPEDERS

In 1972, the Juno Awards earned a new level of respectability, as Marci McDonald noted in *The Toronto Star:* "From an industry that has barely begun to burgeon — scarcely a year since the institution of radio's 30 percent Canadian content quotas — it was a ceremony that lasted not quite an hour, lagged not a second and was carried off with such simple panache and dispatch that it made all those interminable glory shows, the Grammys and the Oscars and even the Canadian film awards, look like amateur night at the high school gym."

Sweet City Woman

1972 JUNO AWARD WINNERS

(For the 1971 voting year)

FEMALE VOCALIST OF THE YEAR	**Anne Murray**
OUTSTANDING PERFORMANCE OF THE YEAR, FEMALE	**Ginette Reno**
MALE VOCALIST OF THE YEAR	**Gordon Lightfoot**
OUTSTANDING PERFORMANCE OF THE YEAR, MALE	**Joey Gregorash**
VOCAL INSTRUMENTAL GROUP OF THE YEAR	**The Stampeders**
OUTSTANDING PERFORMANCE OF THE YEAR, GROUP	**Lighthouse**
FOLK SINGER OF THE YEAR	**Bruce Cockburn**
MALE COUNTRY SINGER OF THE YEAR	**Stompin' Tom Connors**
FEMALE COUNTRY SINGER OF THE YEAR	**Myrna Lorrie**
COUNTRY GROUP OF THE YEAR	**The Mercey Brothers**
COMPOSER OF THE YEAR	**Rich Dodson** (**The Stampeders**)
BEST PRODUCED SINGLE OF THE YEAR	**Mel Shaw** for *Sweet City Woman* by **The Stampeders**
BEST PRODUCED MOR ALBUM	**Brian Ahern** for TALK IT OVER IN THE MORNING by **Anne Murray**
CANADIAN CONTENT COMPANY OF THE YEAR	**GRT of Canada**
RECORD COMPANY IN PROMOTIONAL ACTIVITIES	**Kinney Music Of Canada**
RECORD COMPANY OF THE YEAR	**Kinney Music Of Canada**
BROADCASTER OF THE YEAR	**The CHUM Group**
MUSIC JOURNALIST OF THE YEAR	**Ritchie Yorke**
SPECIAL JUNO FOR CONTRIBUTION TO CANADIAN MUSIC	**George Hamilton IV**

Ginette Reno

Riding the success of their international hit single *Sweet City Woman*, The Stampeders rounded up three Junos, but the names of Anne Murray, Gordon Lightfoot, Bruce Cockburn, Stompin' Tom Connors, Myrna Lorrie, Brian Ahern, and The Mercey Brothers again appeared on the awards.

The short-lived Outstanding Performance categories for male, female, and group were first introduced, while Nashville-based George Hamilton IV became the first foreign performer to win a Juno for recording three albums of all-Canadian material.

1972: Bachman-Turner Overdrive evolves from the Winnipeg country/rock group **Brave Belt**.

1972: Country singer **Dick Damron** appears on the Grand Ole Opry in Nashville.

1972: Journeyman musician **David Foster**, at this point a member of the Vancouver group **Skylark**, heads for Los Angeles with the band in a Volkswagen van to record for Capitol Records. While attending a meeting at the Capitol Tower, the van is broken into and everything is stolen, but Skylark does not leave L.A. empty-handed as their album produces the hit single, *Wildflower*.

1972: Guitarist **Domenic Troiano** and vocalist **Roy Kenner** join the **James Gang**.

1972: Larry Good replaces **James Ackroyd** in **James and the Good Brothers** and the three brothers debut at The Riverboat in Toronto.

1972: While touring Europe in *Catch My Soul*, a stage musical version of Shakespeare's Othello, **Claudja Barry** catches the ear of German producer Jorgen Korduletsch who signs her to his Lollipop label in Munich. She subsequently moves to Munich and her singing career, marked by a number of international hits in the disco field, including the biggest, *Boogie Woogie Dancin' Shoes* (1978), begins in earnest, and she becomes a founding member of European supergroup *Boney M.*

1972: The band **A Foot In Coldwater** — British slang for "bad luck" — which includes former members of Toronto-based groups like **Lords Of London** and **Nucleus**, has its self-titled, debut album released on the Daffodil/Capitol label,

Crowbar with Pierre Trudeau

featuring the classic single *Make Me Do Anything You Want*.

1972: April Wine's cover of the song *You Could Have Been A Lady*, which had been a British hit for Hot Chocolate, marks the group's earliest visit to the U.S. Top 40 chart.

1972: Terry Black and **Laurel Ward**, who began their singing collaboration when they both appeared in the Toronto production of *Hair*, have a hit internationally with their single *Goin' Down (On the Road To L.A.)*.

1972: Los Angeles Mayor Sam Yorty declares February 14th "**Steppenwolf** Day" on the occasion of the group's announced "retirement" which actually becomes a sabbatical as the group returns after a few years with a new line up but still led by John Kay.

1972: Neil Young's HAR-VEST album reaches number one on the *Billboard* album chart, where it remains for three weeks in March, and he tops the Billboard Hot 100 singles chart with *Heart Of Gold*, recorded in Nashville with Linda Ronstadt and James Taylor on back-up vocals.

1972: The Maple Music Junket, a project designed to develop markets in Europe for Canadian pop records, is launched on June 2nd by Canada's music industry with financial support from the federal government which is used in part to entertain a party of 100 leading writers, editors, broadcasters, producers, and filmmakers from more than a dozen European countries at receptions and concerts in Montreal and Toronto.

1972: The tribal love-rock musical *Hair* closes on Broadway on July 1st after 1,729 performances.

1972: Ottawa's **Five Man Electrical Band** (who had topped the Canadian charts in 1967 as **The Staccatos** with *Half Past Midnight*), follow up with their hit *Signs*, which reaches number

three on *Billboard*'s Hot 100, with the top U.S. hit *Absolutely Right*.

1972: Heart forms in Vancouver during August with members of the former Seattle band Hocus Pocus that featured Ann Wilson, Roger Fisher, and Steve Fossen.

1972: Danny Whitten, former member of Neil Young's group Crazy Horse, dies in Los Angeles on November 18th of a heroin overdose, just as Bruce Berry, a former roadie for **Crosby, Stills, Nash & Young**, died of the same drug during this period, tragic events memorialized in Neil Young's TONIGHT'S THE NIGHT album (1975).

1972: **Lighthouse** lead singer **Bob McBride** records his first solo album while still with the group, and **Paul Hoffert** plays his last concert with Lighthouse on New Year's Eve, until their brief reunion some years later.

*L*ast Song 1973

Gordon Lightfoot captured the spirit of this particularly patriotic awards ceremony as he accepted two Junos: "I've been accepted in my native country on a scale I never dreamed possible. I'm going to sing the praises of Canada far and wide for as long as I can."

FEMALE VOCALIST OF THE YEAR	**Anne Murray**
OUTSTANDING PERFORMANCE OF THE YEAR, FEMALE	**Ginette Reno**
MALE VOCALIST OF THE YEAR	**Gordon Lightfoot**
OUTSTANDING PERFORMANCE OF THE YEAR, MALE	**Bob McBride (Lighthouse)**
VOCAL INSTRUMENTAL GROUP OF THE YEAR	**Lighthouse**
OUTSTANDING PERFORMANCE OF THE YEAR, GROUP	**Edward Bear**
FOLK SINGER OF THE YEAR	**Bruce Cockburn**
OUTSTANDING PERFORMANCE OF THE YEAR, FOLK	**Valdy**
MALE COUNTRY SINGER OF THE YEAR	**Stompin' Tom Connors**
FEMALE COUNTRY SINGER OF THE YEAR	**Shirley Eikhard**
COUNTRY GROUP OF THE YEAR	**The Mercey Brothers**
BEST PRODUCED SINGLE	*Last Song* **Edward Bear**; **Gene Martynec**, producer
BEST PRODUCED MOR ALBUM	ANNIE, **Anne Murray**; **Brian Ahern**, producer
CANADIAN CONTENT COMPANY OF THE YEAR	**Capitol Records of Canada**
PROMOTION COMPANY OF THE YEAR	**RCA Ltd.**
RECORD COMPANY OF THE YEAR	**WEA Music of Canada Ltd.**
COMPOSER OF THE YEAR	**Gordon Lightfoot**
BROADCASTER OF THE YEAR	**VOCM**, St. John's, Newfoundland
MUSIC INDUSTRY MAN OF THE YEAR	**Arnold Gosewich**
MUSIC JOURNALIST OF THE YEAR	**Peter Goddard**
OUTSTANDING CONTRIBUTION TO THE CANADIAN MUSIC SCENE	**David Clayton-Thomas**

Stompin' Tom Connors

Other double awards winners were Anne Murray, Edward Bear, and Lighthouse, while Valdy picked up his first Juno in the newly-introduced category of Outstanding Performance of the Year, Folk. David Clayton-Thomas of Blood, Sweat & Tears was honored with a special Juno for his contribution to the Canadian music scene, and the national Film Board documentary, *Rock-A-Bye*, profiling the Canadian pop music business, was premiered.

1973: The Toronto franchise of Chicago's famed comedy institution Second City is opened in Toronto by **Andrew Alexander**, whose alumni includes Canadians **Dan Aykroyd**, **John Candy**, **Martin Short**, **Dave Thomas**, **Eugene Levy**, **Catherine O'Hara**, and **Andrea Martin** as well as U.S. imports Joe Flaherty, Brian Doyle-Murray, and Gilda Radner.

1973: In one of his earliest acting roles, **Victor Garber**, former vocalist of the Canadian group **Sugar Shoppe**, takes the lead role of Jesus in the movie adaptation of Stephen Schwartz's stage musical *Godspell*.

1973: Harmonium, featuring **Serge Fiori**, **Michel Normandeau,** and **Louis Valois**, debut at Montreal's Le Patriote club.

1973: By the time of the release of **April Wine's** sophomore album, *Electric Jewels*, **David** and **Ritchie Henman** had left the group to be replaced by **Jim Clench**, **Jerry Mercer**, and **Gary Moffet**. With the new line-up, the group becomes one of the first Canadian bands to headline in arenas across Canada, playing in 80 towns and cities on their Electric Adventure Tour. The excursion results in a live album, recorded in Halifax, Nova Scotia and produced by fellow-Canadian **Gene Cornish** and Dino Danelli, members of **The Young Rascals** who had first seen them in concert at Massey Hall in Toronto.

1973: **Neil Young** interrupts his Carnegie Hall concert on January 23rd to tell a joyous audience that "peace has come." The Vietnam War is over. Young and the Stray Gators launch into a spirited version of *Southern Man*. Young's documentary film *Journey Through the Past*, based on events in his own life, premieres in April at the U.S. Film Festival in Dallas.

Edward Bear

1973: **Rush** begin recording their debut album in Toronto during March with producer **Terry Brown**.

1973: Vancouver group **Skylark**, featuring keyboardist **David Foster** and vocalist **Donny Gerrard**, begin a five-day stand on April 10th at the Troubadour in Los Angeles with Link Wray as their single *Wildflower* hits the Top 10 on the *Billboard* chart.

1973: **The Diamonds** reunite for the first time in 14 years for a *Midnight Special* show on April 27th that features other golden oldie acts like Ed "Kookie" Byrnes, Little Richard, The Penguins, Little Anthony, Chubby Checker, and host Jerry Lee Lewis.

1973: **Bachman-Turner Overdrive** releases its first, self-titled LP on May Day.

1973: **The DeFranco Family** perform *Heartbeat, It's A Lovebeat* on Dick Clark's *American Bandstand*.

1973: On his show *Let's Be Personal* on radio station CFRB in Toronto, **Gordon Sinclair** delivers an emotional editorial

The Mercey Brothers

Detroit Symphony Orchestra to record it for release as *Americans*, which receives orders of five million copies. Sinclair records a version — *The Americans (A Canadian's Opinion)* — with *Battle Hymn Of the Republic* playing in the background which reaches number 24 on the *Billboard* chart.

1973: At their annual free concert in September at Toronto's Nathan Phillips Square in front of 50,000 people, **Lighthouse** are presented with a platinum record by Toronto Mayor David Crombie for their album LIGHTHOUSE LIVE! They are the first Canadian group to reach the sales plateau of 100,000 records in Canada.

1973: Beau Dommage debut at the University of Quebec at Montreal in October.

1973: Anne Murray appears at the Troubadour in Los Angeles on Thanksgiving and is photographed in the company of audience members John Lennon, Harry Nilsson, Alice Cooper, and Mickey Dolenz of The Monkees.

on the lack of support the American Red Cross is receiving outside of the U.S. as it verges on bankruptcy. A number of American border radio stations pick up the editorial and listener reaction is immediate. **Byron MacGregor**, the 25-year-old news director at powerhouse radio station CKLW Windsor/Detroit, reads it on the air with *America the Beautiful* in the background. So overwhelming is the reaction from CKLW's Detroit/Philadelphia audience that Detroit's Westbound Records takes McGregor into the studio with the

*S*easons In The Sun
1974

4TH ANNUAL JUNO AWARDS
March 25, 1974
Centennial Ballroom, Inn on the Park, Toronto
Host: **George Wilson**, CFRB Toronto

Terry Jacks and **Murray McLauchlan** were the year's big winners as both took home three trophies each. Jacks takes bows for the enormous worldwide success of his single *Seasons In The Sun,* while bemused folkie McLauchlan finds that the success of his *Farmer's Song* single has made him a man outstanding in the country field, joining the company of repeat Juno winners The Mercey Brothers, Stompin' Tom Connors, and Shirley Eikhard.

Seasons In The Sun
1974 JUNO AWARD WINNERS
(For the 1973 Voting Year)

CANADIAN MALE VOCALIST	**Terry Jacks**
CANADIAN FEMALE VOCALIST	**Anne Murray**
CANADIAN GROUP	**Lighthouse**
CANADA'S MOST PROMISING MALE VOCALIST	**Ian Thomas**
CANADA'S MOST PROMISING FEMALE VOCALIST	**Cathy Young**
CANADA'S MOST PROMISING GROUP	**Bachman-Turner Overdrive**
CANADIAN COUNTRY VOCALIST (MALE)	**Stompin' Tom Connors**
CANADIAN COUNTRY VOCALIST (FEMALE)	**Shirley Eikhard**
CANADIAN COUNTRY GROUP	**The Mercey Brothers**
CANADIAN COUNTRY SINGLE	*Farmer's Song*, **Murray McLauchlan**
CANADIAN COUNTRY ALBUM	*To It And At It*, **Stompin' Tom Connors**
CANADIAN COMPOSER	**Murray McLauchlan**
CANADIAN FOLK SINGER	**Valdy**
CANADIAN FOLK SINGLE	**Murray McLauchlan**, *Farmer's Song*
CANADIAN FOLK ALBUM	OLD DAN'S RECORDS, **Gordon Lightfoot**
CANADA'S MOST PROMISING FOLK SINGER	**Dave Nicol**
CANADIAN CONTEMPORARY SINGLE (HIT PARADE)	*Seasons In The Sun*, **Terry Jacks**
CANADIAN POP MUSIC SINGLE (MOR)	*Seasons In The Sun*, **Terry Jacks**
CANADIAN CONTEMPORARY ALBUM (HIT PARADE)	BACHMAN-TURNER OVERDRIVE, **Bachman-Turner Overdrive**
CANADIAN POP MUSIC ALBUM (MOR)	DANNY'S SONG, **Anne Murray**
CANADIAN TOP RECORD COMPANY (MANUFACTURER AND DISTRIBUTOR)	**WEA Music of Canada Ltd.**
CANADIAN RECORD COMPANY IN PROMOTIONAL ACTIVITIES	**A&M Records of Canada Ltd.**
CANADIAN INDEPENDENT LABEL (RECORD LABEL)	**True North Records**
CANADIAN CONTENT RECORD COMPANY	**GRT of Canada Ltd.**

Valdy

This is the first year in which the award winners are not known prior to the awards ceremony. Previously, original awards organizers *RPM Weekly* magazine would publish the names of the winners in advance of the presentations. The musical theme for the evening, *Stars In The North*, performed by the 23-piece orchestra, was composed by Stan Klees, one of the event's organizers. Though not televised, the 1974 Juno Awards were taped as a trial run for future presentations.

1974: Anne Murray's *Send A Little Love My Way* from the movie *Oklahoma Crude* is nominated for an Academy Award as well as a Grammy and a Golden Globe Award.

1974: Bob Dylan and **The Band** open a six-week North American tour on January 3rd at the Chicago Stadium during which they play two concerts at Toronto's Maple Leaf Gardens (January 9 &10). On the second night, they drop by to see **Ronnie Hawkins** playing at The Nickelodeon on Yonge Street to celebrate his 39th birthday. Dylan will later cast Hawkins as "Bob Dylan" in the Rolling Thunder film *Renaldo and Clara*. On February 14th, after 39 shows in 21 cities, the tour comes to an end in Los Angeles at The Forum in front of a star-studded audience which includes Jack Nicholson, **Neil Young**, Carole King, and Ringo Starr. Many of the tracks on Dylan's BEFORE THE FLOOD album are recorded during this concert.

1974: **Terry Jacks** hits the top of the *Billboard* Hot 100 singles chart on March 2nd with *Seasons In The Sun*, an English adaptation (lyrics by Rod McKuen) of the Jacques Brel song *Le Moribond*. The Beach Boys originally recorded the song at Jacks' urging during a recording session with them but they ultimately decided not to release it. Jacks later made some revisions to the song, which he had first heard by **The Kingston Trio** in 1964, and released it himself. Besides becoming an international hit with sales of over 10 million copies, it is one of the biggest selling singles of all time in Canada. In February, *Seasons In The Sun* had become the first Canadian platinum single for sales of over 100,000 copies.

1974: **Rush** release their self-titled debut album on their own Moon Records label in April, and in August,

the album is released by Mercury Records in the U.S. After the departure of original drummer **John Rutsey** for health reasons, St. Catharines, Ontario native **Neil Peart** joins the group before they head out on August 19th on their first U.S. tour, opening for acts like Uriah Heep, Rory Gallagher, and Kiss.

1974: **Ian Thomas** performs with the Hamilton Philharmonic on May 4th in the wake of his hit *Painted Ladies*.

1974: **Alanis Morrissette** is born in Ottawa, Ontario, on June 1st.

1974: On June 29th **Gordon Lightfoot** becomes one of the few artists in rock history to have a single and album hit the top of the influential *Billboard* charts in the U.S. with the album *Sundown* and the single of the same name.

1974: **Neil Young** is back with David Crosby, Stephen Stills, and Graham Nash as the CSN&Y reunion tour begins on July

9th in Seattle. Highlight dates include the Ontario Motor Speedway in California on August 3rd with **The Band**, The Beach Boys, Joe Walsh and Barnstorm, and Jesse Colin Young; Varsity Stadium in Toronto with **The Band** on September 2nd; and Wembley Stadium, London, England with **The Band** and **Joni Mitchell** on September 11th. On November 2nd, the group's SO FAR album hits number one on the *Billboard* album chart.

1974: The **Paul Anka** single *You're Having My Baby*, a duet with Odia Coates, causes a furor with feminist groups who denounce the song for what they consider sexist lyrics. Notwithstanding, the record becomes Anka's first number one single since *Lonely Boy* in 1959.

1974: No stranger to the top of the charts as a songwriter (he co-wrote *Sugar, Sugar*, a number one single for **The Archies**) or as a recording artist (*Baby I Love You, How'd We Ever Get This Way?* and *Be My Baby*), **Andy Kim** has his first number one single on the *Billboard* Hot 100 chart as an artist with *Rock Me Gently*.

1974: CBC Radio's folk series *Touch the Earth*, hosted by **Sylvia Tyson**, debuts on October 1st.

1974: Bachman-Turner Overdrive's NOT FRAGILE hits the number one position on the *Billboard* album chart on October 19th, and the following month both the NOT FRAGILE and BACHMAN-TURNER OVERDRIVE II albums are certified platinum in Canada for sales of over

100,000 copies each, a first for a Canadian group. They round out the year nicely on November 7th with a concert date at New York's Fillmore East and a number one single as two days later *You Ain't Seen Nothin' Yet*, the song that **Randy Bachman** originally didn't want to see released, hits the top of the *Billboard* Hot 100 singles chart.

1974: Having appeared on the cover of *Maclean*'s magazine with an interview by her close friend **Malka Himel** in June, **Joni Mitchell** appears on the cover of *Time* as "Rock 'N' Roll's Leading Lady."

1974: Tom Cochrane makes his recording debut with the album HANG ON TO YOUR RESISTANCE.

1974: Tommy Hunter receives a citiation from the Country Music Hall of Fame in Nashville for "continuous and outstanding contribution to country music."

1974: Having taken up the guitar at age 10, **Kathy Dawn Lang** (a.k.a. **k.d. lang**) begins writing songs in her hometown of Consort, Alberta.

1974: At the age of 60, **Hank Snow** has his seventh number one hit in the U.S. with *Hello Love*.

1974: Domenic Troiano joins **The Guess Who**.

1974: Robert Charlebois collaborates with Frank Zappa on a song titled *Petroleum* in Montreal, and Zappa subsequently guests on Charlebois' 1977 album, SWING CHARLEBOIS SWING.

Joni Mitchell: self-portrait of a superstar

HOW TO OUTWIT A HEART ATTACK

Maclean's

Scientology: pay now, pray later
Why everybody loves to hate the CBC
Secrets of Canada's grand hotels

MURRAY McLAUCHLAN
BOULEVARD

The Homecoming 1975

**5TH
ANNUAL
JUNO
AWARDS**
March 25, 1975
Queen Elizabeth
Theatre, Canadian
National Exhibi-
tion, Toronto
Host:
Paul Anka
Performers:
**Paul Anka,
Stompin' Tom
Connors,
Susan Jacks,
Terry Jacks,
Andy Kim,
Diane Leigh,
Anne Murray,
The Stampeders**

"We owe this occasion to the CBC," Ian Thomas remarked as he received his first Juno award, "and I'm sure they'd like to thank Alcan for the set." The first televised awards were hosted by Paul Anka making a homecoming to Canada just as Hagood Hardy's best-selling single *The Homecoming* was about to hit the charts.

The Homecoming
1975 JUNO AWARD WINNERS
(For the 1974 Voting Year)

CANADIAN MALE VOCALIST	**Terry Jacks**
FEMALE ARTIST OF THE YEAR	**Anne Murray**
MALE ARTIST OF THE YEAR	**Gordon Lightfoot**
GROUP OF THE YEAR	**Bachman-Turner Overdrive**
COUNTRY FEMALE ARTIST OF THE YEAR	**Anne Murray**
COUNTRY MALE ARTIST OF THE YEAR	**Stompin' Tom Connors**
COUNTRY GROUP OF THE YEAR	**The Carlton Showband**
FOLK SINGER (MALE OR FEMALE)	**Murray McLauchlan**
MOST PROMISING NEW FEMALE ARTIST	**Suzanne Stevens**
MOST PROMISING NEW MALE ARTIST	**Gino Vannelli**
MOST PROMISING NEW GROUP	**Rush**
COMPOSER OF THE YEAR	**Paul Anka**
PRODUCER OF THE YEAR	**Randy Bachman**
BEST-SELLING ALBUM OF THE YEAR	NOT FRAGILE, **Bachman-Turner Overdrive**
BEST-SELLING SINGLE OF THE YEAR	*Seasons In The Sun*, **Terry Jacks**
BEST-SELLING INTERNATIONAL ALBUM	BAND ON THE RUN, **Paul McCartney and Wings**
BEST-SELLING INTERNATIONAL SINGLE	*The Night Chicago Died,* **Paper Lace**
BEST ALBUM GRAPHICS	**Bart Schoales** for NIGHT VISION, **Bruce Cockburn**

Andy Kim

Bachman-Turner Overdrive made their first major impression on the Junos as they won three awards, while Anne Murray and Gordon Lightfoot continued their winning ways with two each. As the non-profit industry organization the Canadian Music Awards Association (CMAA) took over the awards presentation, the categories were completely overhauled with sales playing a larger part in the nominations procedure. The actual Juno Award itself was redesigned for television by its original designer, Stan Klees.

1975: Celine Dion's career begins at the age of seven singing the songs of **Ginette Reno** in her parents restaurant in Charlemagne, Quebec. A demo of the song *Ce n'était qu'un reve,* written by Dion's mother, is sent to Reno's manager **René Angelil** who is impressed. He commissions French lyricist Eddy Marnay to write *La Voix du Bon Dieu* for her and supervises Dion's recording of the song.

1975: Kate and Anna McGarrigle record their self-titled debut album for Warner Bros.

1975: Ronnie Prophet takes on the hosting duties of CTV's *Grand Old Country* program.

1975: Rene Simard makes his first appearance at the Olympia in Paris.

1975: *The Homecoming,* originally recorded as a Salada Tea jingle in 1972, is released as a single by its composer **Hagood Hardy** to great acclaim and chart success at home and abroad.

1975: Walter Ostanek earns his title as Canada's Polka King as host of *Polka Time* seen on CKCO-TV in Kitchener, Ontario.

1975: Ofra Harnoy, at age 10, makes her professional debut as a soloist.

1975: Maureen Forrester performs with New York's Metropolitan Opera Company.

1975: Gino Vannelli appears on the long-running U.S. TV show *Soul Train* on January 11th, one of the few white artists ever to do so to that point.

1975: Guitarist **Liona Boyd** makes her New York debut at the Carnegie Recital Hall on March 22nd.

1975: Ian & Sylvia make their last appearance as a duo at Toronto's Horseshoe Tavern in May, and **Sylvia's** first solo album *Woman's World* is released in July, produced by husband **Ian**.

1975: Bachman-Turner Overdrive tour Europe in the spring and kick off their first Canadian tour in Regina on July 28th.

1975: Musician/agent **Billy O'Connor** reunites **The Happy Gang** for one last hoorah at the Canadian National Exhibition in Toronto. Their two concerts, broadcast by the CBC, draw over 30,000 people.

1975: Burton Cummings plays his last gig with **The Guess Who** at the Montreal Forum on September 13th before embarking on a solo career. Since that time, the group with various line-ups, but with original member **Jim Kale** as a constant, has continued to

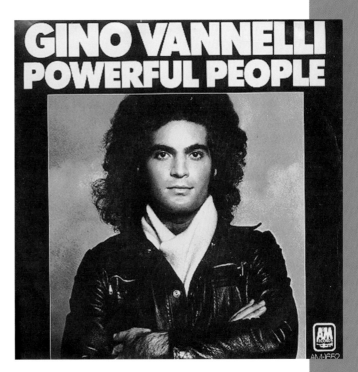

tour and record. There was a short-lived reunion of the original group in 1983.

1975: Canadian comedian and producer **Lorne Michaels'** *Saturday Night Live* is broadcast for the first time on October 11th with George Carlin as guest host. The show's music director is former **Lighthouse** member **Howard Shore** who hires fellow-Canadian **Paul Shaffer** as keyboardist in the band.

1975: Toronto rock trio **Triumph** debut at the Knob Hill Tavern in their hometown on November 12th.

1975: Moxy release their debut, self-titled album fronted by vocalist **Buzz Sherman** who is replaced in 1977 by **Mike Rynoski** (a.k.a. **Mike Reno**), co-founder of **Loverboy** in the early 1980s.

HAGOOD HARDY

Consistently, Canada's Most Successful Instrumental Artist

You Ain't Seen Nothin' Yet
1976

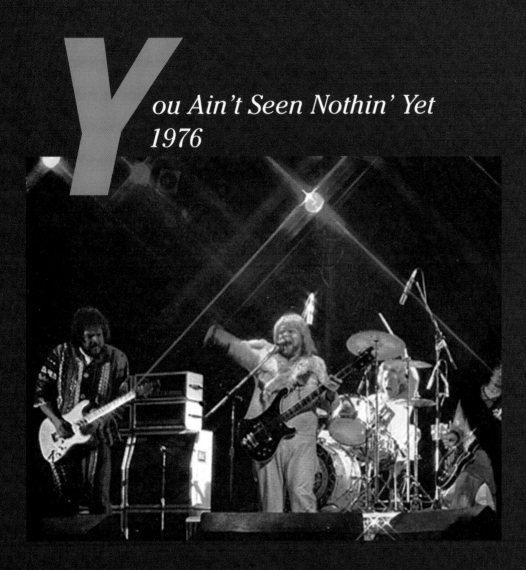

6TH ANNUAL JUNO AWARDS
March 15, 1976
Ryerson
Theatre,
Toronto
Host:
**John Allen
Cameron**
Performers:
**Bachman-
Turner
Overdrive,
Carroll Baker,
Blood, Sweat &
Tears, Hagood
Hardy, Dan Hill,
Michel Pagliaro,
Suzanne
Stevens,
Valdy,
Gino Vannelli.**

Bachman-Turner Overdrive took care of business during the ceremonies, winning three Junos for their FOUR WHEEL DRIVE album project and hit single, *You Ain't Seen Nothin' Yet.* Pianist/composer Hagood Hardy was also involved in three awards, including the new Instrumental Artist of the Year Award for *The Homecoming.*

1976

You Ain't Seen Nothin' Yet
1976 JUNO AWARD WINNERS
(For the Voting Year 1975)

BEST SELLING ALBUM	FOUR WHEEL DRIVE, **Bachman-Turner Overdrive**
BEST SELLING SINGLE	*You Ain't Seen Nothin' Yet*, **Bachman-Turner Overdrive**
FEMALE ARTIST OF THE YEAR	**Joni Mitchell**
MALE ARTIST OF THE YEAR	**Gino Vannelli**
GROUP OF THE YEAR	**Bachman-Turner Overdrive**
COMPOSER OF THE YEAR	**Hagood Hardy** for *The Homecoming*
COUNTRY FEMALE ARTIST OF THE YEAR	**Anne Murray**
COUNTRY MALE ARTIST OF THE YEAR	**Murray McLauchlan**
COUNTRY GROUP OF THE YEAR	**The Mercey Brothers**
FOLK SINGER OF THE YEAR	**Gordon Lightfoot**
BEST NEW FEMALE ARTIST OF THE YEAR	**Patricia Dahlquist**
BEST NEW MALE ARTIST	**Dan Hill**
BEST NEW GROUP	**Myles & Lenny**
INSTRUMENTAL ARTIST OF THE YEAR	**Hagood Hardy**
BEST ALBUM GRAPHICS	**Bart Schoales** for JOY WILL FIND A WAY, **Bruce Cockburn**
PRODUCER OF THE YEAR	**Peter Anastasoff** for *The Homecoming*, **Hagood Hardy**
RECORDING ENGINEER OF THE YEAR	**Michel Ethier** for DOMPIERRE, DOMPIERRE
INTERNATIONAL SINGLE	**Captain & Tennille**, *Love Will Keep Us Together*
INTERNATIONAL ALBUM	**Elton John**, GREATEST HITS

Carroll Baker

Although she didn't win an award, Carroll Baker set her career alight with a stunning rendition of I've Never Been This Far Before, a performance that, in part, led to her subsequent signing to RCA Records. The newly-formed Canadian Academy of Recording Arts & Sciences (CARAS) took over the annual organization and presentation of the Junos, and to mark the transition, Juno founder Walt Grealis was presented with a "People Award" by Randy Bachman, inscribed "You were always there when we needed you," and signed The Musicians of Canada. All categories are now voted on by the CARAS membership, except for the international awards which are based on sales.

1976: *Rough Trade Live!*, produced by **Jack Richardson**, becomes the first direct-to-disc album recorded in Canada.

1976: Prism is organized in Vancouver by producer/horn player **Bruce Fairbairn** and features **Lindsay Mitchell,** vocalist **Ron Tabak,** and various session players, including **Rodney Higgs (Jim Vallance)**, **Tom Lavin,** and **Tom Keenlyside**.

1976: The **T.H.P. Orchestra** (Three Hats Productions Orchestra), a studio project masterminded by producers **Willi Morrison** and **Ian Guenther**, has a number one hit in Canada with *Theme From S.W.A.T.*.

1976: Gordon Lightfoot receives two Grammy Award nominations for *The Wreck of the Edmund Fitzgerald*.

1976: Ralph Cole of **Lighthouse** takes the band out on tour for the last time after the departure of Skip Prokop in 1974.

1976: Fourteen-year-old **Corey Hart**, with the help of **Paul Anka's** organization, records the single *Ooh Baby!* for United Artists records.

1976: Hometown boy **Maynard Ferguson** is the featured soloist at the opening of the Montreal Olympics.

1976: Patsy Gallant has an international hit with *From New York To L.A.*, an English, disco version of Gilles Vigneault's Mon Pays.

1976: Classical guitar broadens its audience as **Liona Boyd** embarks on a North American tour as opening act for **Gordon Lightfoot**.

1976: The **Montreal Symphony Orchestra** makes its Carnegie Hall debut under the direction of **Rafael Frühbeck de Burgos.**

1976: Such is **April Wine's** fan base in Canada that the album *The Whole World's Going Crazy* becomes the first Canadian album to ship platinum — that's music industry talk for 100,000 copies. An extensive Canadian tour follows which grosses over one million dollars.

1976: Rush's ALL THE WORLD'S A STAGE becomes the first live album to be certified gold for sales over 50,000, and the band plays three nights at Massey Hall on June in the wake of this success.

1976: Composer **Percy Faith** (67) dies of cancer in Los Angeles on February 9th.

1976: The Stampeders have their last major hit with *Hit The Road Jack*, a song that features a staged phone conversation between legendary radio deejay **Wolfman Jack** and group member **Ronnie King** under his given name **Cornelius (Van Sprang)**. The single peaks at 40 on *Billboard*'s Hot 100 charton April 4th. King's Dutch heritage had helped to make the group popular in The Netherlands, and With *Hit The Road Jack*, the group has a number one hit there and earns a coveted Edison Award.

1976: Nick Gilder and **Jim McCulloch**, formerly with the Vancouver group **Sweeney Todd**, sign to Chrysalis Records in the U.S. Gilder is initially replaced as vocalist in Sweeney Todd by **Clark Perry** after he records a version of the group's hit *Roxy Roller* for release in the U.S., but it is scrapped in August as Vancouver singer **Bryan Guy Adams** replaces Perry and re-records the single for release on August 27th. Gilder's version peaks at number 90 after two weeks on the *Billboard* singles chart, while Adams' makes a one week visit at number 99.

1976: DREAMBOAT ANNIE, the debut album by Vancouver-based band **Heart**, is certified gold for sales of over 50,000 in Canada.

1976: Bachman-Turner Overdrive embark on a Japanese tour on October 29th which is recorded for the album LIVE IN JAPAN.

1976: The Band performs *Georgia On My Mind* on *Saturday Night Live* in honor of presidential candidate Jimmy Carter who is elected to office a few days later.

1976: Burton Cummings, the former vocalist for **The Guess Who**, plays his first concert as a solo artist on November 8th at the Manitoba Centennial Concert Hall in his hometown of Winnipeg.

1976: "The Last Waltz," **The Band's** swansong performance at Winterland in San Francisco, takes place on Thanksgiving night before the cameras of director Martin Scorsese. Promoter Bill Graham convinces the group to turn the event into a grand affair complete with buffet supper, chandeliers, an orchestra for dancing, and a $25 ticket. Musicians and friends on hand to say goodbye include Bob Dylan, **Ronnie Hawkins**, **Joni Mitchell**, Van Morrison, **Neil Young**, Paul Butterfield, **Bobby Charles**, **Neil Diamond**, Dr. John, **Muddy Waters**, Eric Clapton, Stephen Stills, Ron Wood, and Ringo Starr. The event is later released as the film *The Last Waltz* in 1977 and as a triple album set in 1978.

Roxy Roller *1977*

7TH ANNUAL JUNO AWARDS
March 16, 1977
Canadian Room, Royal York Hotel, Toronto
Host:
David Steinberg
with
Roy Hennessy
(CKLG Vancouver),
Jay Nelson
(CHUM Toronto),
Ralph Lockwood
(CKGM Montreal),
Bob Burns (CKY Winnipeg), **and**
Len Theusen
(CHED Edmonton).
Performers:
Carroll Baker,
Keath Barrie,
Colleen Peterson
and Al Cherney,
Andre Gagnon,
Patsy Gallant,
The Lavender
Hill Mob,
T.H.P. Orchestra
and the
Soul Express
Dancers,
Ian Tyson.

"Don't let anyone tell you that things don't happen fast in Canada," Burton Cummings quipped as he received his second award of the night. "In just 75 minutes, I went from Best New Male Vocalist to the Best Male Vocalist of the Year." The Folk Singer of the Year Award category, which had been dropped earlier in the balloting but was later reinstated due to negative public and industry reaction, was awarded to Gordon Lightfoot, who shared the spotlight with Burton Cummings as top award winner.

1977

1977 JUNO AWARD WINNERS
(For the Voting Year 1976)

FEMALE VOCALIST OF THE YEAR	**Patsy Gallant**
MALE VOCALIST OF THE YEAR	**Burton Cummings**
GROUP OF THE YEAR	**Heart**
COUNTRY FEMALE VOCALIST	**Carroll Baker**
COUNTRY MALE VOCALIST	**Murray McLauchlan**
COUNTRY GROUP OF THE YEAR	**The Good Brothers**
BEST NEW FEMALE VOCALIST	**Colleen Peterson**
BEST NEW MALE VOCALIST	**Burton Cummings**
BEST NEW GROUP	**T.H.P. Orchestra**
BEST SELLING ALBUM	NEIGES, **Andre Gagnon**
BEST SELLING SINGLE	*Roxy Roller,* **Sweeney Todd**
FOLK SINGER OF THE YEAR	**Gordon Lightfoot**
INSTRUMENTAL ARTIST OF THE YEAR	**Hagood Hardy**
PRODUCER OF THE YEAR	**Mike Flicker** for *Dreamboat Annie,* **Heart**
COMPOSER OF THE YEAR	**Gordon Lightfoot**
BEST JAZZ RECORDING	**Phil Nimmons,** NIMMONS 'N NINE PLUS SIX
BEST CLASSICAL RECORDING	**Beethoven Vol. 1, 2 and 3, Anton Kuerti**
BEST ALBUM GRAPHICS	**Michael Bowness** for SELECT, **Ian Tamblyn**
RECORDING ENGINEER OF THE YEAR	**Paul Page** for *Are You Ready For Love?,* **Patsy Gallant**
BEST SELLING INTERNATIONAL SINGLE	*I Love To Love,* **Tina Charles**
BEST SELLING INTERNATIONAL ALBUM	FRAMPTON COMES ALIVE, **Peter Frampton**

Domenic Troiano

Controversy later swirled around Heart's award as Group of the Year when the band's Ann Wilson told a U.S. magazine that they have always been an American act. Bryan Adams of Sweeney Todd appeared with producer Martin Shaer to pick up the band's award as Top New Group. Jazz and Classical categories were introduced.

1977: **Bryan Adams** meets drummer **Rodney Higgs** (a.k.a. **Jim Vallance**) in a Vancouver music store. Higgs is writing material for a new local group, **Prism**. Shortly after their first meeting, they begin a writing collaboration destined to launch both of their careers.

1977: The Raes' single *Que Sera Sera* sells over 65,000 copies, becoming one of A&M Records' biggest Canadian singles in its history.

1977: Rough Trade co-star with U.S. transvestite Divine in the revue *Restless Underwear* at Toronto's Massey Hall and in New York.

1977: *Paper Rosie*, a country hit for its writer **Dallas Harms** in Canada, becomes a U.S. chart-topper for Gene Watson.

1977: The show "100 Years of Recorded Sound" opens at the Canadian National Exhibition in Toronto.

1977: Leonard Cohen collaborates with legendary pop music producer Phil Spector on the album DEATH OF A LADIES MAN, which features a guest appearance by Bob Dylan.

1977: Paul Shaffer takes a break from *Saturday Night Live* to star in the summer comedy series *A Year At the Top*, a 1970s version of The Monkees TV shows.

1977: Hagood Hardy receives a *Billboard* award at presentation ceremonies at the Roxy Theatre in Los Angeles on January 10th as Number One Instrumentalist for Singles in 1976 for *The Homecoming*.

February 1977: Released with very little fanfare in the summer of 1976, **Klaatu**'s

Sweeney Todd Producer and Bryan Adams

first album catches the attention of the world in February 1977 when an article in the *Providence Journal* (Rhode Island) by Steve Smith compared Klaatu to The Beatles and put forward the persuasive argument that members of the Fab Four were indeed involved in the recording project. This led to the extraordinary rumor that Klaatu was The Beatles. Before it was revealed that Klaatu were in fact **John Woloschuk**, **Terry Draper,** and **Dee Long**, three Toronto studio musicians, Klaatu's self-titled debut album had hit number 32 on the *Billboard* album chart. Later that year, The Carpenters had a Top 40 hit with the group's *Calling Occupants Of Interplanetary Craft*, a song that became the anthem of World Contact Day. The group's name was inspired by the 1951 film *The Day The Earth Stood Still* in which Klaatu, an alien peace emissary played by Michael Rennie, travels to earth to warn of the dangers of nuclear power. *Klaatu barada nikto!*

1977: Triumph play their first U.S. concert in February with The Runaways at the Municipal Auditorium in San Antonio, Texas as a replacement for Sammy Hagar.

1977: Frank Marino and **Mahogany Rush** debut in concert in the U.K.

1977: The Rolling Stones, with **April Wine** as opening act, play two nights at Toronto's El Mocambo club on March 4th and 5th. While most of the attention at the time focuses on Keith Richards' recent arrest by Canadian authorities and the presence in the small audience of **Margaret Trudeau**, the wife of the Prime Minister, the real significance of the club concerts becomes apparent in September when LOVE YOU LIVE is released with one side comprised of the vintage R&B the band performed in Toronto.

1977: April Wine open for The Rolling Stones at Rich Stadium in Buffalo, New York on July 4th.

1977: Harmonium tour Europe during the summer with British group Supertramp.

1977: Bachman-Turner Overdrive disbands after the departure of **Randy Bachman**. Bass player **Fred Turner** subsequently moves to guitar, former **April Wine** member **Jim Clench** is brought in on bass, and the band shortens its name to **BTO**, but after recording two more albums the group splits up in 1980.

1977: The Blues Brothers, the original million-dollar gag, are initially formed by comedians Dan Aykroyd and John Belushi to get the crowd in a party mood before the tapings of *Saturday Night Live*, but the act moves into the body of the show, and Jake and Elwood Bluesmania ensues. They surround themselves with the best musicians in the business, including guitarist Steve Cropper and bassist Donald "Duck" Dunn, who had played on some of the original versions of the songs they covered, including Sam & Dave's *Hold On I'm Coming* and *Soul Man*. Their first album BRIEFCASE FULL OF BLUES is recorded live in September 1978, and the record goes on to sell well over a million copies in North America, leading to the biographical film and the soundtrack THE BLUES BROTHERS, co-starring Aretha Franklin, James Brown, Ray Charles, and Cab Calloway.

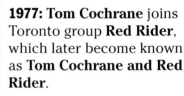

1977: Tom Cochrane joins Toronto group **Red Rider**, which later become known as **Tom Cochrane and Red Rider**.

1977: Maynard Collins' musical revue, "Hank Williams: The Show He Never Gave," premieres in November at the Beacon Arms Hotel in Ottawa with **Sneezy Waters** (a.k.a. Peter Hodgson) in the lead role.

1977: Rush receive gold records for three albums on November 16th — 2112, ALL THE WORLD'S A STAGE, and A FAREWELL TO KINGS.

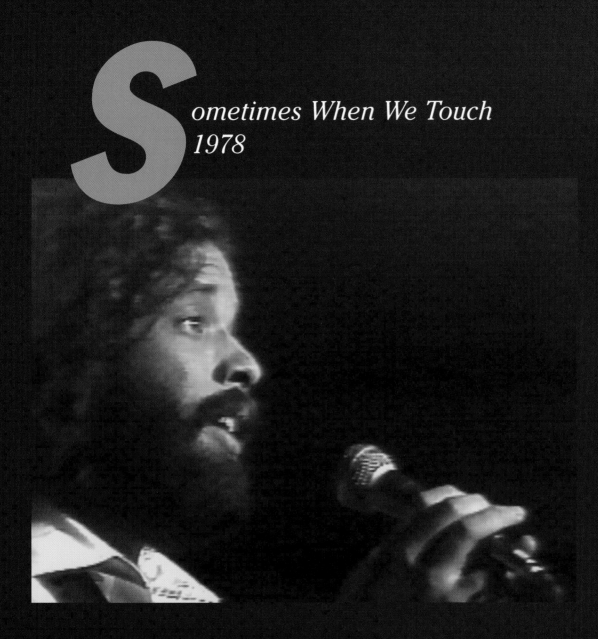

*S*ometimes When We Touch
1978

8TH ANNUAL JUNO AWARDS
March 29, 1978
Harbour Castle
Convention
Centre, Toronto
Host: **David Steinberg**
Performers:
**Burton Cummings,
Lisa Dalbello,
Patsy Gallant,
The Good Brothers,
Grant Smith** and **Barbara Law,
Dan Hill,
The Raes,
Rush**

As Alex Lifeson of Rush accepted their Juno award for Group of the Year, he commented, "We'd like to thank Dan Hill for not being a group." The success of Dan Hill's *Sometimes When We Touch* single from the album LONGER FUSE placed this singer/songwriter in the winner's circle five times during the ceremonies, while Patsy Gallant won her second consecutive Female Vocalist award and Single of the Year honors for *Sugar Daddy* as the evening carried a disco theme.

Sometimes When We Touch

1978 JUNO AWARD WINNERS
(For the Voting Year 1977)

FEMALE VOCALIST OF THE YEAR	**Patsy Gallant**
MALE VOCALIST OF THE YEAR	**Dan Hill**
GROUP OF THE YEAR	**Rush**
COMPOSER OF THE YEAR	**Dan Hill** with **Jeff Barry**
COUNTRY FEMALE VOCALIST OF THE YEAR	**Carroll Baker**
COUNTRY MALE VOCALIST OF THE YEAR	**Ronnie Prophet**
COUNTRY GROUP OF THE YEAR	**The Good Brothers**
BEST NEW FEMALE VOCALIST	**Lisa Dalbello**
BEST NEW MALE VOCALIST	**David Bradstreet**
BEST NEW GROUP	**Hometown Band**
BEST SELLING ALBUM	LONGER FUSE, **Dan Hill**
BEST SELLING SINGLE	*Sugar Daddy*, **Patsy Gallant**
PRODUCER (SINGLE)	**Matt McCauley** and **Fred Mollin** for *Sometimes When We Touch*
PRODUCER (ALBUM)	**Matt McCauley** and **Fred Mollin** for LONGER FUSE
BEST ALBUM GRAPHICS	**Dave Anderson** for SHORT TURN, SHORT TURN
BEST CLASSICAL RECORDING	THREE BORODIN SYMPHONIES, **Toronto Symphony Orchestra**
BEST JAZZ RECORDING	BIG BAND JAZZ, **Rob McConnell and the Boss Brass**
RECORDING ENGINEER OF THE YEAR	*(tie)* **Terry Brown** for *Hope*, **Klaatu;** and **David Greene** for *Big Band Jazz*, **Rob McConnell and the Boss Brass.**
INSTRUMENTAL ARTIST OF THE YEAR	**Andre Gagnon**
FOLK SINGER OF THE YEAR	**Gordon Lightfoot**
INTERNATIONAL BEST SELLING ALBUM	RUMOURS, **Fleetwood Mac**
INTERNATIONAL BEST SELLING SINGLE	*When I Need You*, **Leo Sayer**
HALL OF FAME	**Guy Lombardo** and **Oscar Peterson**

Lisa Dalbello

For the first time, the remarkable achievements of Oscar Peterson and Guy Lombardo were formally recognized by the Academy when they were inducted into the newly created Canadian Music Hall of Fame.

1978: Tommy Banks' Big Band, which features, among others, **Clarence "Big" Miller** and **P.J. Perry**, performs at the Montreux Jazz Festival in Switzerland and records a double live LP of the performance.

1978: The Blues Brothers record two **Downchild Blues Band** numbers, *(I Got Everything I Need) Almost* and *Shot Gun Blues*, on their BRIEFCASE FULL OF BLUES album.

1978: Toronto's **Sharon, Lois & Bram**, who become one of the most popular children/family acts in North America, record their debut album ONE ELEPHANT, DEUX ELÉPHANTS on their own Elephant record label.

1978: Hank Snow is inducted into the Songwriter's Association's Hall of Fame in Nashville.

1978: Melissa Manchester has an international hit with the **Lisa Dalbello** song, *Pretty Girls*.

1978: Denny Doherty, formerly with **The Mamas and the Papas**, becomes the host of the CBC-TV musical variety program, *The Denny Sho'*.

1978: Ginette Reno's exposure in the U.S. is greatly increased by appearances on the Johnny Carson, Merv Griffin, and Dinah Shore TV shows.

1978: The **Toronto Symphony**, conducted by **Andrew Davis**, tours China and Japan with soloists **Maureen Forrester** and pianist **Louis Lortie.**

1978: Swiss-born conductor **Charles Dutoit** becomes artistic director of the **Montreal Symphony Orchestra**.

Blues Brothers

1978: The legendary Riverboat club at 134 Yorkville Ave. in Toronto's Yorkville Village closes on June 25th with a performance by **Murray McLauchlan**.

1978: The Raes (**Cherrill** and **Robbie Rae**) summer special TV series debuts.

1978: Tafelmusik give their first concert in Toronto on July 29th.

1978: Martha and the Muffins have a Top Five single in Canada with the single *Echo Beach,* which sells over 75,000 copies and becomes a number one hit in Australia, Portugal, Spain, and The Netherlands, hitting the Top 10 on the U.K. charts.

1978: The first Vancouver Folk Festival is held on August 11th in Stanley Park, Vancouver.

1978: Keith Richards of The Rolling Stones goes on trial in Toronto after his bust at the Harbour Castle Hilton Hotel for cocaine and heroin possession. He is let off on probation on the promise that he performs a special benefit concert in the area with proceeds going to the Canadian National Institute for the Blind (CNIB).

1978: Nick Gilder, former lead singer of **Sweeney Todd,** hits the top of the *Billboard* Hot 100 chart on October 28th with the single *Hot Child In The City*.

1978: Raffi's *Singable Songs* is certified gold in Canada for sales over 50,000 copies, the first Canadian children's record to achieve this milestone.

1978: Anne Murray has the biggest single of her career as *You Needed Me* from her album LET'S KEEP IT THAT WAY hits the top of the *Billboard* Hot 100 chart on November 4th.

1978: The Last Pogo is held at Toronto's Horseshoe Tavern on December 1st as the venerable Queen St. West venue reverts back to a policy of booking country music after a brief fling with punk/new wave music. The law closes the party early as, in typical punk fashion, it gets well out of hand.

1978: Elvis Presley's cover of **Paul Anka's** *My Way* hits the 500,000 sales mark the year after the King's death, while Sid Vicious of the Sex Pistols films his rendition of the song for the movie *The Great Rock 'n' Roll Swindle*.

1978: Salome Bey writes and stars in *Indigo: A History of the Blues* that plays for close to a year at the Basin Street Club before being produced for television.

Patsy Gallant vaulting onstage

You Needed Me
1979

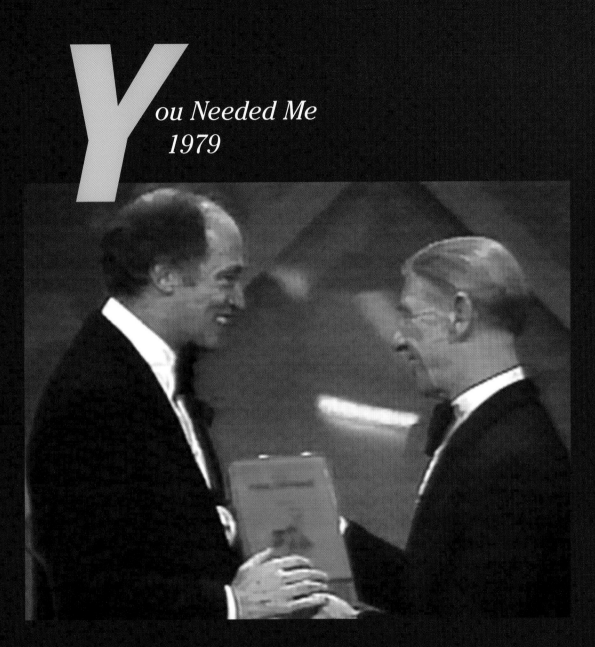

**9TH
ANNUAL
JUNO
AWARDS**
March 21, 1979
Harbour Castle
Convention
Centre, Toronto
Host:
**Burton
Cummings**
Performers:
**Claudja Barry,
Chilliwack,
Burton
Cummings,
Nick Gilder,
Ginette Reno
with Rob
McConnell
and the
Boss Brass,
Myrna Lorrie,
The Mercey
Brothers,
Ronnie
Prophet,
Toulouse,
Gino Vannelli.**

On a night when Anne Murray, Gino Vannelli, and Nick Gilder were multiple award winners, the emotional high point of the evening came with the induction of country legend Hank Snow into the Hall Of Fame by Prime Minister Pierre Elliot Trudeau. In the audience, and introduced by Snow, was A. Hugh Joseph, the RCA Victor record executive who first recorded Snow in an old church in Montreal in October of 1936.

You Needed Me
1979 JUNO AWARD WINNERS
(For the Voting Year 1978)

BEST SELLING ALBUM	*Dream Of A Child,* **Burton Cummings**
BEST SELLING SINGLE	*Hot Child In The City,* **Nick Gilder**
FEMALE VOCALIST	**Anne Murray**
MALE VOCALIST	**Gino Vannelli**
GROUP OF THE YEAR	**Rush**
COMPOSER	**Dan Hill** for *Sometimes When We Touch,* **Dan Hill**
COUNTRY FEMALE VOCALIST	**Carroll Baker**
COUNTRY MALE VOCALIST	**Ronnie Prophet**
COUNTRY GROUP	**The Good Brothers**
MOST PROMISING FEMALE VOCALIST	**Claudja Barry**
MOST PROMISING MALE VOCALIST	**Nick Gilder**
MOST PROMISING GROUP	**Doucette**
PRODUCER(S) OF THE YEAR:	**Gino Vannelli, Joe Vannelli,** and **Ross Vannelli** for *Brother To Brother,* **Gino Vannelli**
RECORDING ENGINEER	**Ken Friesen** for LET'S KEEP IT THAT WAY, **Anne Murray**
INSTRUMENTAL ARTIST	**Liona Boyd**
FOLK ARTIST OF THE YEAR	**Murray McLauchlan**
BEST ALBUM GRAPHICS	**Alan Gee** and **Greg Lawson** for MADCATS, **Madcats**
COMEDY ALBUM	THE AIR FARCE COMEDY ALBUM, **The Royal Canadian Air Farce**
CHILDREN'S ALBUM	*There's A Hippo In My Tub,* **Anne Murray**
INTERNATIONAL BEST-SELLING ALBUM	SATURDAY NIGHT FEVER, **Various Artists**
INTERNATIONAL BEST-SELLING SINGLE	*You're the One That I Want,* **John Travolta** and **Olivia Newton-John**
BEST CLASSICAL RECORDING	HINDEMITH; DAS MARIENLEBEN, **Glenn Gould** and **Roxalana Raslack**
BEST JAZZ RECORDING	JAZZ CANADA MONTREUX, **Tommy Banks Big Band**
HALL OF FAME	**Hank Snow**

A.Hugh Joseph

The Royal Canadian Air Farce and Anne Murray, respectively, won the first Comedy and Children's albums awards. Prime Minister Trudeau took on a comic role himself as he addressed the Air Farce and audience: "Nominees, Juno Award winners, ladies and gentlemen, and Nestor Pistor. I don't mind, Nestor, if you want to be the next Prime Minister, just as long as you're not in too much of a hurry. I'm really not after this job anyhow. I'm after the other one that our Alma Faye Brooks talked about," he quipped, alluding to the fact that she had addressed him from the stage as "Mr. President."

1979: Country singer **Marie Bottrell** begins an eight year consecutive run as a Juno nominee for female country singer.

1979: Marc Connors, **Paul Cooper**, and **Claude Morrison**, collectively known as **The Nylons**, debut at a Toronto cabaret across from the Art Gallery of Ontario.

1979: Anne Murray is named Honorary National Chairperson of the Canadian Save the Children Fund during this, The Year of the Child.

1979: David Foster wins his first Grammy Award in the U.S. for his work on Earth, Wind & Fire's *After the Love Is Gone*. By 1995, he will have racked up over 30 nominations and have 12 Grammys on his mantlepiece.

1979: Brian Eno comes to Canada to record at **Daniel Lanois'** Grant Avenue Studio in Hamilton, Ontario. A close working relationship develops between the two, and in 1984 they begin working with Irish group U2, for whom they co-produce THE UNFORGETTABLE FIRE (1984) and THE JOSHUA TREE (1987).

1979: Paul Hyde and **Bob Rock**, who had first met in high school, form **The Payola$** at Vancouver's Little Mountain Sound where Rock is working as a recording engineer. They initially record the independent *China Boys/Make Some Noise* single on Slophouse Records before signing with A&M.

1979: Trooper's HOT SHOTS greatest hits album becomes the first by a Canadian act to be certified quadruple platinum for sales of over 400,000 copies.

Frank Mills

1979: Hank Snow is inducted into the Country Music Hall of Fame in Nashville during the Country Music Association's (CMA) nationally-televised awards show on CBS.

1979: Anne Murray is given a star in the Country Music Hall of Fame's Walkway of Stars.

1979: Rush are named the country's official "Ambassadors of Music" by the Canadian government on January 9th.

1979: Harpist **Judy Loman** premieres **R. Murray Schafer's** *Crown Of Ariadne* for Toronto's New Music Concerts on March 5th.

1979: Frank Mills, former member of the Montreal group **The Bells** (*Stay Awhile*), makes his solo return to the U.S. single charts in a big way as his piano instrumental

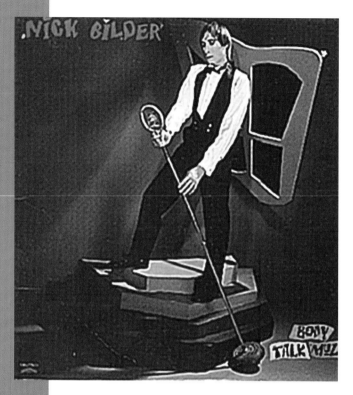

Music Box Dancer reaches number three on the *Billboard* Hot 100 chart. Sheet music sales of the song exceed two million copies, the single sells over three million, and the album of the same name closes in on two million copies.

1979: As part of the sentence handed down by the judge to Keith Richards for his 1977 drug bust in Toronto, the Rolling Stones' guitarist performs a concert to benefit the Canadian National Institute for the Blind at the Oshawa Civic Auditorium with his newly-formed band, **The New Barbarians**.

1979: Rush's Tour Of the Hemispheres comes to a close on June 4th at the Pink Pop Festival in The Netherlands after eight months on the road.

1979: Joni Mitchell appears at the Charlie Mingus tribute during the Playboy Jazz Festival at the Hollywood Bowl in the wake of the recording of her album Mingus with this jazz bass legend.

1979: The movie *Carny*, produced and co-written by **Robbie Robertson**, in which he stars alongside **Jodie Foster** and **Gary Busey**, completes production on July 1st.

1979: The **Neil Young** concert film *Rust Never Sleeps* premieres on July 11th at the Bruin Theater in Westwood, California, and a week later at New York's Palladium.

1979: Anne Murray plays to a standing-room-only audience at New York's Carnegie Hall on September 19th.

1979: Felix Leclerc makes a brief appearance at the first ADISQ gala on September 23rd at Montreal's Expo Theatre and thereafter lends his name to the Felix Awards that are presented as part of the annual event.

1979: *Glenn Gould's* *Toronto*, a TV film that forms part of the CBC Cities series, airs on September 27th.

1979: Sixteen-year-old Montreal disco diva **France Joli** hits the top 15 of the *Billboard* Hot 100 singles chart with *Come To Me*. In 1984, she wins the top song prize at the Tokyo International Song Festival with the **George Duke** song, *Party Lights*.

1979: Raffi's SINGABLE SONGS album is certified platinum in Canada, first for a Canadian-produced children's record.

1979: Loverboy debuts in concert at Vancouver's Pacific Coliseum in November as the opening act for **Kiss**.

1979: *The Village Voice* in New York names **Neil Young** Artist of the Decade.

H

*it Me With Your Best Shot
1980*

**10TH
ANNUAL
JUNO
AWARDS**
April 2, 1980
Harbour Castle
Convention
Centre,
Toronto
Host:
**Burton
Cummings**
Performers:
**Carroll Baker,
Burton
Cummings,
France Joli,
Gordon
Lightfoot,
Max Webster,
Murray
McLauchlan,
Frank Mills.**

Once again The Good Brothers were awarded a Juno for Best Country Group of the Year, the category over which they reigned for 8 consecutive years (1977–1984). Anne Murray dominated the awards, adding four trophies to her already crowded mantlepiece as she received Junos in the categories of Album, Single, Female Vocalist, and Country Female Vocalist of the Year.

Hit Me With Your Best Shot

1980 JUNO AWARD WINNERS
(For the Voting Year 1979)

ALBUM OF THE YEAR	NEW KIND OF FEELING, **Anne Murray**
SINGLE OF THE YEAR	*I Just Fall In Love Again*, **Anne Murray**
FEMALE VOCALIST OF THE YEAR	**Anne Murray**
MALE VOCALIST OF THE YEAR	**Burton Cummings**
GROUP OF THE YEAR	**Trooper**
COMPOSER OF THE YEAR	**Frank Mills** for *Peter Piper*
COUNTRY FEMALE VOCALIST	**Anne Murray**
COUNTRY MALE VOCALIST	**Murray McLauchlan**
COUNTRY GROUP OF THE YEAR	**The Good Brothers**
MOST PROMISING FEMALE VOCALIST	**France Joli**
MOST PROMISING MALE VOCALIST	**Walter Rossi**
MOST PROMISING GROUP	**Streetheart**
INSTRUMENTAL ARTIST OF THE YEAR	**Frank Mills**
FOLK ARTIST OF THE YEAR	**Bruce Cockburn**
COMEDY ALBUM OF THE YEAR	A CHRISTMAS CAROL, **Rich Little**
CHILDREN'S ALBUM OF THE YEAR	SMORGASBORD, **Sharon, Lois & Bram**
INTERNATIONAL ALBUM OF THE YEAR	BREAKFAST IN AMERICA, **Supertramp**
INTERNATIONAL SINGLE OF THE YEAR	*Heart Of Glass*, **Blondie**
PRODUCER OF THE YEAR	**Bruce Fairbairn** for ARMAGEDDON, **Prism**
RECORDING ENGINEER OF THE YEAR	**David Greene** for HOFFERT: CONCERTO FOR CONTEMPORARY VIOLIN, **Paul Hoffert**
BEST JAZZ RECORDING	SACKVILLE 4005, **Ed Bickert** and **Don Thompson**
BEST ALBUM GRAPHICS	**Rodney Bowes** for CIGARETTES, **The Wives**
BEST CLASSICAL RECORDING	THE CROWN OF ARIADNE, **Judy Loman**
HALL OF FAME	**Paul Anka**

Paul Anka

Ken Taylor, the celebrated former Ambassador to Iran who became an American and Canadian hero when he assisted the escape of a number of American citizens from Iran during the hostage crisis, was on hand to induct Paul Anka into the Canadian Music Hall of Fame, but when Anka became stranded somewhere in Colorado in a snowstorm, Taylor presented the Juno for the Male Vocalist of the Year to host Burton Cummings, who found it hard to hide his joy at the honor. Anka's fellow Ottawa native Rich Little won the Comedy Album of the Year award for his amusing version of A CHRISTMAS CAROL.

1980: Rough Trade sign with the Toronto-based True North Records and record *Avoid Freud*.

1980: Bryan Adams' debut album is recorded at Toronto's Manta Sound with help from musicians **Fred Turner** (**BTO**), **Jim Clench** (**April Wine**, **BTO**), and Jeff "Skunk" Baxter (The Doobie Brothers).

1980: Long John Baldry, one of the mainstays of the British blues and R&B boom of the 1960s and influential in the development of the careers of artists like Rod Stewart and Elton John, emigrates from England and becomes a citizen in 1980.

1980: Burton Cummings makes his acting debut co-starring in the movie **Melanie**, for which he composes and performs the original soundtrack.

1980: Bruce Cockburn has one of his biggest hits in the U.S. this year with *Wondering Where the Lions Are*, which goes Top 25 on the Billboard singles chart.

1980: *Je ne suis qu'une chanson*, written by **Diane Juster** and performed by **Ginette Reno**, becomes one of the biggest singles in Quebec music history.

1980: John Kay and Steppenwolf hit the road once more, motivated by the appearance of a group calling itself

Rough Trade

Steppenwolf and fronted by former group members **Nick St. Nicholas** and **Goldy McJohn**. Kay has never stopped touring since.

1980: Canada's *Today Magazine* features **Anne Murray** on the cover of the April 26th issue with the headline, "Anne Wins Big In Vegas: Nova Scotia's Snowbird Is Suddenly Superstar," referring to her success at the Riviera Hotel.

1980: Bill C-36, passed on June 27th in Canada's House of Commons, designates *O Canada* as Canada's national anthem.

1980: The Montreal Jazz Festival/Festival international de jazz de Montréal is established by **Alain Simard** and **André Menard**.

1980: Rush and **Max Webster** get together at Phase One Studios in Toronto to record the track *Battlescar* for Max Webster's new album. During the session, lyricist **Pye Dubois** presents some lyrics to Rush, and they become the foundation for the Rush song *Tom Sawyer*.

1980: The Edmonton Folk Festival, established by **Don Whalen**, is held for the first time on August 8th.

1980: Loverboy's self-titled, debut

album is released in the U.S. in September.

1980: Sharon, Lois & Bram make their U.S. debut at the Lincoln Center Out-of-Doors Festival in New York.

1980: The Lovin' Spoonful, featuring Zal Yanovsky and John Sebastian, briefly re-form to appear in Paul Simon's semi-autobiographical film *One Trick Pony,* which premieres in New York on October 1st.

1980: Toronto singer/songwriter **Eddie Schwartz** has one of his biggest successes as Pat Benatar hits number nine on the Billboard chart with his song *Hit Me With Your Best Shot*. He has similar success a little over seven years later as his co-write of Paul Carrack's *Don't Shed A Tear* goes to number nine, as does the song *Doctor*, recorded by The Doobie Brothers in 1989.

Sharon, Lois & Bram

1980: Levon Helm of **The Band** makes his acting debut as Loretta Lynn's father in *The Coal Miner's Daughter* and goes on to star in *The Right Stuff*, *Dollmaker*, and *Elvis '56*, while **Robbie Robertson** begins a close association with Martin Scorsese working on the soundtrack to *Raging Bull, The King of Comedy*, and *The Color of Money*.

1980: *Country Music News* (initially known as *Capital Country News*) begins publication.

1980: John Lennon is murdered in New York on December 8th.

E*cho Beach 1981*

**11TH
ANNUAL
JUNO
AWARDS**
April 2, 1981
The O'Keefe
Centre, Toronto
Hosts:
John Candy &
Andrea Martin;
Ronnie Hawkins
& Carroll Baker;
Frank Mills &
Ginette Reno
Performers:
Ginette Reno
and Frank Mills,
Graham Shaw
and the Sincere
Serenaders,
Powder Blues,
Ronnie Hawkins
& Carroll Baker,
Diane Tell,
Shari Ulrich

There was a little unrehearsed and unexpected slapstick in the wings as co-hosts Ronnie Hawkins and Carroll Baker arrived on stage in a chauffeur-driven Rolls Royce. The door jammed and in the process of extricating himself from the car, Hawkins ripped his tuxedo pants and almost did his Bo Diddley a mischief as he clambered out as co-host Baker doubled up with laughter.

Echo Beach
1981 JUNO AWARD WINNERS
(For the Voting Year 1980)

ALBUM OF THE YEAR	GREATEST HITS, **Anne Murray**
SINGLE OF THE YEAR	*(tie) Could I Have This Dance*, **Anne Murray**; and *Echo Beach*, **Martha and the Muffins**
FEMALE VOCALIST OF THE YEAR	**Anne Murray**
MALE VOCALIST OF THE YEAR	**Bruce Cockburn**
GROUP OF THE YEAR	**Prism**
COMPOSER OF THE YEAR	**Eddie Schwartz** for *Hit Me With Your Best Shot*, **Pat Benatar**
COUNTRY FEMALE VOCALIST	**Anne Murray**
COUNTRY MALE VOCALIST	**Eddie Eastman**
COUNTRY GROUP OF THE YEAR	**The Good Brothers**
MOST PROMISING FEMALE VOCALIST	**Carole Pope**
MOST PROMISING MALE VOCALIST	**Graham Shaw**
MOST PROMISING GROUP	**Powder Blues**
INSTRUMENTAL ARTIST OF THE YEAR	**Frank Mills**
FOLKSINGER OF THE YEAR	**Bruce Cockburn**
CHILDREN'S ALBUM OF THE YEAR	SINGING 'N' SWINGING, **Sharon, Lois & Bram**
INTERNATIONAL ALBUM OF THE YEAR	THE WALL, **Pink Floyd**
INTERNATIONAL SINGLE OF THE YEAR	*Another Brick In the Wall*, **Pink Floyd**
PRODUCER OF THE YEAR	**Gene Martynec** for *Tokyo*, **Bruce Cockburn**
RECORDING ENGINEER OF THE YEAR	**Mike Jones** for *Factory* and *We're OK*, **Instructions**
BEST JAZZ RECORDING	PRESENT PERFECT, **Rob McConnell and the Boss Brass**
BEST CLASSICAL RECORDING	STRAVINSKY – CHOPIN BALLADS, **Arthur Ozolins**
BEST ALBUM GRAPHICS	**Jeanette Hanna** for WE DELIVER, **Downchild Blues Band**
HALL OF FAME	**Joni Mitchell**

As Joni Mitchell was inducted into the Canadian Music Hall of Fame by Prime Minister Trudeau, she joined in the comic spirit that infused the ceremonies hosted by John Candy and Andrea Martin by remarking, "Well, the Hall of Fame . . . Makes me feel like Boom Boom Geoffrion!" Anne Murray was again a four-time Juno winner for the second year in a row, though her hit single *Could I Have This Dance* shared the spotlight with Martha and the Muffins' first chart topper, *Echo Beach*.

Loverboy

1981: **Rob McConnell and The Boss Brass** make their first U.S. live appearance at the Monterey Jazz Festival in California.

1981: A concert appearance at Toronto's Music Hall by **Bruce Cockburn** becomes the subject of the film *Rumours of Glory*.

1981: Former **Lighthouse** member **Skip Prokop** produces an album for singer/songwriter **Gene MacLellan** recorded live at Attica State Prison.

1981: Hank Snow and **Wilf Carter** tour Canada together.

1981: Loreena McKennitt bases herself in Stratford, Ontario and opens her own independent record label, Quinlan Road.

1981: Murray McLauchlan's *If the Wind Could Blow My Troubles Away* becomes the theme for the International Year of Disabled Persons.

1981: David Clayton-Thomas takes part in a five-city tour with the Cincinnati Pops Orchestra in a Tribute to John Lennon that also includes Sarah Vaughan and Roberta Flack.

1981: Having attended the Berklee School Of Music in Boston, **Neil Osborne** returns to Vancouver and forms the band **54-40** with **Brad Merritt**. Their initial recorded output is the four tracks included on the compilation album, THINGS ARE STILL COMING ASHORE, released by local independent label Mo-Da-Mu.

Powder Blues at the Juno Awards Ceremony

1981: The **Montreal Symphony Orchestra's** first album DAPHNIS ET CHLOE is released in March.

1981: Though **April Wine** had consciously put a harder edge to their rock sound, ironically it is the ballad *Just Between You and Me* from their album NATURE OF THE BEAST that brings the group their first gold album in the U.S.

1981: Raffi plays his first public concert in the U.S. in Portland, Oregon, and the demand for tickets is such that a second show has to be added.

Martha and the Muffins

1981: Loverboy complete the recording of their sophomore album GET LUCKY and are honored with a party on 52nd Street in New York by Columbia Records on May 20th in recognition of their first album going gold for U.S. sales in excess of 500,000 copies. In Canada, sales have passed the 300,000 mark. The group subsequently sets out on a two-month U.S. tour with **ZZ Top**.

1981: In August, MTV debuts in the U.S. and the first video played is *Video Killed The Radio Star* by **Buggles**.

1981: Anne Murray, who appears at the CNE Grandstand in Toronto for the first time since 1972, receives the highest guarantee to this point for an appearance at the venue, a sum reportedly well in excess of $100,000.

1981: Tafelmusik make their New York debut at the Metropolitan Museum of Art as part of a wider North American tour.

1981: Bob and Doug McKenzie (Canadian SCTV cast members Rick Moranis and Dave Thomas) make their *Tonight Show* debut on December 1st, and upon its release, their album GREAT WHITE NORTH becomes one of the fastest selling debut albums in the history of the Canadian recording industry. **Rush**, with **Geddy Lee** on vocals, guest on their single *Take Off*.

1981: The Canadian music trade paper *The Record* is launched under the direction of **David Farrell.**

*T*urn Me Loose
1982

12TH ANNUAL JUNO AWARDS

April 14, 1982
Harbour Castle
Hilton
Convention
Centre, Toronto
Host:
**Burton
Cummings**
Performers:
**Liona Boyd,
Carole Pope
and Rough
Trade,
Chilliwack,
Burton
Cummings,
B.B. Gabor,
Ronnie
Hawkins and
Carroll Baker,
The Rovers**

When Neil Young was inducted into the Canadian Music Hall of Fame at the 12th annual Juno Awards, he recognized his Canadian roots: "I have this one feeling tonight. I'm proud to be a Canadian." But the ceremonies belonged to a new generation of artists as Loverboy's self-titled debut album set a new standard for most wins at the Junos, taking six trophies, or a quarter of all the awards.

Turn Me Loose
1982 JUNO AWARD WINNERS
(For the Voting Year 1981)

ALBUM OF THE YEAR	LOVERBOY, **Loverboy**
SINGLE OF THE YEAR	*Turn Me Loose,* **Loverboy**
INTERNATIONAL ALBUM OF THE YEAR	DOUBLE FANTASY, **John Lennon**
INTERNATIONAL SINGLE OF THE YEAR	*Bette Davis Eyes,* **Kim Carnes**
COMPOSER OF THE YEAR	**Mike Reno** and **Paul Dean** for *Turn Me Loose,* **Loverboy**
FEMALE VOCALIST OF THE YEAR	**Anne Murray**
MALE VOCALIST OF THE YEAR	**Bruce Cockburn**
GROUP OF THE YEAR	**Loverboy**
COUNTRY FEMALE VOCALIST	**Anne Murray**
COUNTRY MALE VOCALIST	**Ronnie Hawkins**
COUNTRY GROUP OF THE YEAR	**The Good Brothers**
MOST PROMISING FEMALE VOCALIST	**Shari Ulrich**
MOST PROMISING MALE VOCALIST	**Eddie Schwartz**
MOST PROMISING GROUP	**Saga**
INSTRUMENTAL ARTIST OF THE YEAR	**Liona Boyd**
FOLK ARTIST OF THE YEAR	**Bruce Cockburn**
COMEDY ALBUM OF THE YEAR	THE GREAT WHITE NORTH, **Bob & Doug McKenzie**
RECORDING ENGINEER OF THE YEAR	*(tie)* **Keith Stein/Bob Rock** for *When It's Over and It's Your Life,* **Loverboy**; and **Gary Gray** for *Attitude* and *For Those Who Think Young,* **Rough Trade**
PRODUCER OF THE YEAR	**Paul Dean/Bruce Fairbairn** for WORKING FOR THE WEEKEND and *When It's Over,* **Loverboy**
BEST CHILDREN'S ALBUM	INCH BY INCH, **Sandra Beech**
BEST ALBUM GRAPHICS	**Hugh Syme & Debra Samuels**, MOVING PICTURES
BEST JAZZ ALBUM	THE BRASS CONNECTION, **The Brass Connection**
BEST CLASSICAL ALBUM	RAVEL: DAPHNIS ET CHLOE (COMPLETE BALLET), **L'Orchestre symphonique de Montreal, Charles Dutoit**, conductor.
HALL OF FAME AWARD	**Neil Young**

Oscar Peterson

The Technics All-Star Band Award, voted on by record-buyers and fans and presented to outstanding Canadian musicians, is introduced. First winners are Ken "Spider" Sinnaeve (bass), Neil Young (rhythm guitar), Rob McConnell (trombone), Neil Peart (drums), Burton Cummings (keyboards), Rik Emmett (lead guitar), Moe Koffman (sax), and Mark Hasselbach (trumpet).

1982: Kathy Dawn Lang, who had appeared in the musical *Country Chorale* in Edmonton, Alberta and had begun singing at the Sidetrack Cafe there, answers an ad in a local newspaper placed by **Larry Wanagas** looking for a vocalist for a "Texas swing, twin-fiddle band." She gets the job, Wanagas becomes her manager, and she becomes **k.d. lang**, who will reign as the queen of "country-cow-punk."

Bruce Cockburn and Robbie Robertson

1982: Platinum Blonde plays the Toronto club circuit, initially as a tribute to The Police.

1982: Zal Yanovsky and John Sebastian, formerly of **The Lovin' Spoonful**, reunite for the CBC-TV special, *Heart Of Gold*.

1982: The Family Brown appear on the long-running U.S. country show, *Hee Haw*.

1982: Kim Mitchell of **Max Webster** embarks on a solo career.

1982: The **Montreal Jubilation Choir** is formed by **Trevor Payne** for a concert commemorating the 75th anniversary of Union United Church, Montreal's oldest black community church.

1982: Bruce Cockburn receives the USC Gold Pin from the Unitarian Service Committee for his on-going work with Third World countries. He also wins an Edison Award in the Netherlands for the album INNER CITY FRONT and makes a five city tour of Italy.

1982: Lisa Dalbello wins first and second prize at the American Song Festival in the Top 40 category with the songs *Can I*

Do It? and *Don't Get Mad*, co-written with Tim Thorney.

1982: Celine Dion tours Japan, has a couple of hits in Germany, and is a gold medal winner at Tokyo's World Popular Music Festival before appearing on the French TV variety show Champs Elysees and returning to Montreal to sing with the **Montreal Symphony Orchestra**.

1982: At age 17, cellist **Ofra Harnoy** becomes the youngest first prize winner in the history of the New York Concert Artists Guild Award.

1982: The **Robert Gordon** cover of **Jack Scott's** *The Way I Walk* is the catalyst for a reissue of Scott's early material by Attic Records.

1982: Los Angeles mayor Tom Bradley declares January 18th **Bob** and **Doug McKenzie** Day in honor of the two Canadian characters ("hosers") portrayed by **Rick Moranis** and **Dave Thomas** on the TV comedy program SCTV. Back bacon sandwiches and Molson Ale are served at the celebration.

1982: Saga sell out a 12,000-seat concert hall in Budapest, Hungary as part of a triumphant European tour during which they record their Munich, Germany date.

1982: NBC-TV's *Late Night with David Letterman* debuts on February 1st. His side-kick and band leader (**World's Most Dangerous Band**) is multi-talented Canadian musician **Paul Shaffer**, who had previously worked in the band on NBC-TV's *Saturday Night Live*.

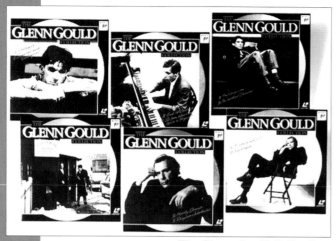

The Glenn Gould Collection

1982: The re-formed **Mamas and the Papas**, with original members John Phillips and **Denny Doherty** joined by Phillips' actress daughter MacKenzie and Spanky McFarlane of the 1960s folk/pop group Spanky And Our Gang, play the first show of their brief reunion tour at New York's Other End club on March 3rd.

1982: John Belushi, **Dan Aykroyd's** partner in **The Blues Brothers**, dies of an accidental drug overdose on March 5th at the Chateau Marmont Hotel in Los Angeles.

1982: Sass Jordan embarks on a solo singing career as the popular Montreal group **The Pinups**, which she has fronted as vocalist/bassist for over three years, play their last gig at The Pretzel in Montreal.

1982: Loverboy appear in a segment of the TV soap opera, *Guiding Light*.

Sass Jordan

1982: The Nylons make their concert debut on May 4th at Massey Hall.

1982: The National Film Board feature *Anna and Kate McGarrigle*, directed by **Carolyn Leaf**, airs on CBC-TV on May 19th.

1982: The Montreal duo of **Rosalind Milligan Hunt** and **Lyn Cullerier**, collectively known as **Cheri**, have a Top 40 U.S. hit with the single *Murphy's Law*.

1982: Pianist **Jane Vasey** of **Downchild Blues Band**, who wrote the group's *Trying To Keep Her 88s Straight*, dies of leukemia at age 33 on July 7th.

1982: Lighthouse plays a two-night reunion at Toronto's Ontario Place.

1982: The **Glenn Gould** Society is founded in Groningen, The Netherlands, on October 1st, three days before he dies, following a severe stroke, at Toronto General Hospital.

1982: *Up Where We Belong*, written by **Buffy Sainte-Marie**, her husband Jack Nitzsche, and Will Jennings and performed by Joe Cocker and Jennifer Warnes, tops the *Billboard* Hot 100 singles chart on November 6th. In 1983, the song is heard on the soundtrack of the movie *An Officer and A Gentleman* and wins an Academy Award as Best Song.

1982: Bruce Cockburn is appointed a Member of the Order of Canada.

1982: Canadian model **Denise Matthews** (a.k.a. **D.D. Winters**) meets Prince backstage at the American Music Awards, and they develop a working relationship during which she changes her name to **Vanity** and launches her recording and acting career. She appears on the cover of *Playboy* in 1988.

E yes Of A Stranger 1983

13TH ANNUAL JUNO AWARDS
April 5, 1983
Toronto Hilton
Harbour Castle
Hotel, Toronto
Hosts:
Burton Cummings and **Alan Thicke**
Performers:
Claude Dubois, The Family Brown, Gordon Lightfoot, The Nylons, David Roberts, The Spoons

When the Right Honorable Edward Schreyer, Governor General of Canada, inducted Glenn Gould into the Canadian Music Hall of Fame, he recognized Gould's enormous contribution to Canadian and international music: "This honors a man whose talent burned so brightly that he transcended all categories of craft and lifestyle or even nationhood in the sense that his talent was truly of international caliber."

Eyes Of A Stranger
1983 JUNO AWARD WINNERS
(For the Voting Year 1982)

ALBUM OF THE YEAR	GET LUCKY, **Loverboy**
SINGLE OF THE YEAR	*Eyes Of A Stranger*, **Payola$**
INTERNATIONAL ALBUM	*Business As Usual*, **Men At Work**
INTERNATIONAL SINGLE	*Eye Of the Tiger*, **Survivor**
COMPOSERS OF THE YEAR	**Bob Rock**, **Paul Hyde** for *Eyes Of A Stranger*, **The Payola$**
FEMALE VOCALIST OF THE YEAR	**Carole Pope**
MALE VOCALIST OF THE YEAR	**Bryan Adams**
GROUP OF THE YEAR	**Loverboy**
COUNTRY FEMALE VOCALIST	**Anne Murray**
COUNTRY MALE VOCALIST	**Eddie Eastman**
COUNTRY GROUP	**The Good Brothers**
INSTRUMENTAL ARTIST	**Liona Boyd**
BEST CHILDREN'S ALBUM	WHEN YOU DREAM A DREAM, **Bob Schneider**
MOST PROMISING FEMALE VOCALIST	**Lydia Taylor**
MOST PROMISING MALE VOCALIST	**Kim Mitchell**
MOST PROMISING GROUP	**Payola$**
PRODUCER OF THE YEAR	**Bill Henderson**, **Brian McLeod** for *Whatcha Gonna Do* and *Secret Information*, **Chilliwack** (Solid Gold)
RECORDING ENGINEER	**Bob Rock** for *No Stranger To Danger*, **Payola$**
BEST ALBUM GRAPHICS	**Dean Motter** for *Metal On Metal*, **Anvil**
BEST CLASSICAL ALBUM	*Bach: The Goldberg Variations*, **Glenn Gould**
BEST JAZZ ALBUM	*I Didn't Know About You*, **Fraser MacPherson**, **Oliver Gannon**
HALL OF FAME	**Glenn Gould**

The Vancouver-based group Payola$ won four Junos, including Most Promising Group and Best Single for *Eyes Of A Stranger*, and fellow Vancouver artist Bryan Adams won his first Juno Award for Male Vocalist of the Year. Anne Murray's absence from the show again caused a certain amount of controversy and an on-stage comment from Burton Cummings' co-host, Alan Thicke, a friend of Murray's, who quipped, "Anne Murray is in Los Angeles, conducting herself, as usual, in a manner that does honor to the Canadian recording industry." Jazz legend Count Basie was on hand to introduce the nominees for Best Jazz Album.

1983: The Tommy Banks Quintet becomes the first foreign jazz group to tour in the People's Republic Of China.

1983: Rough Trade embarks on a European tour after opening for David Bowie on a number of his Canadian dates.

1983: Loverboy become the first international artist in CBS Records' history to sell over three million albums in the U.S. The band's sophomore album GET LUCKY is at that point the biggest-selling LP ever to come out of Canada.

1983: Gordon Lightfoot makes his silver screen debut in the Bruce Dern/Helen Shaver film *Harry Tracy, Desperado*.

1983: Rush prove to be kings of the magazine polls as they place first in Britain's *Sounds* magazine's poll in the album (SIGNALS) and group categories. *Circus* magazine in the U.S. also makes them number one in the same categories as well as in the categories of songwriters, bassist (**Geddy Lee**), and drummer (**Neil Peart**).

1983: Walter Ostanek is inducted into the International Polka Hall of Fame in Chicago.

1983: Jackie Mittoo tours with British band UB40.

1983: Barney Bentall, the Toronto-born son of a Baptist minister, who had recorded in the late 1970s for A&M under the name Brandon Wolf, reverts back to his given name and begins working the British Columbia bar scene with **The Revengers** (later **The Legendary Hearts**).

1983: Honeymoon Suite takes top prize in the Homegrown contest run by Toronto radio station Q107.

1983: While in high school, guitarist **Jeff Healey** is chosen as a Canadian Stage Band Festival All-Star for two consecutive years.

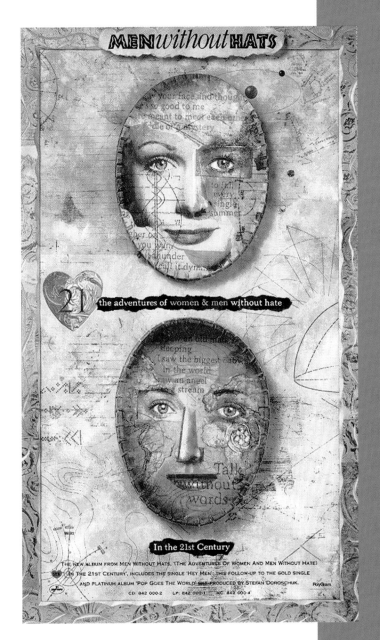

1983: Corey Hart signs to Aquarius Records in his hometown of Montreal and heads for England to record his debut album. Eric Clapton guests on the track *Jenny Fay*.

1983: A&M Records releases **Bryan Adams'** CUTS LIKE A KNIFE album in January. Through the rest of the year, Adams tours with Aerosmith, Journey, and The Police (in Australia and New Zealand) and headlines his own shows in Japan.

1983: Bruce Cockburn and **Nancy White** travel to Nicaragua and Mexico

Parachute Club

on an Oxfam-sponsored fact-finding tour. His Nicaragua experience and his subsequent anger explode in the song *If I Had A Rocket Launcher* released on November 8, 1984, the day after Ronald Reagan was elected for a second term as president.

1983: Brian MacLeod and **Ab Bryant** leave **Chilliwack** to become full-time members of **The Headpins**.

1983: Triumph's album *Never Surrender* premieres simultaneously at seven radio stations across Canada on April 29th via the first nationwide live radio network of its type in Canada. In the April issue of *Hit Parader* magazine, the group's guitarist **Rik Emmett** makes the Top 15 list of Great Guitar Heroes along with artists like Jeff Beck, Eric Clapton, Ritchie Blackmore, and Jimi Hendrix.

1983: A cover story in *Canadian Business* on **Anne Murray**'s business empire reveals that to this point she has sold over 18 million records internationally for Capitol Records from 19 albums and 30 singles.

1983: "Metal Queen" **Lee Aaron**, with interim backing group **Sam Thunder**, debuts in England on May 4th at London's Marquee Club.

1983: Singer/songwriter **Stan Rogers** dies on June 2nd in a plane fire aboard an Air Canada DC-9 at Cincinnati airport on his way home to Toronto from the

Kerrville Folk Festival in Texas. Rogers leaves a musical legacy of six highly-acclaimed albums recorded for his own Fogarty's Cove record label.

1983: Buzz Shearman (**Douglas Stewart Shearman**), former lead singer for Toronto groups **Leigh Ashford** and **Moxy**, dies on June 16th following a motorcycle accident.

1983: The **Men Without Hats** techno-pop single *The Safety Dance* lands at number three on the *Billboard* Hot 100 chart, and earns the group a Grammy Award for 1984 in the category of Best New Artist.

1983: Powder Blues appear at the Montreux Jazz Festival in Switzerland and the North Sea Jazz/Blues Festival. Portions of the Montreux concert are featured on the group's album LIVE AT MONTREUX.

1983: Major country music festival The Big Valley Jamboree is held for the first time in **Buffy Sainte-Marie**'s hometown of Craven, Saskatchewan.

1983: *Strange Brew*, the **Bob and Doug McKenzie** film, shot in "Hoserama" by **Dave Thomas** and **Rick Moranis**, premieres on August 26th with the title song performed by **Ian Thomas**, Dave's brother.

1983: Corey Hart's debut single *Sunglasses At Night* is released in the fall but does not make the charts in Canada until February of 1984, peaking outside of the Top 20. In the U.S., where his video is getting regular airplay on MTV, the single soars into the Top 10.

1983: Loverboy Day is proclaimed on October 16th in Shreveport, Louisiana, and they appear as musical guests on NBC-TV's *Saturday Night Live* on November 19th.

1983: The National Library of Canada acquires **Glenn Gould's** private legacy from his estate.

R ise Up
1984

14TH ANNUAL JUNO AWARDS

December 5, 1984

Automotive Building, Exhibition Place, Toronto

Hosts: **Andrea Martin** and **Joe Flaherty**

Performers: **Veronique Beliveau, The Crew Cuts, The Diamonds, The Four Lads, Honeymoon Suite, Sherry Kean, The Parachute Club, Platinum Blonde, Rob McConnell and the Boss Brass, Rough Trade, Bob Schneider, Jane Siberry, Diane Tell**

"I'd like to thank CBS and True North Records," Carole Pope said while accepting her second consecutive Female Vocalist award, "and my creator, Max Factor."

Bryan Adams "arrived" as a bonafide star this year, winning four awards for his CUTS LIKE A KNIFE album project.

Rise Up
1984 JUNO AWARD WINNERS
(For the Voting Year 1983)

ALBUM OF THE YEAR	CUTS LIKE A KNIFE, **Bryan Adams**
SINGLE OF THE YEAR	*Rise Up*, **Parachute Club**
COMPOSER OF THE YEAR	**Bryan Adams/Jim Vallance** for *Cuts Like A Knife*, **Bryan Adams**
INTERNATIONAL ALBUM OF THE YEAR	SYNCHRONICITY, **The Police**
INTERNATIONAL SINGLE OF THE YEAR	*Billie Jean*, **Michael Jackson**
FEMALE VOCALIST	**Carole Pope**
MALE VOCALIST	**Bryan Adams**
COUNTRY MALE VOCALIST	**Murray McLauchlan**
COUNTRY FEMALE VOCALIST	**Anne Murray**
MOST PROMISING MALE VOCALIST	**Zappacosta**
MOST PROMISING FEMALE VOCALIST	**Sherry Kean**
GROUP OF THE YEAR	**Loverboy**
MOST PROMISING GROUP	**Parachute Club**
COUNTRY GROUP	**The Good Brothers**
INSTRUMENTAL ARTIST	**Liona Boyd**
BEST JAZZ ALBUM	ALL IN GOOD TIME, **Rob McConnell & the Boss Brass**
BEST CLASSICAL ALBUM	BRAHMS: BALLADES & RHAPSODIES, **Glenn Gould**
BEST COMEDY ALBUM	STRANGE BREW, **Bob & Doug McKenzie**
BEST CHILDREN'S ALBUM	RUGRAT ROCK, **The Rugrats**
PRODUCER OF THE YEAR	**Bryan Adams** for CUTS LIKE A KNIFE, **Bryan Adams**
RECORDING ENGINEER OF THE YEAR	**John Naslen** for *Stealing Fire*, **Bruce Cockburn**
BEST ALBUM GRAPHICS	**Dean Motter, Jeff Jackson & Debra Samuels** for SEAMLESS, **The Nylons**
BEST VIDEO	**Rob Quartly** for *Sunglasses At Night*, **Corey Hart**
HALL OF FAME	**The Crew Cuts, The Diamonds, The Four Lads**
WALT GREALIS SPECIAL ACHIEVEMENT AWARD	**J. Lyman Potts**

The Diamonds

Parachute Club took the honors for Most Promising Group and for their single *Rise Up*, while Corey Hart's *Sunglasses At Night* video, directed by Rob Quartly, received the first Juno in the Best Video category. The inaugural Walt Grealis Special Achievement Award, named after the *RPM Weekly* publisher/editor and Juno co-founder, was presented to record executive J. Lyman Potts of the Canadian Talent Library. The induction of The Crew Cuts, The Diamonds, and The Four Lads into the Canadian Music Hall Of Fame was the highlight of the show as the 12 members of the three doo-wop groups performed a medley of their hits from the 1950s.

1984: Canada's first fully-animated video, *Can't Stand Still* for **The Extra's** first single, is produced by **Peter Sandler,** who had worked on Yellow Submarine.

1984: Daniel Lanois co-produces the soundtrack to Alan Parker's film *Birdy* with Peter Gabriel, who composes and performs the music.

1984: k.d. lang makes her U.S. debut at the Bottom Line in New York.

1984: After playing at a farewell party for Canada's U.S. ambassador **Ken Taylor** in New York, **The Nylons** leave for a tour of the Far East, Australia, and New Zealand.

1984: Sharon, Lois & Bram's *Elephant Show* is first telecast by CBC-TV and appears on the Nickelodeon cable channel beginning in 1987.

1984: Leonard Cohen, singer/musician/songwriter **Lewis Furey,** and actress/singer **Carole Laure** collaborate on the film *Night Magic*. Cohen's *Book of Mercy*, a collection of psalms, is released as his ambitious, long-form video, *I Am A Hotel*, written, scored, and directed by Cohen and featuring appearances by dancer/choreographer Ann Ditchburn and figure skater Toller Cranston, among others. It wins the Gold Rose Award at the Montreux International Television Festival.

1984: Fred Penner begins hosting the popular CBC-TV children's show *Fred Penner's Place*, which is introduced in the U.S. on Nickelodeon in 1989.

1984: At age 10, **Alanis Morissette** is in the cast of the kids series *You Can't Do That On Television* seen on the Nickelodeon network, and she cuts an indie single titled *Fate Stay With Me*.

1984: Before taking a two-year sabbatical from the music business to go through the image perception transformation from child star to mature

Liona Boyd

recording artist, **Celine Dion** plays six weeks at the Olympia in Paris and sings at Montreal's Olympic Stadium for the Pope and an audience of 65,00 people.

1984: Lisa Dalbello drops her first name professionally and moves to England, where she is managed by Roger Davies, whose other clients include Olivia Newton-John and Tina Turner.

1984: Tafelmusik become the first North American baroque orchestra to be invited to tour Europe.

1984: Blue Rodeo play their first gig at the Rivoli in Toronto on February 14th.

Corey Hart

1984: M+M (formerly **Martha and the Muffins**), led by **Martha Johnson** and **Mark Gane**, find that social commentary and pop music do in fact mix as their single *Black Stations, White Stations,* from their Daniel Lanois-produced Mystery Walk album becomes a hit in Canada, the U.S., and the U.K. during the summer.

1984: Celebrated Canadian jazz guitarist **Lenny Breau** is murdered in Los Angeles on August 12th.

Jane Siberry

1984: Corey Hart tours with Hall and Oates and Rick Springfield in August, and later in the year is nominated by MTV as one of the hot new acts of 1984.

1984: MuchMusic, the Nation's Music Station, is launched in Toronto on August 31st.

1984: Eleanor Townsend is inducted into the Fiddler's Hall of Fame at Oceola, New York.

1984: Jane Siberry makes her U.S. concert debut at The Ritz in New York on September 17th.

1984: Bryan Adams gives a free concert at the 2700-seat Orpheum Theatre in Vancouver in order to complete filming of his five-song video-cassette, and his manager, **Bruce Allen,** buys $1000 worth of pizza to feed many of the 6000 people who are waiting in line.

1984: Rush tours Japan, Hawaii, Canada, and the U.S. during their 100-date Grace Under Pressure tour.

1984: Ron Tabak, former lead singer of Vancouver group **Prism**, dies on December 26th from a brain hemorrhage after falling off his bicycle.

1984: Corey Hart plays a hometown concert at The Spectrum in Montreal on December 28th which heats up the blood of the local teeny-bop set.

1984: In the middle of an extensive North American tour, **Bryan Adams** takes time out to co-host MTV's New Years' Eve Bash.

Never Surrender
1985

15TH ANNUAL JUNO AWARDS
November 4, 1985
Harbour Castle
Convention
Centre, Toronto
Host:
Andrea Martin
and **Martin Short**
Performers:
**Bryan Adams,
The Box,
The Canadian
Brass,
k. d. lang and
the reclines,
Luba,
Kim Mitchell,
Liberty Silver,
Tina Turner**

With his three Juno wins, a scorching live duet with Tina Turner on *It's Only Love*, and his integral involvement in *Tears Are Not Enough*, the benefit project song for Ethiopian famine relief, Bryan Adams was center stage, though he was up-staged when k.d. lang made a dash for the stage to accept her award as Most Promising Female Vocalist in a frothy, white wedding dress.

Never Surrender

1985 JUNO AWARD WINNERS
(For the Voting Year 1984)

ALBUM OF THE YEAR	RECKLESS, **Bryan Adams**
SINGLE OF THE YEAR	*Never Surrender*, **Corey Hart**
COMPOSER OF THE YEAR	**Bryan Adams/Jim Vallance**
MALE VOCALIST OF THE YEAR:	**Bryan Adams**
FEMALE VOCALIST OF THE YEAR	**Luba**
GROUP OF THE YEAR	**The Parachute Club**
COUNTRY MALE VOCALIST	**Murray McLauchlan**
COUNTRY FEMALE VOCALIST	**Anne Murray**
COUNTRY GROUP	**The Family Brown**
MOST PROMISING MALE VOCALIST	**Paul Janz**
MOST PROMISING FEMALE VOCALIST	**k.d. lang**
MOST PROMISING GROUP	**Idle Eyes**
PRODUCER OF THE YEAR	**David Foster** for CHICAGO 17, **Chicago**
RECORDING ENGINEER OF THE YEAR	**Hayward Parrott** for UNDERWORLD, **The Front**
BEST VIDEO	**Rob Quartly** for *Criminal Mind*, **Gowan**
INTERNATIONAL ALBUM OF THE YEAR	BORN IN THE U.S.A., **Bruce Springsteen**
INTERNATIONAL SINGLE OF THE YEAR	*I Want To Know What Love Is*, **Foreigner**
INSTRUMENTAL ARTIST	**The Canadian Brass**
BEST R&B/SOUL RECORDING	LOST SOMEWHERE INSIDE YOUR LOVE, **Liberty Silver**
BEST REGGAE/CALYPSO RECORDING	HEAVEN MUST HAVE SENT YOU, **Liberty Silver & Otis Gayle**
BEST CHILDREN'S ALBUM	MURMEL MURMEL MUNSCH, **Robert Munsch**
BEST CLASSICAL ALBUM (SOLO OR CHAMBER ENSEMBLE)	W.A. MOZART: STRING QUARTETS, **The Orford String Quartet**
BEST CLASSICAL ALBUM (LARGE ENSEMBLE)	RAVEL: MA MÈRE L'OYE/PAVANE POUR UN INFANTE DEBUNTE/TOMBEAU DE COUPERIN and VALSES NOBLES ET SENTIMENTALES, **L'Orchestre symphonique de Montréal, Charles Dutoit, conductor**
BEST JAZZ ALBUM	A BEAUTIFUL FRIENDSHIP, **Don Thompson**
BEST ALBUM GRAPHICS	**Rob MacIntyre/Dimo Safari** for STRANGE ANIMAL, **Gowan**
HALL OF FAME	**Wilf Carter**
WALT GREALIS SPECIAL ACHIEVEMENT AWARD	**A.H. Joseph**

Prime Minister Brian Mulroney recognized the generosity of Canadian musicians as he accepted a special Juno awarded to the Canadian people for their support of the Northern Lights for Africa initiative: "Tonight is a double celebration. A celebration of the tremendous generosity of the Canadian people inspired in many ways by the creativity of the Canadian artistic community, so I accept on behalf of the Canadian people this tremendous award, but tonight is also a celebration of the unique and splendid talent of Canada's recording artists and the strength and vibrancy of this industry." Country legend Wilf Carter (a.k.a. Montana Slim) was inducted into the Canadian Music Hall of Fame.

k.d. lang

1985: Glass Tiger, formerly **Tokyo**, signs to Capitol Records and open for Culture Club at Maple Leaf Gardens.

1985: Luba and group travel to Japan where their song *How Many (Rivers To Cross)* is an entry at the 16th World Popular Music Song Festival.

1985: The Tragically Hip, named after a line from Michael Nesmith's *Animal Parts* video, is formed in Kingston, Ontario by Queen's University alumni **Gord Downie**, **Bobby Baker,** and **Gord Sinclair**.

1985: On February 4th, **Bruce Cockburn** begins a five-week tour of Czechoslovakia, Austria, and East and West Germany with back-to-back dates in West and East Berlin.

1985: *Tears Are Not Enough*, a song by **Bryan Adams**, **Jim Vallance**, and **David Foster** (with the title conceived by **Bob Rock** and **Paul Hyde** and the French verse by **Rachel Paiement)** written to raise funds for Ethiopian famine relief and domestic food banks, is recorded on February 10th at Toronto's Manta Sound Studios under the name **Northern Lights** with **Bruce Allen** and **Maureen Jack** working as the co-ordinators of the project. The instrumental track had previously been recorded in Vancouver at Little Mountain Sound Studios (Engineer: **Bob Rock** with assistant **Mike Fraser)**

and at the Lion Share Recording Studio (Engineer: **Humberto Gatica** with assistant **Tom Fouce**) with a group that consists of **David Foster** (keyboards), **Paul Dean** (guitar), **Jim Vallance** (drums), **David Sinclair** (guitar), **Steve Denroche** (French horn), and **Doug Johnson** (keyboards). In Toronto, the Canadian recording artists, entertainers, and sports personalities involved include **Bryan Adams**, **Carroll Baker**, **Veronique Beliveau**, **Salome Bey**, **Liona Boyd**, **John Candy**, **Robert Charlebois**, **Tom Cochrane**, **Bruce Cockburn**, **Burton Cummings**, **Dalbello**, **Paul Dean**, **Gordon Deppe**, **Claude Dubois**, **Robin Duke**, **Rik Emmett**, **David Foster**, **Donny Gerrard**, **Brian Good**, **Corey Hart**, **Ronnie Hawkins**, **Dan Hill**, **Mark Holmes**, **Tommy Hunter**, **Paul Hyde**, **Martha Johnson**, **Marc Jordan**, **Geddy Lee**, **Eugene Levy**, **Gordon Lightfoot**, **Baron Longfellow**, **Loverboy**, **Luba**, **Richard Manuel**, **Murray McLauchlan**, **Frank Mills**, **Joni Mitchell**, **Kim Mitchell**, **Anne Murray**, **Bruce Murray**, the 1985 National Hockey League All-Stars, **Aldo Nova**, **Catherine O'Hara**, **Rachel Paiement**, **Oscar Peterson**, **Colina Phillips**, **Carole Pope**, **Mike Reno**, **Lorraine Segato**, **Paul Shaffer**, **Graham Shaw**, **Leroy Sibbles**, **Jane Siberry**, **Liberty Silver**, **Wayne St. John**, **Alan Thicke**, **Dave Thomas**, **Ian Thomas**, **Sylvia Tyson**, **Jim Vallance**, **Sharon Lee Williams**, **Neil Young**, and **Zappacosta**.

1985: Triumph sets out on their 17-date Thunder Seven tour on March 16th.

1985: k.d. lang appears with the **Edmonton Symphony Orchestra** in Edmonton, Alberta, on March 31st, and when record executive Seymour Stein sees k.d. lang at New York's Bottom Line later in the spring, he signs her to his Sire record label, which at the time is also the recording home of Madonna.

1985: Corey Hart's single/video *Never Surrender* from his sophomore album BOY IN THE BOX becomes his first number one single in Canada and his biggest hit in the U.S., where it reaches number three.

1985: Toronto (a.k.a. **Holly Woods and Toronto**), one of only a handful of groups from Canada to have four straight platinum albums, play their last date on April 18th in Hanover, Ontario.

1985: Sheriff play their last gig on June 15th, but it is not the last heard of the band as group members **Arnold Lanni** and **Wolf Hassel** later form the band **Frozen Ghost**.

1985: Bryan Adams' single *Heaven*, a song originally written by Adams and **Jim Vallance** for the 1983 film *A Night In Heaven* starring Lesley Ann Warren and Christopher Atkins, begins a two-week run at the top of the *Billboard* Hot 100 chart on June 22nd. His concert at the CNE Stadium in Toronto results in the largest gross by a Canadian artist in the Canadian marketplace in history ($914,163.50), and he receives a diamond award in December for sales of over one million copies of his RECKLESS album in Canada, the first for a Canadian artist.

1985: Kim Mitchell Day is proclaimed on August 28th in Sarnia, Ontario.

1985: Loverboy receives a Golden Globe Award in New York from Columbia Records for selling in excess of five million albums outside of the artist's country of origin (Canada).

1985: The Band, with **The Revols**, play a benefit in Stratford, Ontario at, and for, the Shakespeare Festival Theatre. It is the 25th anniversary reunion of the Rockin' Revols, with whom The Band's **Richard Manuel** began his career.

1985: The Payola$ play their last gig in December at Vancouver's Club Soda.

Don't Forget Me (When I'm Gone) *1986*

16TH ANNUAL JUNO AWARDS
November 10, 1986
Harbour Castle Convention Centre, Toronto
Host: **Howie Mandel**
Performers: **Glass Tiger, Kenny Hamilton, Corey Hart, Honeymoon Suite, Gordon Lightfoot, Luba, Kim Mitchell, Billy Newton-Davis, Glen Ricketts, Liberty Silver, Erroll Starr, Martine St-Clair**

"So this is where you hold this thing every year!" Anne Murray remarked as she returned to the Juno ceremonies after a lengthy absence. "Finally found it! As some of you know, I've won a great many of these. I just want you to know that I'm very proud of every one."

Don't Forget Me (When I'm Gone)
1986 JUNO AWARD WINNERS
(For the Voting Year 1985)

BEST SELLING INTERNATIONAL ALBUM	BROTHERS IN ARMS, **Dire Straits**
BEST SELLING INTERNATIONAL SINGLE	*Live Is Life*, **Opus**
ALBUM OF THE YEAR	THE THIN RED LINE, **Glass Tiger**
SINGLE OF THE YEAR	*Don't Forget Me (When I'm Gone)*, **Glass Tiger**
FEMALE VOCALIST OF THE YEAR	**Luba**
MALE VOCALIST OF THE YEAR	**Bryan Adams**
GROUP OF THE YEAR	**Honeymoon Suite**
COUNTRY MALE VOCALIST	**Murray McLauchlan**
COUNTRY FEMALE VOCALIST	**Anne Murray**
COUNTRY GROUP OR DUO	**Prairie Oyster**
INSTRUMENTAL ARTIST	**David Foster**
MOST PROMISING FEMALE VOCALIST	**Kim Richardson**
MOST PROMISING MALE VOCALIST	**Billy Newton-Davis**
MOST PROMISING GROUP	**Glass Tiger**
COMPOSER OF THE YEAR	**Jim Vallance**
BEST CHILDREN'S ALBUM	10 CARROT DIAMOND, **Charlotte Diamond**
BEST CLASSICAL ALBUM (SOLO OR CHAMBER ENSEMBLE)	STOLEN GEMS, **James Campbell** (clarinet) and **Eric Robertson** (keyboard)
BEST CLASSICAL ALBUM (LARGE ENSEMBLE OR SOLOISTS WITH LARGE ENSEMBLE ACCOMPANIMENT)	HOLST: THE PLANETS, **Toronto Symphony Orchestra, Andrew Davis**, conductor
BEST JAZZ ALBUM	LIGHTS OF BURGUNDY, **Oliver Jones**
BEST REGGAE/CALYPSO RECORDING	REVOLUTIONARY TEA PARTY, **Lillian Allen**
BEST R&B/SOUL RECORDING	LOVE IS A CONTACT SPORT, **Billy Newton-Davis**
PRODUCER OF THE YEAR	**David Foster** for ST. ELMO'S FIRE Soundtrack, Various Artists
RECORDING ENGINEER OF THE YEAR	**Joe and Gino Vannelli**, BLACK CARS, **Gino Vannelli**
BEST ALBUM GRAPHICS	**Hugh Syme/Dimo Safari** for POWER WINDOWS, **Rush**
BEST VIDEO	**Greg Masuak** for *How Many (Rivers To Cross)*, **Luba**
HALL OF FAME	**Gordon Lightfoot**
WALT GREALIS SPECIAL ACHIEVEMENT AWARD	**Jack Richardson**

Luba

Glass Tiger were three-time winners, and Rick "The Man in Motion" Hansen, the inspiration for David Foster's song *St. Elmo's Fire*, presented the Group of the Year Award to Honeymoon Suite.

The appearance of Bob Dylan to help induct Gordon Lightfoot into the Canadian Music Hall of Fame added the touch of excitement only a music legend can generate.

1986: Liona Boyd once again broadens her audience as she releases the album PERSONA featuring rock guitarists **Eric Clapton and David Gilmour**.

1986: Luba's *Let It Go* and *The Best Is Yet To Come* is included on the soundtrack of the Mickey Rourke/Kim Basinger film *9 1/2 Weeks*.

1986: Rough Trade end their 14-year career in 1986 with their Deep Six In 86 mini-tour with guests Nona Hendryx, Dusty Springfield, and Taborah Johnson and a show at the RPM Club in Toronto.

1986: Long involved in the fund-raising efforts of the Canadian Cerebral Palsy Association, **Neil Young** and son Ben are featured on a poster released by the organization.

1986: Randy Bachman joins the exclusive Million Air Club for having had his songs broadcast over a million times over the North American airwaves.

1986: Jennifer Warnes, one of **Leonard Cohen**'s former back-up singers, records an album of his songs titled FAMOUS BLUE RAINCOAT. The subsequent single and video *First We Take Manahattan* creates a renewed surge of interest in Cohen and his music, and in 1988, after receiving the Crystal Globe Award from CBS Records for the sale of over five million copies of his record outside of America, the album I'M YOUR MAN is released.

Gordon Lightfoot and Bob Dylan

1986: Honeymoon Suite record the theme for the Mel Gibson film *Lethal Weapon*.

1986: On January 26th, **Corey Hart** becomes only the second Canadian artist in history to sell over a million copies of an album in Canada for BOY IN THE BOX.

1986: Richard Manuel of **The Band** commits suicide on March 4th after a gig with the group in Winter Park, Florida. **Robbie Robertson** dedicates a future solo track, *Fallen Angel*, to him. Eric Clapton's tribute to Manuel is *Holy Mother*.

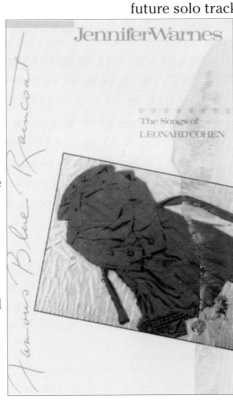

1986: Former Toronto carpet salesman turned internationally renowned comedian **Howie Mandel** releases the album FITS LIKE A GLOVE and the single *I Do the Watusi*.

1986: The **Glenn Gould** Prize is inaugurated on April 24th as "a tribute by the people of Canada to the life and work of Glenn Gould."

Glass Tiger

1986: David Foster is named songwriter of the year at the BMI Awards in New York.

1986: Peter Gabriel's SO album, co-produced by Gabriel and **Daniel Lanois**, debuts at number one on the British album chart in May.

1986: Bryan Adams, U2, Sting, Peter Gabriel, and Lou Reed open Amnesty International's a Conspiracy of Hope tour on May 31st at the Cow Palace in San Francisco.

1986: The **Loverboy** single/video *Heaven In Your Eyes* is featured in the soundtrack of the film *Top Gun*, recorded without the participation of group member **Doug Johnson** who objects to the militaristic content of the film.

1986: Honeymoon Suite's *What Does It Take* is featured in the Warner Bros. film *One Crazy Summer,* and the band are finalists at the Yamaha World Popular Music Festival in Tokyo with the Ray Coburn song *Those Were The Days.*

1986: Ian & Sylvia reunite on August 18th for a concert at the Kingswood Music Theatre in Maple, Ontario, and the evening's proceedings, which also include performances from guests **Gordon Lightfoot**, Judy Collins, Emmylou Harris, and **Murray McLauchlan**, are filmed by the CBC.

1986: *Throb*, a TV sitcom that takes a comedic look at the youth-oriented record business, is released to syndication with the theme written by **Paul Cooper** of **The Nylons** and performed by the group, who make several guest appearances.

1986: French music video network MusiquePlus, sister station to MuchMusic, goes on the air in Quebec on September 2nd.

1986: Glass Tiger's *Don't Forget Me (When I'm Gone)* peaks at number two on the *Billboard* singles chart on October 11th.

1986: Powder Blues win the W.C Handy Award as Best Foreign Blues Group at the National Blues Foundation Convention in Memphis, Tennessee.

1986: The release of **Rita MacNeil's** album FLYING ON YOUR OWN in December, produced by **Declan O'Doherty** and **Ralph Dillon** for her own Lupins record label, proves to be a major turning point in MacNeil's career. Virgin Records subsequently sign her and, in 1988, fellow Nova Scotian **Anne Murray** releases the title song as the debut single from her album ASIAM.

*S*hakin' Like A Human Being
1987

17TH ANNUAL JUNO AWARDS
November 2, 1987
O'Keefe Centre, Toronto
Host:
Howie Mandel
Performers:
Erroll Starr and Kim Richardson, Gowan, Oliver Jones, Luba, The Nylons, The Partland Brothers, Rock & Hyde, Gino Vannelli

Randy Bachman, Burton Cummings, Garry Peterson, and Jim Kale, the four original members of the night's Hall Of Fame inductees The Guess Who, inadvertently had their acceptance speeches cut off by a commercial break during the telecast, and the resulting kerfuffle produced a half- hour profile on the group by the CBC on December 29, 1987. The inaugural Entertainer of the Year award, voted on by the public, was won by Bryan Adams, who accepted with his band via satellite from London, England, while Kim Mitchell's SHAKIN' LIKE A HUMAN BEING became the first release on a Canadian independent label (Alert) to win in the category of Album of the Year.

Shakin' Like A Human Being

1987 JUNO AWARD WINNERS
(For the Voting Year 1986)

CANADIAN ENTERTAINER OF THE YEAR	**Bryan Adams**
BEST SELLING INTERNATIONAL ALBUM	TRUE BLUE, **Madonna**
BEST SELLING INTERNATIONAL SINGLE	*Venus*, **Bananarama**
ALBUM OF THE YEAR	SHAKIN' LIKE A HUMAN BEING, **Kim Mitchell**
SINGLE OF THE YEAR	*Someday*, **Glass Tiger**
FEMALE VOCALIST OF THE YEAR	**Luba**
MALE VOCALIST OF THE YEAR	**Bryan Adams**
GROUP OF THE YEAR	**Tom Cochrane & Red Rider**
COUNTRY FEMALE VOCALIST OF THE YEAR	**k.d. lang**
COUNTRY MALE VOCALIST OF THE YEAR	**Ian Tyson**
COUNTRY GROUP OF THE YEAR	**Prairie Oyster**
INSTRUMENTAL ARTIST OF THE YEAR	**David Foster**
MOST PROMISING FEMALE VOCALIST	**Rita MacNeil**
MOST PROMISING MALE VOCALIST	**Tim Feehan**
MOST PROMISING GROUP OF THE YEAR	**Frozen Ghost**
COMPOSER OF THE YEAR	**Jim Vallance**
BEST CHILDREN'S ALBUM	DRUMS, **Bill Usher**
BEST CLASSICAL COMPOSITION	*(tie)* ATAYOSKEWIN, **Edmonton Symphony Orchestra**, **Uri Mayer**, conductor, **Malcolm Forsyth**, composer; and PAGES OF SOLITARY DELIGHTS, **Maureen Forrester** with the **McGill Symphony Orchestra**, **Donald Steven**, composer
BEST CLASSICAL ALBUM (SOLO OR ENSEMBLE)	SCHUBERT: QUINTET IN C, **Orford String Quartet**, **Ofra Harnoy**, cello
BEST CLASSICAL ALBUM (LARGE ENSEMBLE)	HOLST: THE PLANETS, **L'Orchestre symphonique de Montréal**, **Charles Dutoit**, conductor
BEST JAZZ ALBUM	IF YOU COULD SEE ME NOW, **The Oscar Peterson Four**
BEST R&B/SOUL RECORDING	PEEK-A-BOO, **Kim Richardson**
BEST REGGAE/CALYPSO RECORDING	MEAN WHILE, **Leroy Sibbles**
PRODUCER OF THE YEAR	**Daniel Lanois** for SO, **Peter Gabriel**; and THE JOSHUA TREE, **U2**
RECORDING ENGINEER OF THE YEAR	**Joe & Gino Vannelli** for WILD HORSES and YOUNG LOVER, **Gino Vannelli**
BEST ALBUM GRAPHICS	**Jamie Bennett & Shari Spier** for SMALL VICTORIES, **The Parachute Club**
BEST VIDEO	**Ron Berti** for *Love Is Fire*, **The Parachute Club**
HALL OF FAME	**The Guess Who**
WALT GREALIS SPECIAL ACHIEVEMENT AWARD	**Bruce Allen**

Bruce Allen

1987: After close to two years away from the music business, **Celine Dion** returns as a dance music artist and wins the Eurovision Song Contest with *Ne partez pas sans moi*, which sells over 200,000 copies in Europe in a couple of days. Her album *INCOGNITO* becomes one of the biggest sellers of the year in Quebec.

1987: Daniel Lanois co-produces **Robbie Robertson's** self-titled, debut solo album.

1987: k.d. lang records her sophomore album ANGEL WITH A LARIAT in England with Dave Edmunds in the producer's chair. lang performs the **Patsy Cline** classic *Three Cigarettes And An Ash Tray* on *The Tonight Show*, which is seen by Cline's producer Owen Bradley, who subsequently produces her third album.

1987: The Nylons' *That Kind Of Man* is heard on the soundtrack of the Disney movie, *Tin Men*.

1987: Vancouver's **Skinny Puppy** has their album CLEANSE, FOLD AND MANIPULATE listed in the Top 10 of *Melody Maker's* year-end poll in the U.K.

1987: Ross Vannelli, who wrote the hit *I Just Wanna Stop* for brother Gino, becomes the producer behind the California Raisins records that include the single *I Heard It Through the Grapevine* with Buddy Miles on vocals.

1987: The track *Overload* by Toronto's **Zappacosta** is included on the sound-track of the film *Dirty Dancing*, which sells over 10 million copies.

1987: Peterborough, Ontario native **Sebastein**

Bruce Cockburn

Bierk (a.k.a. **Sebastien Bach**) joins American group **Skid Row** as vocalist.

1987: MuchMusic, with Britain's Sky Channel, organizes the first World Music Video Awards.

1987: King Lou and Capital Q become the **Dream Warriors**.

1987: Dan Hill's *Can't We Try* is named the number one adult contemporary hit of the year by *Billboard* magazine.

1987: Bryan Adams fourth album, INTO THE FIRE, is released, and eventually becomes the first CD by a Canadian artist to be certified gold for sales of 50,000 copies.

1987: Lucille Starr becomes the first woman inducted into the Canadian Country Music Hall of Honor.

Cowboy Junkies

Kim Mitchell

David Foster

1987: Bruce Cockburn's WAITING FOR A MIRACLE becomes the first double CD to be issued by a Canadian artist.

1987: Bryan Adams records a live version of *Run Rudolph Run* on June 3rd at the Marquee in London, England for inclusion on a Special Olympics charity album, and a few days later, he joins artists like George Harrison, Elton John, and Ringo Starr in the fifth annual Prince's Trust Rock Gala at Wembley Arena in London.

1987: Neil Young is reunited with members of his Kelvin High School days group **The Squires** as he appears at the Shakin' All Over concert on June 27th at Winnipeg's Main Street Club, organized by writer/music historian **John Einarson**. The event, which reunites ten of Winnipeg's early rock bands, features artists like **Randy Bachman**, **Burton Cummings**, **Fred Turner**, **Chad Allan**, and **Kurt Winter**.

1987: Liona Boyd becomes the first solo classical artist to go platinum in Canada for the album A GUITAR FOR CHRISTMAS. The Montreal Symphony Orchestra had received a platinum album for a recording of Ravel's *Bolero* in 1985.

1987: Corey Hart plays a Montreal Forum concert date on September 25th that is filmed for a CBC-TV special, which airs on December 13, 1987.

1987: Cowboy Junkies' THE TRINITY SESSION album, recorded on November 27th at the Church of the Holy Trinity in Toronto pretty much live off the floor, produces a cover of Lou Reed's *Sweet Jane* which opens the floodgate of critical praise on both sides of the Atlantic. In 1988, the *Los Angeles Times* votes the album one of the ten best of the year.

T*ry 1988–89*

18TH ANNUAL JUNO AWARDS
March 12, 1989
O'Keefe Centre, Toronto
Host:
Andre-Philippe Gagnon
Performers:
The Band (Robbie Robertson, Rick Danko, Garth Hudson),
Blue Rodeo,
Crowded House,
Glass Tiger with **Dalbello**,
The Jeff Healey Band,
Colin James,
k.d. lang,
Rita MacNeil with **Men Of The Deeps**,
Tom Cochrane and **Red Rider**

The 18th Annual Juno Awards recognized in effect two years of Canadian music history because no ceremonies were held in 1988 as the awards season shifted from autumn to late winter. The highlight of the evening was the induction of The Band into the Hall of Fame. Robbie Robertson (winner of three Junos), Garth Hudson, and Rick Danko performed *The Weight* with back-up provided by the members of Blue Rodeo, also three-time Juno winners. But the show-stopper was Rita MacNeil's performance of *Working Man* with the full roster of the Men of the Deeps male choir.

1988
1989

Try
1988–89 JUNO AWARD WINNERS
(For the Voting Year 1987–88)

CANADIAN ENTERTAINER OF THE YEAR	**Glass Tiger**
INTERNATIONAL ENTERTAINER OF THE YEAR	**U2**
BEST SELLING INTERNATIONAL ALBUM	DIRTY DANCING, Various Artists
BEST SELLING INTERNATIONAL SINGLE	*Pump Up the Volume*, **M.A.R.R.S.**
ALBUM OF THE YEAR	ROBBIE ROBERTSON, **Robbie Robertson**
SINGLE OF THE YEAR	*Try*, **Blue Rodeo**
FEMALE VOCALIST OF THE YEAR	**k.d. lang**
MALE VOCALIST OF THE YEAR	**Robbie Robertson**
GROUP OF THE YEAR	**Blue Rodeo**
COUNTRY FEMALE VOCALIST	**k.d. lang**
COUNTRY MALE VOCALIST	**Murray McLauchlan**
COUNTRY GROUP OR DUO	**The Family Brown**
INSTRUMENTAL ARTIST	**David Foster**
MOST PROMISING FEMALE VOCALIST	**Sass Jordan**
MOST PROMISING MALE VOCALIST	**Colin James**
MOST PROMISING GROUP	**Barney Bentall & the Legendary Hearts**
COMPOSER OF THE YEAR	**Tom Cochrane**
BEST ROOTS & TRADITIONAL ALBUM	THE RETURN OF THE FORMERLY BROTHERS, The Amos Garrett, Doug Sahm, Gene Taylor Band
BEST CHILDREN'S ALBUM	*(tie)* FRED PENNER'S PLACE, **Fred Penner**; and LULLABY BERCEUSE, **Connie Kaldor & Carmen Campagne**
BEST CLASSICAL ALBUM (SOLO OR CHAMBER ENSEMBLE)	SCHUBERT: ARPEGGIONE SONATA, Ofra Harnoy
BEST CLASSICAL ALBUM (LARGE ENSEMBLE OR SOLOIST WITH LARGE ENSEMBLE)	BARTOK: CONCERTO FOR ORCHESTRA: MUSIC FOR STRINGS, PERCUSSION AND CELESTA, **Montreal Symphony Orchestra**, **Charles Dutoit**, conductor
BEST CLASSICAL COMPOSITION	Songs of Paradise, **Alexina Louie**
BEST JAZZ ALBUM	LOOKING UP, **The Hugh Fraser Quartet**
BEST R&B/SOUL RECORDING	ANGEL, **Erroll Starr**
BEST REGGAE/CALYPSO RECORDING	CONDITION CRITICAL, **Lillian Allen**
PRODUCER OF THE YEAR	**Daniel Lanois & Robbie Robertson** for *Showdown At Big Sky* and *Somewhere Down the Crazy River*, **Robbie Robertson**
RECORDING ENGINEER OF THE YEAR	**Mike Fraser** for *Calling America and Different Drummer*, **Tom Cochrane and Red Rider**
BEST ALBUM DESIGN	**Hugh Syme** for LEVITY, **Ian Thomas**
BEST VIDEO	**Michael Buckley** for *Try*, **Blue Rodeo**
HALL OF FAME	**The Band**
WALT GREALIS SPECIAL ACHIEVEMENT AWARD	**Sam Sniderman**
LIFETIME ACHIEVEMENT AWARD	**Pierre Juneau**

When k.d. lang accepted her Female Vocalist award after performing *Crying*, her hit duet with the late Roy Orbison, she said,

Pierre Juneau

"Roy deserves a piece of this too." And when the tears wouldn't stop: "I feel like Wayne Gretzky when he got traded."

1988: Stompin' Tom Connors, newly-signed to Capitol Records, returns to the recording scene after a decade away with the CD FIDDLE AND SONG.

1988: k.d. lang's duet with Roy Orbison, *Crying*, becomes an international hit and earns the duo a Grammy Award. lang also appears with Orbison in the full-length concert movie, *A Black and White Evening*, and records her SHADOWLAND album, featuring a collaboration with country legends Loretta Lynn, Kitty Wells, and Brenda Lee on *Honky Tonk Angels Medley*. She travels to the U.K. on the Country Music Association's Route 88 tour with Randy Travis and the Sweethearts Of the Rodeo, and on March 10th she is named best female performer in a Rolling Stone magazine poll.

1988: Platinum Blonde play alien bikers in an episode of Paramount Pictures' *War of the Worlds* series, and in Mr. T's *T and T* series. Frontman Mark Holmes is seen in the film *Eddie and the Cruisers II — Eddie Lives*.

1988: David Wilcox catches the ear of the movie studios as his *Hypnotizing Blues* is heard on the soundtrack of the popular Tom Cruise flick *Cocktail*, while his *Cabin Fever* is heard on *The Great Outdoors* starring fellow Canadians **Dan Aykroyd** and the late **John Candy**. Reggae band **Messenjah** appears in the film *Cocktail* and also contribute to the soundtrack.

1988: Ian Thomas receives the Danny Kaye Medal from UNICEF in recognition of his fund-raising efforts.

Blue Rodeo

1988: Jane Siberry makes her European debut at the Institute of Contemporary Art in London.

1988: Walter Ostanek is inducted into the National Cleveland-Style Polka Hall of Fame in Euclid, Ohio.

1988: Priscilla Wright becomes the first Canadian female singer to re-record a hit and have it top the charts again with a new version of her 1955 hit *The Man In A Raincoat*.

1988: The Jeff Healey Band signs a worldwide record deal with Arista Records in the U.S., and appear on *Late Night with David Letterman* as well as *The Tonight Show*.

1988: Bryan Adams plays five sold-out shows before 65,000 people in Tokyo, Japan, where he is presented with a platinum record for his INTO THE FIRE album.

1988: The Raffi video featuring songs like *Baby Beluga* and *Down By the Bay* is certified platinum after selling over 55,000 copies in the U.S.

k.d. lang

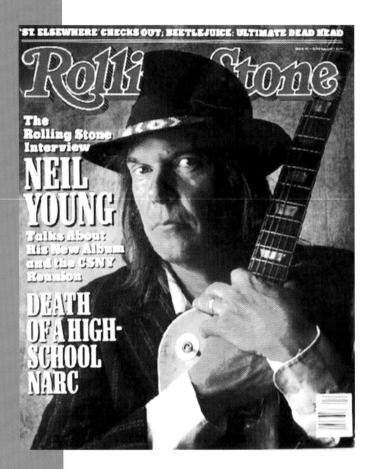

in the wake of the release of their debut CD OUTSKIRTS and the single *Try. Rolling Stone* magazine states in their year-end wrap-up: "The best new American band of the year (1988) may very well be Canadian."

1988: R. Murray Schafer's *Concerto For Harp and Orchestra*, commissioned by the **Toronto Symphony** for harpist **Judy Loman**, premieres on April 6th.

1988: Honeymoon Suite have their first Top 10 hit in Canada with *Love Changes Everything*.

1988: The Parachute Club plays its final concert on July 21st at Toronto's Ontario Place.

1988: Kim Mitchell makes Toronto music history as he sells out two shows at the Kingswood Music Theatre at Canada's Wonderland, and adds a third show, ultimately playing to close to 40,000 people.

1988: *Don't Shed A Tear*, the Paul Carrack single co-written by **Eddie Schwartz,** hits the Top 10 in February.

1988: As part of the opening ceremonies for the 1988 Winter Olympic Games in Calgary, **Ian Tyson** and **Gordon Lightfoot** join together to sing Tyson's *Four Strong Winds* and Lightfoot's *Alberta Bound*. **Liona Boyd** performs with **Rik Emmett** of **Triumph** and **Alex Lifeson** of **Rush** on *Hands Of Man*, the song which featured Boyd singing her own lyrics for the first time on record.

1988: Leonard Cohen is presented with an award on March 9th by CBS Records in New York to commemorate the sale of more than five million of his albums outside of the U.S. market.

1988: Blue Rodeo showcase at New York's Bottom Line club on March 17th

1988: Quebec mourns the loss of one of its cultural giants as **Félix Leclerc** passes away on August 8th.

1988: The original members of **Triumph** play their last concert at the Kingswood Music Theatre on September 3rd as guitarist **Rik Emmett** departs after the show.

1988: Mary Margaret O'Hara's debut album MISS AMERICA is released in October, and in England O'Hara basks in the glow of wide critical acclaim and SRO concerts.

1988: Neil Young reunites with Crosby, Stills and Nash in November to record AMERICAN DREAM, a Top 20 album in the U.S.

1988: After a benefit show for Nashville's songwriters, **Anne Murray** is presented with a Lifetime Achievement

Award, becomes an honorary citizen of Tennessee, and receives the key to Nashville. The **Anne Murray** Christmas special on CBC-TV draws an impressive 4.2 million viewers, the highest rated entertainment TV show in the network's history.

1989: The Diamonds are part of the Royalty of Doo Wop Tour with the Belmonts, The Chiffons, The Flamingos, and The Silhouettes.

1989: Roch Voisine sweeps the major Felix awards at the annual ADISQ gala in Montreal, including Male Singer, Pop Song (*Hélène*), Pop Rock Album (HÉLÈNE), and Discovery. As a presenter, he hands **Sass Jordan** her Felix as Top Quebec Artist Working in English.

1989: Daniel Lanois' first album, ACADIE, is released.

1989: The Pursuit of Happiness spend 80 days on the road opening for artists like Duran Duran, The Replacements, Mike and the Mechanics, and Melissa Etheridge. Britain's *Melody Maker* calls the group's frontman **Moe Berg**, "Woody Allen with a groin."

1989: Soul Asylum, Nick Cave, and Pixies are among the artists contributing to a tribute album to **Neil Young** titled THE BRIDGE TO NEIL YOUNG, with the proceeds going to The Bridge, a California foundation for handicapped children headed up by Young and his wife Peggy.

1989: Gary Fjellgaard receives the Gram Award in The Netherlands as Most Promising New International artist.

1989: Daniel MacMaster, from Barrie, Ontario, joins Bonham as lead vocalist.

1989: The Jeff Healey Band appears in the film *Road House,* starring Patrick

Swaze, and contribute four songs to the soundtrack.

1989: Anne Murray appears on George Bush's list of all-time favorite recording artists.

1989: Bryan Adams' late-1987 tour of Europe produces the TV special *Live In Belgium*, which airs on CBC-TV on January 15th.

1989: Ofra Harnoy makes world premiere recordings of several Vivaldi Cello Concertos, which subsequently top the *Billboard* classical chart.

1989: Almost six years after the single hit the *Billboard* Hot 100 chart and four years after the group had broken up, **Sheriff's** *When I'm With You* hits the top of the charts in America on February 4th. **Arnold Lanni** and **Wolf Hassell**, two of the original members of Sheriff, had already formed a new group, **Frozen Ghost**, which had charted on the Billboard Hot 100 in May 1987 with the single *Should I See* and had no interest in retracing their steps and reforming Sheriff. The success of the single was the catalyst though for former Sheriff members vocalist **Freddy Curci** and guitarist **Steve DeMarchi** to get together with former **Heart** guitarist **Roger**

Fisher to form the group **Alias**. The group hit number two on the *Billboard* Hot 100 chart with their first single, *More Than Words Can Say,* in 1990.

1989: With the release of their sophomore album *Diamond Mine*, **Blue Rodeo** showcase at Soho's Borderline Club in London, England on February 15th.

1989: The Jeff Healey Band's album SEE THE LIGHT receives Holland's Edison Award for Best Foreign Rock Recording.

1989: Tom Cochrane and Red Rider's performance on March 17th with the **Edmonton Symphony Orchestra** is recorded as the group's final album, THE SYMPHONY SESSIONS, and the band appear on the *David Letterman Show* before heading for Europe to open for German star Herbert Gronmeyer.

1989: Kon Kan, the Toronto dance music duo of **Barry Harris** and **Kevin Wynne**, have a number one dance hit and a top 15 song on the *Billboard* Hot 100 with the single *I Beg Your Pardon*, which freely samples the Lynn Anderson country hit, *Rose Garden*.

1989: Rita MacNeil makes her U.S. concert debut at the Berklee Performance Center on April 14th to great critical praise.

1989: Bryan Adams makes music history on April 14th when he and guitarist **Keith Scott** perform *Kids Want To Rock* with the Russian group Aureole (Halo) live from Moscow on the internationally broadcast World Video Music Awards.

1989: David Clayton-Thomas is among the featured performers at the opening of The Skydome in Toronto on June 3rd.

1989: The Montreal Jazz Festival/ Festival international de jazz de Montréal introduces the Prix **Oscar Peterson** for Canadian musicians of international renown. Peterson receives the Prix in its inaugural year.

1989: Blue Rodeo are one of the featured groups at the Montreux Jazz Festival in Switzerland as part of a European tour with Edie Brickell and the New Bohemians. During this period, the group is selected by actress Meryl Streep and music director **Howard Shore** to play her back-up band in a climactic scene from the movie *Postcards From the Edge*.

1989: The **Anne Murray** Centre opens on July 28th in Springhill, Nova Scotia.

1989: While touring Europe, **Andrew Cash** joins Melissa Etheridge, Joe Cocker, and several German bands for a free concert at the Berlin Wall on November 12th as citizens are allowed to move freely between East and West Germany.

1989: *See the Light*, a one-hour Global TV special on **The Jeff Healey Band**, airs on December 15th.

1989: Dan Hill appears at the NAACP 80th anniversary benefit gala in New York on a bill that includes Stevie Wonder.

FAMILY BROWN
LIFE AND TIMES 1962-89

A seven year retrospective featuring A new Canadian Country Classic
PIONEERS

Black Velvet
1990

**19TH
ANNUAL
JUNO
AWARDS**
March 18, 1990
The O'Keefe
Centre, Toronto
Host:
Rick Moranis
Performers:
**Cowboy Junkies,
The Jeff Healey
Band with Tom
Cochrane and
Sass Jordan,
Lyle Lovett** and
**Margo Timmins,
Maestro
Fresh Wes,
Milli Vanilli,
Kim Mitchell,
Alannah Myles,
Rod Stewart**

From her show-opening performance of *Still Got This Thing* to her closing acceptance of the Album of the Year award, her fifth award of the evening, this was Alannah Myles' Juno night. The Jeff Healey Band won the prestigious Canadian Entertainer of the Year award, the only category voted on by the public. Kim Mitchell commented while accepting the Male Vocalist award: "I think of myself more as a white boy yelling." George Fox on accepting his Country Male Vocalist Juno: "I'll tell you folks, a couple of years ago it was a big deal for me to take the cow into the vet."

1990

Black Velvet
1990 JUNO AWARD WINNERS
(For the Voting Year 1989)

CANADIAN ENTERTAINER OF THE YEAR	**The Jeff Healey Band**
INTERNATIONAL ENTERTAINER OF THE YEAR	**Melissa Etheridge**
INTERNATIONAL ALBUM OF THE YEAR	GIRL YOU KNOW IT'S TRUE, **Milli Vanilli**
INTERNATIONAL SINGLE OF THE YEAR	*Swing the Mood*, **Jive Bunny and the Mixmasters**
ALBUM OF THE YEAR	ALANNAH MYLES, **Alannah Myles**
SINGLE OF THE YEAR	*Black Velvet*, **Alannah Myles**
FEMALE VOCALIST OF THE YEAR	**Rita MacNeil**
MALE VOCALIST OF THE YEAR	**Kim Mitchell**
GROUP OF THE YEAR	**Blue Rodeo**
COUNTRY FEMALE VOCALIST	**k.d. lang**
COUNTRY MALE VOCALIST	**George Fox**
COUNTRY GROUP OR DUO	**The Family Brown**
INSTRUMENTAL ARTIST	**Manteca**
MOST PROMISING FEMALE VOCALIST	**Alannah Myles**
MOST PROMISING MALE VOCALIST	**Daniel Lanois**
MOST PROMISING GROUP	**The Tragically Hip**
COMPOSER OF THE YEAR	**David Tyson and Christopher Ward**
BEST ROOTS/TRADITIONAL ALBUM	JE VOUDRAIS CHANGER D'CHAPEAU, **La Bottine Souriante**
BEST CHILDREN'S ALBUM	BEETHOVEN LIVES UPSTAIRS, **Susan Hammond and Barbara Nichol**
BEST CLASSICAL ALBUM (SOLO OR CHAMBER ENSEMBLE)	20TH CENTURY ORIGINAL PIANO TRANSCRIPTIONS, **Louis Lortie**
BEST CLASSICAL ALBUM (LARGE ENSEMBLE OR SOLOIST WITH LARGE ENSEMBLE ACCOMPANIMENT)	BOCHERINI: CELLO CONCERTOS AND SYMPHONIES, **Tafelmusik Baroque Orchestra.**
BEST CLASSICAL COMPOSITION	CONCERTO FOR HARP AND CHAMBER ORCHESTRA AND MORAWETZ HARP CONCERTOS, **Oskar Morawetz**
BEST DANCE RECORDING	*I Beg Your Pardon (I Never Promised You A Rose Garden)*, **Kon Kan**
BEST JAZZ ALBUM	SKYDANCE, **Jon Ballantyne Trio featuring Joe Henderson**
BEST R&B/SOUL RECORDING	SPELLBOUND, **Billy Newton-Davis**
BEST REGGAE/CALYPSO RECORDING	TOO LATE TO TURN BACK NOW, **The Sattalites**
PRODUCER OF THE YEAR	**Bruce Fairbairn**
RECORDING ENGINEER OF THE YEAR	**Kevin Doyle**
BEST ALBUM DESIGN	**Hugh Syme** for PRESTO, **Rush**
BEST VIDEO	**Cosimo Cavallaro** for *Boomtown,* **Andrew Cash**
HALL OF FAME	**Maureen Forrester**
WALT GREALIS SPECIAL ACHIEVEMENT AWARD	**Raffi**

1990: Celine Dion launches an international career singing in English with the release of her album *Unison,* produced by **David Foster** in Los Angeles, Chris Neal in London, and Andy Goldmark in New York.

1990: The success of rap artist **Maestro Fresh Wes'** debut album SYMPHONY IN EFFECT and accompanying single/video *Let Your Backbone Slip* makes rap music popular in Canada.

1990: Luc Plamondon and the late **Michel Berger's** rock opera LA LÉGENDE DE JIMMY, starring **Diane Tell, Renaud Hantson,** and **Nanette Workman,** premieres at the Mogador in Paris. The rock opera, based on the life of James Dean, plays for five months.

1990: Musician/author **Paul Quarrington**, formerly with **Joe Hall and the Continental Drift**, wins the Governor General's Award for Fiction for his novel, *Whale Music*, which becomes the basis for the critically-acclaimed film of the same name.

1990: Rush, Bryan Adams, and **k.d. lang** are named artists of the decade by the Canadian Recording Industry Association (CRIA).

1990: Dallas Harms' country standard *Paper Rosie* is heard on the soundtrack of the film *Another 48 Hours.*

1990: Tommy Hunter takes his place in the Country Music Hall of Fame's Walkway of Stars.

1990: David Clayton-Thomas sues the writers of Milli Vanilli's *All Or Nothing* for not giving him credit (or paying royalties) for the song's similarity to *Spinning Wheel.*

The Jeff Healey Band

1990: Ofra Harnoy's recording of *Vivaldi Concertos* becomes one of the biggest-selling classical albums of the year internationally.

1990: During Grammy week in Los Angeles, **Bryan Adams** headlines his own intimate concert for 600 music industry VIPs at the Soundstage on A&M Records' lot (formerly **Charlie Chaplin's** movie studio).

1990: Music critics at *Rolling Stone* give **Neil Young's** FREEDOM the 1989 Critic's Award for Best Album.

1990: Alannah Myles' recording of the **Christopher Ward/Dave Tyson** song *Black Velvet* tops the *Billboard* Hot 100 singles chart on March 24th. The self-titled album on which the song appears goes on to sell over one million copies in Canada alone, making it the top-selling debut record for a Canadian artist in history. She appears on the Arsenio Hall Show on May 9th, and picks up an Elvis Award as Best Newcomer on June 6th at the 2nd International Rock Awards.

Maureen Forrester

1990: Neil Young is among the artists appearing at the Nelson Mandela — An International Tribute To A Free South Africa concert at Wembley Stadium, London, on April 16th.

1990: Cattle country radio stations in the U.S. drop **k.d. lang**'s records after she participates in a "Meat Stinks" campaign for the Washington-based advocacy group People For the Ethical Treatment of Animals, and folks back in Alberta burn the sign that once identified Consort as lang's hometown.

1990: The Quebec music world loses one of its most-beloved "rockers" when **Gerry Boulet** dies on July 18th following a battle with cancer.

1990: Bryan Adams, **Joni Mitchell,** and **The Band** are among the artists to take

George Fox

part in Roger Waters' performance of *The Wall* at the site of the Berlin Wall on July 21st.

1990: The Family Brown give their final performance at the Kanata Kounty Fair in Kanata, Ontario.

1990: Paul Anka becomes an American citizen in a federal court ceremony in Las Vegas.

1990: Joni Mitchell's paintings form a major part of *Canada in the City*, an exhibition of Canadian art, music, and culture at the Broadgate Centre in London during the fall.

1990: Tom Cochrane and Canadian TV personality **Terry David Mulligan** tour four African countries with the international relief and development agency, World Vision Canada.

1990: Rita MacNeil is the first solo female recording artist to place more than two albums on the Australian charts.

1990: Stompin' Tom Connors, whose hit anthology *A Proud Canadian*, becomes the biggest-selling album of his career, completes a 70-city tour of Canada with two concerts at Toronto's Massey Hall in December.

1990: Bryan Adams is named a Member of the Order of Canada.

1990: BMG Music Canada releases the CD set MADE IN CANADA: OUR ROCK 'N' ROLL HISTORY.

Rita MacNeil

Symphony In Effect 1991

20TH ANNUAL JUNO AWARDS
March 3, 1991
Queen Elizabeth
Theatre,
Vancouver
Host:
Paul Shaffer
Performers:
**Alias,
Blue Rodeo,
Holly Cole,
Patricia Conroy,
Celine Dion,
MC Hammer,
Colin James,
Sue Medley,
Mae Moore,
Aaron Neville,
Northern Pikes,
Prairie Oyster,
Lorraine Segato,
Suzanne Vega,
Jennifer Warnes,
Michelle Wright**

One of the most riveting acceptance speeches in Juno history came with Leonard Cohen's acknowledgments following his induction into the Hall Of Fame as he recited the lyrics to his *Tower Of Song*. Celine Dion, Colin James, and songwriter/producer David Tyson were all double awards winners as the Junos were first staged in Vancouver. Blue Rodeo accepted Group of the Year honors for the third year in a row, while The Tragically Hip saw their extensive touring pay off as they are selected by the fans as Canadian Entertainers of the Year. The Rap Recording of the Year category was introduced with Maestro Fresh Wes' *Symphony In Effect* the first winner.

Symphony In Effect
1991 JUNO AWARD WINNERS
(For the Voting Year 1990)

CANADIAN ENTERTAINER OF THE YEAR	**The Tragically Hip**
INTERNATIONAL ENTERTAINER OF THE YEAR	**The Rolling Stones**
BEST SELLING INTERNATIONAL ALBUM	PLEASE HAMMER, DON'T HURT 'EM, **MC Hammer**
BEST SELLING INTERNATIONAL SINGLE	*Vogue*, **Madonna**
ALBUM OF THE YEAR	UNISON, **Celine Dion**
SINGLE OF THE YEAR	*Just Came Back*, **Colin James**
FEMALE VOCALIST OF THE YEAR	**Celine Dion**
MALE VOCALIST OF THE YEAR	**Colin James**
GROUP OF THE YEAR	**Blue Rodeo**
COUNTRY FEMALE VOCALIST	**Rita MacNeil**
COUNTRY MALE VOCALIST	**George Fox**
COUNTRY GROUP OR DUO	**Prairie Oyster**
INSTRUMENTAL ARTIST OF THE YEAR	**Ofra Harnoy**
RAP RECORDING OF THE YEAR	SYMPHONY IN EFFECT, **Maestro Fresh Wes**
MOST PROMISING FEMALE VOCALIST	**Sue Medley**
MOST PROMISING MALE VOCALIST	**Andy Curran**
MOST PROMISING GROUP	**Leslie Spit Treeo**
SONGWRITER OF THE YEAR	**David Tyson**
BEST CHILDREN'S ALBUM	MOZART'S MAGIC FANTASY, Classical Kids — **Sue Hammond**
BEST CLASSICAL ALBUM (SOLO OR CHAMBER ENSEMBLE)	SCHAFERFIVE STRING QUARTETS, **Orford String Quartet**
BEST CLASSICAL ALBUM (LARGE ENSEMBLE OR SOLOIST WITH LARGE ENSEMBLE ACCOMPANIMENT)	DEBUSSY: IMAGES, NOCTURNES, **L'Orchestre symphonique de Montréal, Charles Dutoit**, conductor
BEST CLASSICAL COMPOSITION	SCHAFER: STRING QUARTET NO. 5 "ROSALIND", **R. Murray Schafer**
BEST DANCE RECORDING	*Don't Wanna Fall In Love*, **Jane Child**
BEST HARD ROCK/METAL ALBUM	PRESTO, **Rush**
BEST JAZZ ALBUM	TWO SIDES, **Mike Murley**
BEST R&B/SOUL RECORDING	*Dance To the Music (Work Your Body)*, **Simply Majestic** featuring **B. Kool**
BEST REGGAE/CALYPSO RECORDING	*Soldiers We Are All*, **Jayson & Friends**
BEST ROOTS & TRADITIONAL ALBUM	DANCE & CELEBRATE, **Bill Bourne & Alan MacLeod**
PRODUCER OF THE YEAR	**David Tyson**
RECORDING ENGINEER OF THE YEAR	**Gino Vannelli/Joe Vannelli**
BEST ALBUM DESIGN	**Robert Lebeuf** for **Sue Medley, Sue Medley**
BEST VIDEO	**Joel Goldberg** for *Drop the Needle* by **Maestro Fresh Wes**
HALL OF FAME	**Leonard Cohen**
WALT GREALIS SPECIAL ACHIEVEMENT AWARD	**Mel Shaw**

1991: Paul Anka briefly becomes one of the original owners of the Ottawa Senators' National Hockey League franchise.

1991: Wilf Carter announces that a nine-concert tour of Nova Scotia, New Brunswick, Ontario, and Manitoba would be his last.

1991: A number of Canadian recording artists, including **Barenaked Ladies, B-Funn, Cottage Industry,** and **Rebecca Jenkins,** record a tribute album to **Bruce Cockburn** titled KICK AT THE DARK-NESS. And a number of international recording artists, including John Cale, Nick Cave, The Pixies, and R.E.M., get together to record a tribute album to **Leonard Cohen** titled I'M YOUR FAN.

1991: Bonnie Raitt records the **Shirley Eikhard** song *Something To Talk About,* which hits the top of the charts interna-tionally.

1991: Exactly two decades after it was a hit for Ottawa's **Five Man Electrical Band,** Tesla top the charts with the song *Signs*, which is included on their FIVE MAN ACOUSTICAL JAM album.

1991: Oscar Peterson is named Chancellor of York University in Toronto.

1991: Madonna gets busted at the Skydome for being too sexy, **Guns 'n' Roses** cause a riot as they cut short a show in Montreal, and **The Barenaked Ladies** are banned from playing at Toronto's City Hall by Mayor June Rowlands.

1991: Fiddle player **Ashley MacIsaac** emerges from Cape Breton, Nova Scotia for the first time to play the Memphis Celtic Festival and to perform alongside **The Rankin Family** at the Mariposa Folk Festival.

1991: Seventeen-year-old **Alanis Morissette**, known initially by her first name, has her first, self-titled album released by MCA Records in Canada.

1991: Pianist **Stan Szelest**, a former member of **The Hawks,** dies from a heart attack while touring with **The Band** just after co-writing a tribute with **Levon Helm** to **Richard Manuel** and Paul Butterfield titled *Too Soon Gone*.

Prairie Oyster

Maestro Fresh Wes

The Nylons

1991: Celine Dion makes her third appearance on the *Tonight Show* in January.

1991: Susan Aglukark gives her first live public performance at a festival in her hometown of Arviat, North West Territories.

1991: Vancouver-based heavy metal act **Annhilator** opens a 45-date European tour on January 31st with Judas Priest, and **Dream Warriors** embark on a 35-city European tour in February.

1991: David Foster and wife Linda Thompson-Jenner organize the recording of a charity record titled *Voices That Care* to benefit the American Red Cross Gulf Crisis Fund.

1991: Larry Good leaves **The Good Brothers** after 17 years and is replaced by **Bruce Good**'s son **Travis**, and the group changes its name to **The Goods**.

1991: Rod Stewart's *Rhythm Of My Heart*, written by **Marc Jordan**, tops the charts in Canada in May.

1991: Ricky Van Shelton records the **Charlie Major** song *Backroads* and takes it to number one on the U.S. country charts in June.

1991: Bryan Adams has his second consecutive number one single on the *Billboard* Hot 100 chart on July 27th with *(Everything I Do) I Do It For You,* the theme song for the film *Robin Hood: Prince Of Thieves*, co-written by Adams, Michael Kamen, and his co-producer Robert John "Mutt" Lange. In the U.K., the song's 16-week run at the top of the charts is unprecedented in British chart history and the first British chart-topper by a Canadian artist.

1991: Tommy Banks is made an Officer of the Order of Canada.

Life Is A Highway
1992

21ST ANNUAL JUNO AWARDS

Sunday, March 29, 1992

The O'Keefe Centre, Toronto

Host: **Rick Moranis**

Performers: **Bryan Adams, Blue Rodeo, Tom Cochrane, Crash Test Dummies, George Fox, Ofra Harnoy, Molly Johnson, Kashtin, Andy Maize (Skydiggers), Loreena McKennitt, Sarah McLachlan, Neil Osborne (54-40), Jane Siberry**

"Ian Tyson," host Rick Moranis requested at the close of this year's ceremonies, "would you please move your horse so Tom Cochrane can get his U-Haul out of here." Tom Cochrane's MAD, MAD WORLD album and the hit single *Life Is A Highway* garnered four Juno awards for him, while Ian Tyson was inducted along with Sylvia Tyson into the Canadian Music Hall of Fame. The surprise of the night was Cochrane's win in the Single of the Year category, displacing Bryan Adams and his international smash hit *(Everything I Do) I Do It For You*, which led the *Globe and Mail* to headline the ceremonies as *"The Shootout at Juno Corral."* There was talk of a possible backlash from the industry to Adams' much-publicized comments that the Canadian Content regulations foster mediocrity, but he left town with three Junos, including a Special Achievement Award, and the controversy ended.

1992

Life Is A Highway
1992 JUNO AWARD WINNERS
(For the Voting Year 1991)

CANADIAN ENTERTAINER OF THE YEAR	**Bryan Adams**
FOREIGN ENTERTAINER OF THE YEAR	**Garth Brooks**
BEST SELLING ALBUM BY A FOREIGN ARTIST	TO THE EXTREME, **Vanilla Ice**
BEST SELLING SINGLE BY A FOREIGN ARTIST	*More Than Words,* **Extreme**
BEST SELLING FRANCOPHONE ALBUM	SAUVEZ MON AMIE, **Luc De Larochelliere**
ALBUM OF THE YEAR	MAD MAD WORLD, **Tom Cochrane**
SINGLE OF THE YEAR	*Life Is A Highway,* **Tom Cochrane**
FEMALE VOCALIST OF THE YEAR	**Celine Dion**
MALE VOCALIST OF THE YEAR	**Tom Cochrane**
GROUP OF THE YEAR	**Crash Test Dummies**
MOST PROMISING FEMALE VOCALIST	**Alanis**
MOST PROMISING MALE VOCALIST	**Keven Jordan**
MOST PROMISING GROUP OF THE YEAR	**Infidels**
COUNTRY FEMALE VOCALIST OF THE YEAR	**Cassandra Vasik**
COUNTRY MALE VOCALIST OF THE YEAR	**George Fox**
COUNTRY GROUP OR DUO	**Prairie Oyster**
SONGWRITER OF THE YEAR	**Tom Cochrane**
INSTRUMENTAL ARTIST OF THE YEAR	**Shadowy Men on a Shadowy Planet**
BEST ROOTS/TRADITIONAL ALBUM	*(tie)* THE VISIT, **Loreena McKennitt,** and SATURDAY NIGHT BLUES: THE GREAT CANADIAN BLUES PROJECT, **Various Artists.**
BEST CHILDREN'S ALBUM	VIVALDI'S RING OF MYSTERY, A TALE OF VENICE AND VIOLINS, **Classical Kids, Susan Hammond,** producer
BEST CLASSICAL ALBUM (SOLO OR CHAMBER ENSEMBLE)	FRANZ LISZT: ANNEES DE PELERINAGE: ITALIE, **Louis Lortie**
BEST CLASSICAL ALBUM (LARGE ENSEMBLE OR SOLOIST WITH LARGE ENSEMBLE ACCOMPANIMENT)	DEBUSSY: PELLEAS ET MELISANDE, **L'Orchestre symphonique de Montréal, Charles Dutoit,** conductor
BEST CLASSICAL COMPOSITION	CONCERTO FOR PIANO & CHAMBER ORCHESTRA, **Michael Conway Baker**
BEST JAZZ ALBUM	*(three-way tie)* IN TRANSITION, **Brian Dickinson;** THE BRASS IS BACK, **Rob McConnell and the Boss Brass;** and FOR THE MOMENT, **Renee Rosnes**
BEST R&B/SOUL RECORDING	CALL MY NAME, **Love & Sas**
BEST DANCE RECORDING	EVERYONE'S A WINNER (THE CHOCOLATE MOVEMENT MIX), **Bootsauce**
BEST WORLD BEAT RECORDING	THE GATHERING, **Various Artists**
PRODUCER OF THE YEAR	**Bryan Adams** for *Everything I Do (I Do It For You)* and *Can't Stop This Thing We Started,* **Bryan Adams**
RECORDING ENGINEER OF THE YEAR	**Mike Fraser** for *Thunderstruck* and *Money Talks,* **AC/DC**
BEST ALBUM DESIGN	**Hugh Syme** for ROLL THE BONES, **Rush**
BEST VIDEO	**Philip Kates** for *Into the Fire,* **Sarah McLachlan**
BEST HARD ROCK ALBUM	ROLL THE BONES, **Rush**
RAP RECORDING OF THE YEAR	*My Definition Of A Boombastic Jazz Style,* **Dream Warriors**
HALL OF FAME	**Ian & Sylvia**
WALT GREALIS SPECIAL ACHIEVEMENT AWARD	**Wm. Harold Moon**
SPECIAL ACHIEVEMENT AWARD	**Bryan Adams**

Ian Tyson

Tom Cochrane

1992: During a press conference in Sydney, Nova Scotia to kick-off a 13-date Canadian tour, **Bryan Adams** lets fly a barrage of criticism at Canadian content regulations for radio airplay in response to having one of his songs labeled "Un-Canadian" because it didn't meet CanCon requirements. Later in the month, he picks up an unprecedented (for a Canadian artist) six Grammy Award nominations, but at the awards **David Foster** spends more time at the podium, though Adams does pick up the trophy for Best Song Written Specifically for a Motion Picture or Television for *(Everything I Do) I Do It For You*, which was also nominated for an Oscar in the Best Original Song category.

1992: Roch Voisine, a certified superstar in Quebec and the French-speaking countries of Europe, sets out in January on a three-month, 50-city European tour which includes four sold-out shows at the 16,000-seat Palais Omnisports de Paris-Bercy. On July 1st, he is decorated as a Chevalier dans l'Ordre des Arts et

des Lettres by France's ambassador to Canada, and later that day, he premieres a new song co-written with **David Foster,** who joins him for the first live performance of *I'll Always Be There (You and I)*.

1992: Barenaked Ladies, whose independent cassette has already sold well over 50,000 copies in Canada, sign with

R O B   M c C O N N E L L   &   T H E   B O S S   B R A S S

ROB McCONNELL (1)
valve trombone

MOE KOFFMAN (7)
flute, soprano & alto
saxophones

JOHN JOHNSON (3)
flute, clarinet, soprano
& alto saxophones

ALEX DEAN (20)
flute, clarinet, tenor
saxophone

RICK WILKINS (21)
clarinet, tenor saxophone

BOB LEONARD (17)
flute, clarinet, bass clarinet,
baritone saxophone

ARNIE CHYCOSKI (13)
lead trumpet, flugelhorn

STEVE McDADE (11)
assoc. lead trumpet,
flugelhorn

JOHN MacLEOD (15)
trumpet, flugelhorn

GUIDO BASSO (9)
trumpet, flugelhorn

DAVE WOODS (2)
trumpet, flugelhorn

ALASTAIR KAY (12)
lead trombone

BOB LIVINGSTON (14)
trombone

JERRY JOHNSON (4)
trombone, bass trombone
on "Overtime"

ERNIE PATTISON (10)
bass trombone

GARY PATTISON (16)
french horn

JAMES MacDONALD (8)
french horn

DAVID RESTIVO (5)
piano

ED BICKERT (6)
guitar

JIM VIVIAN (19)
bass

TED WARREN (18)
drums

Loreena McKennitt

Sire Records, and their debut album GORDON reaches number one on the album charts.

1992: Michelle Wright's *Take It Like A Man* becomes the first number one single on *The Record*'s country music chart since **Anne Murray** held down top position in 1986 with *Now And Forever (You And Me)*. Wright makes her debut at the Grand Ole Opry, where she is introduced to fellow-Canadian **Hank Snow**.

1992: Bryan Adams becomes the first Canadian artist to have two albums certified diamond in Canada as his WAKING UP THE NEIGHBOURS disc sells over one million copies.

1992: On Canada's 125th birthday Molson Canadian Rocks and MCA Concerts present the Great Canadian Party at major venues in St. John's; Ottawa; and Vancouver. Artists featured on the show that was broadcast live by MuchMusic include **Kim Mitchell**, **The Tragically Hip**, **The Jeff Healey Band**, **Crash Test Dummies**, **Colin James**, **54-40**, **Lee Aaron**, **Sass Jordan**, **Chrissy Steele**, and **Spinal Tap**.

1992: The Band perform their version of *When I Paint My Masterpiece* as part of Sony Records' 30th anniversary tribute to Bob Dylan at Madison Square Gardens in New York, where **Neil Young** meets Pearl Jam for the first time.

W aking Up The Neighbours 1993

22ND
ANNUAL
JUNO
AWARDS
March 21, 1993
The O'Keefe
Centre, Toronto
Host:
Celine Dion
Performers:
Celine Dion with
Kaleefah and
the Killer Choir,
Devon,
Leonard Cohen
with the Friday
Night House
Band and
Robert
Desrosiers and
the Desrosiers
Dance Group,
Barenaked
Ladies, Glen
Campbell,
Jazz All-Star
Ensemble,
Gordon
Lightfoot,
Rita MacNeil,
Pure,
Slik Toxik,
The Tragically
Hip,
The Watchmen,
Michelle Wright

"My cup runneth over," Leonard Cohen mused while accepting one of two awards he received. "It's only in a country like this that I could get the Male Vocalist of the Year award." Celine Dion and k.d. lang topped the list of honored artists, with Dion taking home four and lang snagging three. Bryan Adams became the first Canadian to win the Juno in the category of Best-Selling Album (Foreign or Domestic), and The Tragically Hip picked up their second Canadian Entertainer of the Year Juno. The star-studded tribute to Anne Murray as she was inducted into the Hall of Fame included well-wishes from Gordon Lightfoot, Burt Reynolds, Kenny Rogers, Glen Campbell, Gene MacLellan, Alan Thicke, k.d. lang, Rita MacNeil, and Jerry Seinfeld.

1993

Waking Up The Neighbours
1993 JUNO AWARD WINNERS
(For the Voting Year 1992)

CANADIAN ENTERTAINER OF THE YEAR	**The Tragically Hip**
INTERNATIONAL ENTERTAINER OF THE YEAR	**U2**
BEST SELLING ALBUM (FOREIGN OR DOMESTIC)	WAKING UP THE NEIGHBOURS, **Bryan Adams**
BEST SELLING SINGLE (FOREIGN OR DOMESTIC)	*Achy Breaky Heart*, **Billy Ray Cyrus**
BEST SELLING FRANCOPHONE ALBUM	DION CHANTE PLAMONDON, **Celine Dion**
ALBUM OF THE YEAR	INGENUE, **k.d. lang**
SINGLE OF THE YEAR	*Beauty and the Beast,* **Celine Dion/Peabo Bryson**
FEMALE VOCALIST OF THE YEAR	**Celine Dion**
MALE VOCALIST OF THE YEAR	**Leonard Cohen**
GROUP OF THE YEAR	**Barenaked Ladies**
INSTRUMENTAL ARTIST OF THE YEAR	**Ofra Harnoy**
HARD ROCK ALBUM OF THE YEAR	DOIN' THE NASTY, **Slik Toxik**
RAP RECORDING OF THE YEAR	KEEP IT SLAMMIN', **Devon**
COUNTRY FEMALE VOCALIST	**Michelle Wright**
COUNTRY MALE VOCALIST	**Gary Fjellgaard**
COUNTRY GROUP OR DUO	**Tracey Prescott & Lonesome Daddy**
MOST PROMISING FEMALE VOCALIST	**Julie Masse**
MOST PROMISING MALE VOCALIST	**John Bottomley**
MOST PROMISING GROUP	**Skydiggers**
SOCAN JUNO FOR SONGWRITER OF THE YEAR	**k.d. lang/Ben Mink**
BEST CHILDREN'S ALBUM	WAVES OF WONDER, **Jack Grunsky**
BEST CLASSICAL ALBUM (SOLO OR CHAMBER ENSEMBLE)	BEETHOVEN: PIANO SONATAS, **Louis Lortie**
BEST CLASSICAL ALBUM (LARGE ENSEMBLE OR SOLOIST WITH LARGE ENSEMBLE)	HANDEL: EXCERPTS FROM FLORIDANTE, **Tafelmusik with Alan Curtis, Catherine Robbin, Linda Maguire, Nancy Argenta, Ingrid Attrot, Mel Braun,** and **Jean Lamon,** (leader)
BEST CLASSICAL COMPOSITION	CONCERTO FOR FLUTE AND ORCHESTRA FROM R. MURRAY SCHAFER CONCERTOS, **R. Murray Schafer**
BEST DANCE RECORDING	LOVE CAN MOVE MOUNTAINS (CLUB MIX), **Celine Dion**
BEST JAZZ ALBUM	MY IDEAL, **P.J. Perry**
BEST R&B/SOUL RECORDING	ONCE IN A LIFETIME, **Love & Sas**
BEST ROOTS & TRADITIONAL ALBUM	JUSQU'AUX P'TITES HEURES, **La Bottine Souriante**
BEST WORLD BEAT RECORDING	SPIRITS OF HAVANA, **Jane Bunnett**
PRODUCER OF THE YEAR	**k.d. lang/Ben Mink (Greg Penny**, co-producer) for *Constant Craving* and *The Mind Of Love*
RECORDING ENGINEER OF THE YEAR	**Jeff Wolpert/John Whynot** for *The Lady Of Shallott* from THE VISIT, **Loreena McKennitt**
BEST VIDEO	**Curtis Wehrfritz** for *Closing Time*, **Leonard Cohen**
BEST ALBUM DESIGN	**Rebecca Baird/Kenny Baird**, co-art directors for LOST TOGETHER, **Blue Rodeo**
HALL OF FAME	**Anne Murray**
WALT GREALIS SPECIAL ACHIEVEMENT AWARD	**Brian Robertson**

1993: The CBC-TV special *Anne Murray In Nova Scotia* attracts 2.67 million viewers.

1993: Steppenwolf play the Harley-Davidson 90th birthday bash in Milwaukee, Wisconsin.

1993: The **Bryan Adams'** single *Everything I Do (I Do It For You)* becomes the biggest selling-single of all time.

1993: Pearl Jam, who are touring with **Neil Young** as his opening act, appear with him at the MTV Video awards.

1993: In the hit movie *Sleepless In Seattle* starring Tom Hanks and Meg Ryan, **Celine Dion** is heard singing the main theme *When I Fall In Love*.

1993: Ronnie Hawkins and **The Band**, who invite **Bob Dylan** to appear with them, are among the artists on hand for a concert dubbed "The Blue Jeans Bash" celebrating the presidential inauguration of Bill Clinton.

1993: Toronto raggamuffin rapper **Snow** hits the top of the charts around the world with the single *Informer* from his debut 12 INCHES OF SNOW album.

1993: The Tragically Hip set out across Canada on their Another Roadside Attraction tour.

1993: Toronto vocalist **Molly Johnson** (**Alta Moda**, **Infidels**, **Blue Monday**) organizes the first of her Kumbaya Festivals to raise funds for Canadian AIDS hospices.

1993: *Billboard* magazine names **David Foster** Top Singles Producer and Top R&B Singles Producer for the year.

Celine Dion

The Tragically Hip

Michelle Wright

Snow

*H*arvest Moon 1994

23RD ANNUAL JUNO AWARDS
Sunday, March 20, 1994
The O'Keefe Centre, Toronto
Host:
Roch Voisine
Performers:
Blue Rodeo, Devon, Celine Dion, Kanatan Aski, James Keelaghan, Claudette LeBlanc, Colin Linden, Lawrence Martin, Walter Ostanek, The Rankin Family, Snow, Roch Voisine

Once again the Hall of Fame induction was a star-studded affair as Rush well-wishers included members of Soundgarden, Primus, and Barenaked Ladies as well as Mike Myers, Sebastian Bach of Skid Row, Vernon Reid of Living Color, Kim Mitchell, Toronto Blue Jays Joe Carter and Paul Molitor, long-time manager Ray Danniels, and Alexis Lifeson, son of Rush guitarist Alex Lifeson. Cape Breton's The Rankin Family were awarded four Junos, including the coveted Entertainer of the Year prize. Newcomer Jann Arden was the only other multiple winner, taking home the newly-introduced Best New Artist award and sharing Best Video honors with Jeff Weinrich. Robbie Robertson was on hand to present the first ever Best Music of Aboriginal Canada Recording Juno to Lawrence Martin (Wapistan).

Harvest Moon
1994 JUNO AWARD WINNERS
(For the Voting Year 1993)

CANADIAN ENTERTAINER OF THE YEAR	**The Rankin Family**
BEST SELLING ALBUM (FOREIGN OR DOMESTIC)	THE BODYGUARD, **Various Artists** featuring **Whitney Houston**
BEST SELLING FRANCOPHONE ALBUM	L'ALBUM DU PEUPLE, TOME 2, **François Perusse**
ALBUM OF THE YEAR	HARVEST MOON, **Neil Young**
SINGLE OF THE YEAR	*Fare Thee Well Love,* **The Rankin Family**
FEMALE VOCALIST OF THE YEAR	**Celine Dion**
MALE VOCALIST OF THE YEAR	**Roch Voisine**
GROUP OF THE YEAR	**The Rankin Family**
INSTRUMENTAL ARTIST OF THE YEAR	**Ofra Harnoy**
HARD ROCK ALBUM OF THE YEAR	DIG, **I Mother Earth**
RAP RECORDING OF THE YEAR	ONE TRACK MIND, **TBTBT**
COUNTRY FEMALE VOCALIST	**Cassandra Vasik**
COUNTRY MALE VOCALIST	**Charlie Major**
COUNTRY GROUP OR DUO	**The Rankin Family**
BEST NEW SOLO ARTIST (SPONSORED BY FACTOR)	**Jann Arden**
BEST NEW GROUP (SPONSORED BY FACTOR)	**The Waltons**
SOCAN JUNO FOR SONGWRITER OF THE YEAR	**Leonard Cohen**
BEST CHILDREN'S ALBUM	TCHAIKOVSKY DISCOVERS AMERICA, **Susan Hammond**/Classical Kids
BEST CLASSICAL ALBUM (SOLO OR CHAMBER ENSEMBLE)	BEETHOVEN: THE PIANO SONATAS, OP. 10, NO. 1-3, **Louis Lortie**
BEST CLASSICAL ALBUM (LARGE ENSEMBLE OR SOLOIST WITH LARGE ENSEMBLE)	HANDEL: CONCERTI GROSSI, OP. 3, NO. 1-6, **Tafelmusik**; **Jeanne Lamon**, director
BEST CLASSICAL ALBUM (VOCAL OR CHORAL PERFORMANCE)	DEBUSSY SONGS, **Claudette Leblanc**, soprano; **Valerie Tryon**, piano
BEST CLASSICAL COMPOSITION	AMONG FRIENDS, **Chan Ka Nin** with **AMICI**; **Joaquin Valdepenas**, clarinet; **David Hetherington**, cello; **Patricia Parr**, piano
BEST DANCE RECORDING	THANKFUL (RAW CLUB MIX), **Red Light**
BEST CONTEMPORARY JAZZ ALBUM	DON'T SMOKE IN BED, **Holly Cole Trio**
BEST MAINSTREAM JAZZ ALBUM	FABLES AND DREAMS, **Dave Young/Phil Dwyer Quartet**
BEST R&B/SOUL RECORDING	I'LL BE THERE FOR YOU: THE TIME IS RIGHT, **Rupert Gayle**
BEST ROOTS & TRADITIONAL ALBUM	MY SKIES, **James Keelaghan**
BEST REGGAE RECORDING	INFORMER, **Snow**
BEST MUSIC OF ABORIGINAL CANADA RECORDING	WAPISTAN, **Lawrence Martin**
BEST BLUES/GOSPEL ALBUM	SOUTH AT EIGHT, NORTH AT NINE, **Colin Linden**
BEST GLOBAL RECORDING	EL CAMINO REAL, **Ancient Cultures**
PRODUCER OF THE YEAR	**Steven Mackinnon, Marc Jordan** (**Greg Penny,** co-producer) for *Waiting For A Miracle* from RECKLESS VALENTINE, **Marc Jordan**
RECORDING ENGINEER OF THE YEAR	**Kevin Doyle** for *Old Cape Cod* and *Cry Me A River*, **Anne Murray**
BEST VIDEO	**Jeff Weinrich** for *I Would Die For You*, **Jann Arden**
BEST ALBUM DESIGN	**Marty Dolan** for FAITHLIFT, **Spirit Of the West**
HALL OF FAME	**Rush**
WALT GREALIS SPECIAL ACHIEVEMENT AWARD	**John V. Mills**

1994: Celine Dion's CD *The Colour Of My Love* is certified diamond in Canada for sales of over one million copies.

1994: Inuit singer/songwriter **Susan Aglukark** is honored with the first Aboriginal Achievement Award in the Arts & Entertainment field.

1994: Tom Cochrane wins the Governor General's medal for cultural contributions.

1994: Anne Murray and **Celine Dion**, betting on the stock of The Bay, become TV spokespersons for the Canadian retail giant.

1994: In Los Angeles, **Alanis Morissette** begins her collaboration with Glen Ballard, a protégé of producer Quincy Jones and, among other things, the co-writer of Michael Jackson's *Man In the Mirror*.

1994: At Nashville's Opryland Hotel on March 5th, country singer **Lisa Brokop** sets over 1,000 country broadcasters assembled at the Country Radio Seminar on their heels with a showcase performance that brings a lengthy standing ovation and a solid kick-off for her first U.S.-released single, *Give Me A Ring Sometime*. The same month, *Harmony Cats*, the film in which Brokop plays the female lead role, premieres.

1994: Michelle Wright co-hosts The Nashville Network's top-rated show *Music City Tonight* with Charlie Chase on March 15th.

1994: Randy Bachman donates his archives and memorabilia, including one of the largest collections of vintage rock guitars in the world, to the National Library in Ottawa.

1994: On **Hank Snow**'s 80th birthday, he is presented with an honorary Doctor of

The Rankin Family

Letters from Saint Mary's University in Halifax.

1994: The soundtrack album *The Crow*, containing the **Jane Siberry** track *It Can't Rain All the Time*, hits the top of the U.S. album charts.

1994: Montreal bass player **Melissa Auf Der Maur**, daughter of local politician and Montreal *Gazette* columnist Nick Auf Der Maur, joins the Seattle band Hole fronted by Courtney Love, the widow of Nirvana mainman Kurt Cobain.

Charlie Major

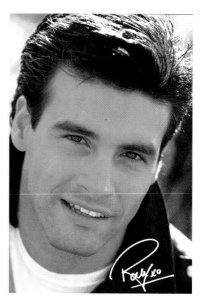

Roch Vosine

1994: Blue Rodeo's FIVE DAYS IN JULY disc, the group's fifth consecutive platinum album in Canada, gets a U.S. release on September 5th as they sign with Discovery Records.

1994: On its release on September 24th, **The Tragically Hip** CD DAY FOR NIGHT becomes the fastest selling Canadian album in history.

1994: Rita MacNeil's CBC-TV musical variety series *Rita And Friends* debuts on October 29th with guests **Roch Voisine**, **Jann Arden**, **Real World,** and **Punjabi By Nature**, drawing 1.7 million viewers.

1994: Bryan Adams tours Europe with The Rolling Stones in November, and he is named best male star over Prince, Seal, and Bruce Springsteen at the publicly-voted European Music Awards in Berlin.

1994: Roch Voisine signs a record deal with BMG

International as his first English-language album I'LL ALWAYS BE THERE has to this point sold over 500,000 copies in Canada and over 1.5 million worldwide.

1994: *Spin* magazine calls Halifax-band **Sloan's** TWICE REMOVED CD one of the "Ten Best Albums You Didn't Hear In 1994."

1994: Following the release of her FREE-DOM SESSIONS album, **Sarah McLachlan** has a private audience on December 16th with The Pope as she takes part in the Christmas At the Vatican concert. Her FUMBLING TOWARDS ECSTASY CD has at this point sold over one million copies in North America.

1994: Celine Dion marries her manager René Angelil on December 17th in a gala ceremony in Montreal.

1994: NCN — New Country Network — debuts on December 31st.

Robbie Robertson and Lawrence Martin

Colour Of My Love
1995

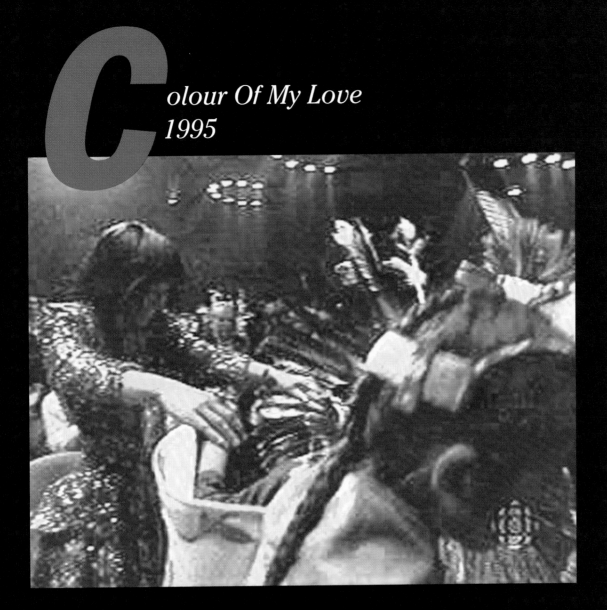

24TH ANNUAL JUNO AWARDS

March 26, 1995
Copps Coliseum, Hamilton, Ontario
Hosts:
Cathy Jones, Rick Mercer, Greg Thomey and **Mary Walsh** of the CBC-TV program *This Hour Has 22 Minutes.*
Performers:
Susan Aglukark, Barenaked Ladies, Bass Is Base with **Ashley MacIsaac, Celine Dion** with **David Foster and the Hamilton Philharmonic Orchestra, Crash Test Dummies, Colin James, Charlie Major, Sarah McLachlan, Moist, Prairie Oyster, Quartette, Stoney Park Singers** and **Six Nations Dancers**

Women were front and center at this year's Junos as artists like Jann Arden, Celine Dion, and Susan Aglukark were all multiple award winners. The Tragically Hip picked up their third Entertainer of the Year Juno and the Group of the Year award. This was only the second Juno Awards show presented outside of Toronto and the first in a venue the size of Hamilton, Ontario's Copps Coliseum as 8,000 seats were made available to the fans of Canadian music. An emotional tribute to Anne Murray's critically-ill manager Leonard Rambeau, who received a special Global Achievement Award, was balanced on the night by the joyous celebration that accompanied the induction of Buffy Sainte-Marie into the Hall of Fame.

1995

Colour Of My Love
1995 JUNO AWARD WINNERS
(For the Voting Year 1994)

ENTERTAINER OF THE YEAR	**The Tragically Hip**
BEST SELLING ALBUM (FOREIGN OR DOMESTIC)	COLOUR OF MY LOVE, **Celine Dion**
BEST SELLING FRANCOPHONE ALBUM	COUP DE TETE, **Roch Voisine**
ALBUM OF THE YEAR	COLOUR OF MY LOVE, **Celine Dion**
SINGLE OF THE YEAR	*Could I Be Your Girl?*, **Jann Arden**
FEMALE VOCALIST OF THE YEAR	**Jann Arden**
MALE VOCALIST OF THE YEAR	**Neil Young**
GROUP OF THE YEAR	**The Tragically Hip**
INSTRUMENTAL ARTIST OF THE YEAR	**André Gagnon**
BEST NEW SOLO ARTIST (SPONSORED BY FACTOR)	**Susan Aglukark**
BEST NEW GROUP (SPONSORED BY FACTOR)	**Moist**
SOCAN JUNO FOR SONGWRITER OF THE YEAR	**Jann Arden**
COUNTRY FEMALE VOCALIST OF THE YEAR	**Michelle Wright**
COUNTRY MALE VOCALIST OF THE YEAR	**Charlie Major**
COUNTRY GROUP OR DUO OF THE YEAR	**Prairie Oyster**
BEST CHILDREN'S ALBUM	BANANAPHONE, **Raffi**
BEST CLASSICAL ALBUM: SOLO OR CHAMBER ENSEMBLE	ERICA GOODMAN PLAYS CANADIAN HARP MUSIC, **Erica Goodman**, Harp
BEST CLASSICAL ALBUM: LARGE ENSEMBLE OR SOLOIST(S) WITH LARGE ENSEMBLE ACCOMPANIMENT	BACH: BRANDENBURG CONCERTOS NOS. 1-6, **Tafelmusik, Jeanne Lamon**, musical director
BEST CLASSICAL ALBUM VOCAL OR CHORAL ERLIOZ PERFORMANCE	LES TROYENS, **Choeur et Orchestre** B **symphonique de Montréal, Charles Dutoit**, conductor
BEST CLASSICAL COMPOSITION	SKETCHES FROM NATAL, **Malcolm Forsyth**; *Milhaud*, **Maurice, Forsyth & Sowande — CBC Vancouver Orchestra**.
BEST ALTERNATIVE ALBUM	SHIVER, **Rose Chronicles**
BEST DANCE RECORDING	HIGHER LOVE (CLUB MIX), **Capital Sound**
BEST HARD ROCK ALBUM	SUFFERSYSTEM, **Monster Voodoo Machine**
BEST CONTEMPORARY JAZZ ALBUM	THE MERLIN FACTOR, **Jim Hillman & The Merlin Factor**
BEST MAINSTREAM JAZZ ALBUM	FREE TRADE, **Free Trade**
BEST R&B/SOUL RECORDING	FIRST IMPRESSIONS FOR THE BOTTOM JIGGLERS, **Bass Is Base**
BEST RAP RECORDING	CERTIFIED, **Ghetto Concept**
BEST REGGAE RECORDING	CLASS AND CREDENTIAL, **Carla Marshall**
BEST MUSIC OF ABORIGINAL CANADA	ARCTIC ROSE, **Susan Aglukark**
BEST ROOTS/TRADITIONAL ALBUM	THE MASK AND MIRROR, **Loreena McKennitt**
BEST BLUES/GOSPEL RECORDING	JOY TO THE WORLD, JUBILATION V, **The Montreal Jubilation Gospel Choir**
BEST GLOBAL RECORDING	AFRICA +, **Eval Manigat**
PRODUCER OF THE YEAR	**Robbie Robertson** for *Skin Walker, It Is A Good Day To Die (Music For The Native Americans)*, **Robbie Robertson & the Red Road Ensemble**
RECORDING ENGINEER OF THE YEAR	**Lenny DeRose** for *Lay My Body Down, Charms (The Philosopher Kings)*, **The Philosopher Kings**
BEST VIDEO	*Tunnel Of Trees*, **Gogh Van Go**; director, **Lyne Charlebois**
BEST ALBUM DESIGN	**Andrew MacNaughton/Our Lady Peace** for *Naveed*, **Our Lady Peace**
GLOBAL ACHIEVEMENT AWARD	**Leonard Rambeau**
HALL OF FAME	**Buffy Sainte-Marie**
WALT GREALIS SPECIAL ACHIEVEMENT AWARD	**Louis Applebaum**

1995: Neil Young's 38th album MIRROR BALL features Pearl Jam as his backing band.

1995: With the appearance of NCN, the Nashville-based CMT: Country Music Television is taken off the air, and a cross-border trade war begins as CMT drops all Canadian country artists without U.S. recording deals off their playlist.

1995: The Rankin Family kick-off a tour of Scotland and England in January with a SRO concert in Glasgow, where they are one of the headliners for the Celtic Connections Festival.

1995: Singer/songwriter **Gene MacLellan**, best known for his songs *Snowbird* and *Put the Hand In the Hand*, which were career launching hits for Anne Murray and Ocean, respectively, dies at his rural Prince Edward Island home on January 19th after an apparent suicide.

1995: Jann Arden, whose LIVING UNDER JUNE CD has sold over 100,000 copies in Canada, sets out on a three-week tour of Europe on January 23rd.

1995: Vocalist/guitarist **Colin James** signs a worldwide record deal with Warner Music/Elektra.

1995: Charlie Major becomes the first country artist to have six number one songs from the same album in Canada as he hits the top of the country chart in February with *I'm Here* from his platinum album THE OTHER SIDE.

1995: Leonard Rambeau, longtime manager of **Anne Murray** as well as **George Fox** and **Rita MacNeil**, dies on April 13th following a lengthy battle with cancer.

1995: Hot on the heels of **Michelle Wright**'s cross-Canada The Reasons

Jann Arden

Why tour in May with guests **John Berry** and **One Horse Blue**, the CD for which the tour is named is certified platinum for sales of over 100,000 copies in Canada.

Buffy Sainte-Marie

Susan Aglukark

1995: Ian Tyson celebrates another milestone in his career as his COWBOY-OGRAPHY album is certified platinum in Canada for sales of over 100,000.

1995: Shania Twain becomes only the third Canadian artist to top the *Billboard* country singles chart in the U.S. as her song *Any Man Of Mine* puts her into the select company of **Anne Murray** and **Hank Snow**. Murray has hit the heights ten times, while Snow has had seven number one hits in the U.S. By the end of the year, Twain's album THE WOMAN IN ME has sold close to five million copies internationally, establishing her as one of the hottest stars in country music.

1995: George Fox is immortalized in his hometown of Cochrane, Alberta as

Crash Test Dummies

the civic leaders rename a street George Fox Trail in his honor.

1995: The Bay's Big Sky Canada Concert, a three day celebration marking the The Bay's 325th anniversary, begins on August 5th at Rocky Mountain Ranch in High River, Alberta, featuring more than 30 Canadian acts, including **Bryan Adams**, **Susan Aglukark**, **Jann Arden**, **Blue Rodeo**, **Burton Cummings**, **Celine Dion**, **David Foster**, **Colin James**, **Ashley MacIsaac**, **Sarah McLachlan**, **Anne Murray**, **Fred Penner**, **The Rankin Family**, **Buffy Sainte-Marie**, and **Michelle Wright**.

1995: *Only One Moon* becomes **Prairie Oyster**'s fourth number one song from their album of the same name.

1995: As **The Tragically Hip** prepare to tour the U.S. with Page & Plant in September, it is revealed that they have hit the three million mark for total albums sales in Canada.

1995: Tom Cochrane's MAD MAD WORLD album is certified diamond for sales of over one million copies in Canada. He joins the select company of Canadian artists **Bryan Adams, Corey Hart, Alannah Myles,** and **Celine Dion** in reaching the milestone.

1995: Ronnie Hawkins launches his video and CD LET IT ROCK with a concert on September 15th at The Canadian Embassy Theatre in Washington, D.C., with special guest **Jeff Healey**, where Hawkins is presented a gold album for sales of 50,000 in Canada.

1995: Twenty-one-year-old **Alanis Morissette** becomes the first Canadian woman to top *Billboard*'s influential Top 200 albums chart on September 28th with her CD JAGGED LITTLE PILL. Morissette is the first Canadian to accomplish the feat since **Bryan Adams'** RECKLESS CD hit the penthouse position of the same chart in 1984. She appears on the cover of both *Rolling Stone* and *Spin* in November.

Shania Twain

1995: Celine Dion, whose THE COLOUR OF MY LOVE disc has sold over ten million copies worldwide, kicks off a 50-date European tour in October.

1995: Beau Dommage take home four Felix Awards at the 17th annual ADISQ gala in November.

1995: Calling themselves Canadian Recording Artists for Copyright Reform, **Bryan Adams, Tom Cochrane, Bruce Cockburn, Celine Dion, k.d. lang, Anne Murray, Oscar Peterson, Rush, Buffy Sainte-Marie**, and **Michelle Wright** send an open letter to Prime Minister Jean Chretien and all federal MPs on December 1st urging swift passage of revisions to the Copyright Act.

1995: The **Canadian Academy of Recording Arts & Sciences** announces that the 25th anniversary of the Juno Awards will be celebrated on March 10, 1996 at Copps Coliseum in Hamilton, and that a four-CD box set of vital Canadian music, a seven-hour radio documentary on the history of the Juno Awards, and a book chronicling Canada's music heritage will all be produced under the title *Oh What a Feeling* as part of the celebrations.

Ronnie Hawkins

JUNO WINNERS ALPHABETICALLY

BRYAN ADAMS
1983 - Male Vocalist of the Year
1984 - Male Vocalist of the Year
1984 - Album of the Year: *Cuts Like A Knife*
1984 - Producer of the Year: *Cuts Like A Knife* (Bryan Adams)
1985 - Male Vocalist of the Year
1985 - Album of the Year: *Reckless*
1986 - Male Vocalist of the Year
1987 - Male Vocalist of the Year
1987 - Canadian Entertainer of the Year
1992 - Global Achievement Award
1992 - Canadian Entertainer of the Year
1992 - Producer of the Year (Robert John "Mutt" Lange, co-producer): *(Everything I Do) I Do It For You; Can't Stop This Thing We Started* from *Waking Up The Neighbours*, Bryan Adams
1993 - Best Selling Album (Foreign or Domestic):*Waking Up the Neighbours*

BRYAN ADAMS and JIM VALLANCE
1984 - Composer(s) of the Year
1985 - Composer(s) of the Year
(see also Bryan Adams or Jim Vallance)

SUSAN AGLUKARK
1995 - Best New Solo Artist (Sponsored by FACTOR)
1995 - Best Music Of Aboriginal Canada Recording: *Arctic Rose*

BRIAN AHERN
1971 - Best Produced Single: *Snowbird*, Anne Murray
1971 - Best Produced MOR Album: *Honey, Wheat & Laughter*, Anne Murray
1972 - Best Produced MOR Album: *Talk It Over In The Morning*, Anne Murray
1973 - Best Produced MOR Album: *Annie*, Anne Murray

THE AIR FARCE
1979 - Comedy/Spoken Word Album of the Year: *The Air Farce Album*

ALAN GEE AND GREG LAWSON
1979 - Best Album Design: *Madcats* , Madcats

ALANIS
1992 - Most Promising Female Vocalist

BRUCE ALLEN
1987 - Walt Grealis Special Achievement Award (Industry Builder)

LILLIAN ALLEN
1986 - Best Reggae/Calypso Recording: *Revolutionary Tea Party*
1989 - Best Reggae/Calypso Recording: *Conditions Critical*

THE AMOS GARRETT-DOUG SAHM-GENE TAYLOR BAND
1989 - Best Roots/Traditional Album: *The Return of The Formerly Brothers*

A&M RECORDS OF CANADA
1974 - Canadian Record Company In Promotional Activities

PETER ANASTASOFF
1976 - Producer of the Year: *The Homecoming* , Hagood Hardy

ANCIENT CULTURES
1994 - Best Global Recording: *El Camino Real*

DAVE ANDERSON
1978 - Best Album Design: *Short Turn*, Short Turn

ANDREW MACNAUGHTON/ OUR LADY PEACE
1995 - Best Album Design for *Naveed*, Our Lady Peace

PAUL ANKA
1975 - Composer of the Year
1980 - Hall Of Fame Award

LOUIS APPLEBAUM
1995 - Walt Grealis Special Achievement Award (Industry Builder)

JANN ARDEN
1994 - Best New Solo Artist
1994 - Best Video: *I Would Die For You* (Jeff Weinrich, director)
1995 - Single of the Year, *Could I Be Your Girl?*
1995 - Female Vocalist of the Year
1995 - Songwriter of the Year

RANDY BACHMAN
1975 - Producer of the Year

BACHMAN-TURNER OVERDRIVE
1974 - Most Promising Group
of the Year
1974 - Contemporary Album of the
Year: *Bachman-Turner Overdrive*
1975 - Group of the Year
1975 - Best-Selling Album of the Year:
Not Fragile
1976 - Group of the Year
1976 - Best-Selling Album of the Year:
Four Wheel Drive
1976 - Best-Selling Single of the Year:
You Ain't Seen Nothin' Yet

CARROLL BAKER
1977 - Country Female Vocalist
of the Year
1978 - Country Female Vocalist
of the Year
1979 - Country Female Vocalist
of the Year

MICHAEL CONWAY BAKER
1992 - Best Classical Composition:
*Concerto For Piano & Chamber
Orchestra*, Robert Silverman,
piano - CBC Vancouver Orchestra,
Kazuyoshi Akiyama, conductor.

BANANARAMA
1987 - Best-Selling International
Single: *Venus*

THE BAND
1989 - Hall Of Fame Award

BARENAKED LADIES
1993 - Group of the Year

**BARNEY BENTALL
AND THE LEGENDARY HEARTS**
1989 - Most Promising Group
of the Year

CLAUDJA BARRY
1979 - Most Promising Female
Vocalist

BASS IS BASE
1995 - Best R&B/Soul Recording: *First
Impressions For the Bottom Jigglers*

SANDRA BEECH
1982 - Best Children's Album:
Inch By Inch

THE BEE GEES
1979 - International Best-Selling
Album: *Saturday Night Fever*

RON BERTI
1987 - Best Video: *Love Is The Fire*,
The Parachute Club

BILL BOURNE & ALLAN MACLEOD
1991 - Best Roots/Traditional Album:
Dance & Celebrate

**BILL HENDERSON
AND BRIAN MACLEOD**
1983 - Producer of the Year: *Watcha
Gonna Do* and *Secret Information*,
Chilliwack

DAVE BIST
1971: Music Journalist of the Year
(Montreal Gazette)

BLONDIE
1979 - International Single of the
Year: *Heart Of Glass*

BLUE RODEO
1989 - Group of the Year
1989 - Single of the Year: *Try*
1989 - Best Video: *Try*, Blue Rodeo
(Blue Rodeo and Mike Buckley,
directors)
1990 - Group of the Year
1991 - Group of the Year
(see also Rebecca Baird And Kenny
Baird)

**BLUE RODEO
AND MIKE BUCKLEY**
1989 - Best Video: *Try*, Blue Rodeo

BOB ROCK AND PAUL HYDE
1983 - Composer (s) of the Year:
for *Eyes Of A Stranger*, The Payola$
(see also Payola$)
(see also Keith Stein And Bob Rock)
(see also Bob Rock)

BOOTSAUCE
1992 - Best Dance Recording:
*Everyone's A Winner (The Chocolate
Movement Mix)*

JOHN BOTTOMLEY
1993 - Most Promising Male Vocalist

RODNEY BOWES
1980 - Best Album Design: *Cigarettes*,
The Wives

MICHAEL BOWNESS
1977 - Best Album Design: *Ian
Tamblyn*, Ian Tamblyn

LIONA BOYD
1979 - Instrumental Artist of the Year
1982 - Instrumental Artist of the Year
1983 - Instrumental Artist of the Year
1984 - Instrumental Artist of the Year

DAVID BRADSTREET
1978 - Best New Male Vocalist

THE BRASS CONNECTION
1982 - Best Jazz Album: *The Brass
Connection*

GARTH BROOKS
1992 - International Entertainer
of the Year

TERRY BROWN
1978 - Recording Engineer of the
Year: *Hope*, Klaatu (tie with David
Greene)

MIKE BUCKLEY
1989 - Best Video: *Try*, Blue Rodeo
(Mike Buckley and Blue Rodeo,
directors)

JANE BUNNETT
1993 - Best World Beat Recording:
Spirits Of Havana

THE CANADIAN BRASS
1985 - Instrumental Artist of the Year

CAPITAL SOUND
1995 - Best Dance Recording: *Higher
Love (Club Mix)*

CAPITOL RECORDS OF CANADA
1971 - Top Record Company in
Promotional Activities
1971 - Top Record Company
1973 - Canadian Content Record
Company of the Year

THE CAPTAIN & TENNILLE
1976 - International Single: *Love Will
Keep Us Together*

KIM CARNES
1982 - International Single: *Bette
Davis Eyes*

CARLTON SHOWBAND
1975 - Country Group of the Year

WILF CARTER
1985 - Hall Of Fame Award

ANDREW CASH
1990 - Best Video: *Boomtown,*
Andrew Cash (Cosimo Cavallaro,
director)

COSIMO CAVALLARO
1990 - Best Video: *Boomtown,*
Andrew Cash

CHAN KA NIN
1994 - Best Classical Composition:
Among Friends, with AMICI, Joaquin
Valdepenas, clarinet; David
Hetherington, cello; Patricia Parr,
piano

LYNE CHARLEBOIS
1995 - Best Video: *Tunnel Of Trees,*
Gogh Van Go

TINA CHARLES
1977 - Best-Selling International
Single: *I Love To Love*

JANE CHILD
1991 - Best Dance Recording: *Don't
Wanna Fall In Love (Knife Feels Good
Mix)*

CHILLIWACK
(see also Bill Henderson and Brian
MacLeod)

**CHOEUR ET ORCHESTRE
SYMPHONIQUE DE MONTREAL**
1995 - Best Classical Album: Vocal or
Choral Performance: *Berlioz: Les
Troyens* (Charles Dutoit, conductor)
(See also Orchestre Symphonique de
Montréal, Charles Dutoit)

CHUM GROUP
1973 - Broadcaster of the Year

**AUDETTE LEBLANC, SOPRANO;
VALERIE TRYON, PIANO**
1994 - Best Classical Album (Vocal or
Choral Performance): *Debussy Songs*

DAVID CLAYTON-THOMAS
1973 - Outstanding Contribution To
the Canadian Music Scene

TOM COCHRANE
1989 - Composer of the Year
1992 - Male Vocalist of the Year
1992 - Album of the Year: *Mad Mad
World*
1992 - Single of the Year: *Life Is A
Highway*

1992 - Songwriter of the Year
(see also Red Rider)

BRUCE COCKBURN
1971- Top Folk Singer (Or Group)
1972 - Folksinger of the Year
1973 - Folksinger of the Year
1980 - Folksinger of the Year
1981 - Folk Artist of the Year
1981 - Folksinger of the Year
1982 - Male Vocalist of the Year
1982 - Folk Artist of the Year
(see also Gene Martynec)
(see also John Naslen)
(see also Bart Schoales)

LEONARD COHEN
1991 - Hall Of Fame Award
1993 - Male Vocalist of the Year
1993 - Best Video: *Closing Time,*
Leonard Cohen (Curtis Wehrfritz,
director)
1994 - Songwriter of the Year

**CONNIE KALDOR
AND CARMEN CAMPAGNE**
1989 - Best Children's Album: *Lullaby
Berceuse* (tie Fred Penner)

STOMPIN' TOM CONNORS
1971 - Top Country Singer, Male
1972 - Male Country Singer of the
Year
1973 - Male Country Singer of the
Year
1974 - Canadian Country Vocalist,
Male
1974 - Canadian Country Album: *To It
And At It*
1975 - Country Male Artist of the
Year

CRASH TEST DUMMIES
1992 - Group of the Year

THE CREW CUTS
1984 - Hall Of Fame Award

BURTON CUMMINGS
1977 - Best New Male Vocalist
1977 - Male Vocalist of the Year
1979 - Best-Selling Album: *Dream Of
A Child*
1980 - Male Vocalist of the Year

ANDY CURRAN
1991 - Most Promising Male Vocalist

BILLY RAY CYRUS
1993 - Best-Selling Single (Foreign or
Domestic): *Achy Breaky Heart*

PATRICIA DAHLQUIST
1976 - Best New Female Artist

LISA DALBELLO
1978 - Best New Female Vocalist

**DANIEL LANOIS
AND ROBBIE ROBERTSON**
1989 - Producer of the Year:
Showdown At Big Sky and *Somewhere
Down the Crazy River,* Robbie
Robertson
(see also Daniel Lanois)
(see also Robbie Robertson)

**DAVE YOUNG/
PHIL DWYER QUARTET**
1994 - Best Mainstream Jazz Album:
Fables And Dreams

**DAVID TYSON
AND CHRISTOPHER WARD**
1990 - Composer(s) of the Year

**DEAN MOTTER, JEFF JACKSON
AND DEBRA SAMUELS**
1984 - Best Album Design: *Seamless,*
The Nylons
(see also Dean Motter)
(see also Hugh Syme
and Debra Samuels)

LUC DE LAROCHELLIERE
1992 - Best Selling Francophone
Album: *Sauvez Mon Ame*

LENNY DEROSE
1995 - Recording Engineer of the Year
for *Lay My Body Down, Charms,*
The Philosopher Kings

DEVON
1993 - Rap Recording of the Year:
Keep It Slammin'

THE DIAMONDS
1984 - Hall Of Fame Award

CHARLOTTE DIAMOND
1986 - Best Children's Album:
Ten Carrot Diamond

BRIAN DICKINSON
1992 - Best Jazz Album: *In Transition*
(tie with Rob McConnell and the
Boss Brass and Renee Rosnes)

CELINE DION
1991 - Female Vocalist of the Year
1991 - Album of the Year: *Unison*
1992 - Female Vocalist of the Year
1993 - Female Vocalist of the Year
1993 - Best-Selling Francophone
Album: *Dion Chante Plamondon*
1993 - Single of the Year: *Beauty And
The Beast* (with Peabo Bryson)
1993 - Best Dance Recordings: *Love
Can Move Mountains (Club Mix)*
1994 - Female Vocalist of the Year
1995 - Best-Selling Album (Foreign or
Domestic): *Colour Of My Love*
1995 - Album of the Year: *Colour
Of My Love*

DIRE STRAITS
1986 - Best-Selling International
Album: *Brothers In Arms*

RICH DODSON
1972 - Composer of the Year

MARTY DOLAN
1994 - Best Album Design: *Faithlift* ,
Spirit of the West

DOMPIERRE
(see Michel Ethier)

DOUCETTE
1979 - Most Promising Group
of the Year

DOWNCHILD BLUES BAND
(see Jeanette Hanna)

KEVIN DOYLE
1990 - Recording Engineer of the
Year: *Alannah Myles*, Alannah Myles
1994 - Recording Engineer of the
Year: *Old Cape Cod* and *Cry Me A
River* from *Croonin'*, Anne Murray

DREAM WARRIORS
1992 - Rap Recording of the Year: *My
Definition Of A Boombastic Jazz Style*

EDDIE EASTMAN
1981 - Country Male Vocalist
of the Year
1983 - Country Male Vocalist
of the Year

EDWARD BEAR
1973 - Outstanding Performance
of the Year, Group
(see also Gene Martynec)

ED BICKERT
AND DON THOMPSON
1980 - Best Jazz Album: *Sackville
4005*

SHIRLEY EIKHARD
1973 - Female Country Singer
of the Year
1974 - Canadian Country Vocalist,
Female

MELISSA ETHERIDGE
1990 - International Entertainer
of the Year

MICHEL ETHIER
1976 - Recording Engineer
of the Year: *Dompierre* , Dompierre

EXTREME
1992 - Best Selling Single by a
Foreign Artist: *More Than Words*

BRUCE FAIRBAIRN
1980 - Producer of the Year:
Armageddon, Prism
1990 - Producer of the Year: *Pump*,
Aerosmith
(see also Paul Dean And Bruce
Fairbairn)

THE FAMILY BROWN
1985 - Country Group or Duo
of the Year
1989 - Country Group or Duo
of the Year
1990 - Country Group or Duo
of the Year

TIM FEEHAN
1987 - Most Promising Male Vocalist

FLEETWOOD MAC
1977 - International Best-Selling
Album: *Rumours*

MIKE FLICKER
1977 - Producer of the Year:
Dreamboat Annie, Heart

GARY FJELLGAARD
1993 - Country Male Vocalist
of the Year

FOREIGNER
1985 - International Single of the
Year: *I Want To Know What Love Is*

MAUREEN FORRESTER
1990 - Hall of Fame Award

MALCOLM FORSYTH
1987 - Best Classical Composition:
(tie with Donald Steven) *Atayoskewin*,
the Edmonton Symphony Orchestra;
Uri Mayer, conductor.
1995 - Best Classical Composition:
Sketches From Natal, Milhaud,
Maurice, Forsythe & Sowande - CBC
Vancouver Orchestra

DAVID FOSTER
1985 - Producer of the Year:
Chicago 17, Chicago
1986 - Instrumental Artist of the Year
1986 - Producer of the Year: *St. Elmo's
Fire Soundtrack*, John Parr and
Various Artists
1987 - Instrumental Artist of the
Year
1989 - Instrumental Artist of the
Year

THE FOUR LADS
1984 - Hall of Fame Award

GEORGE FOX
1990 - Country Male Vocalist
of the Year
1991 - Country Male Vocalist
of the Year
1992 - Country Male Vocalist
of the Year

PETER FRAMPTON
1977 - Best Selling International
Album: *Frampton Comes Alive*

MIKE FRASER
1989 - Recording Engineer of the
Year: *Calling America* and *Different
Drummer*, Tom Cochrane
& Red Rider
1992 - Recording Engineer of the
Year: *Thunderstruck* and *Money Talks*
from *The Razor's Edge*, AC/DC

FRASER MACPHERSON
AND OLIVER GANNON
1983 - Best Jazz Album: *I Didn't Know
About You*

FREE TRADE
1995 - Best Mainstream Jazz Album:
Free Trade

KEN FRIESEN
1979 - Recording Engineer of the
Year: *Let's Keep It That Way,* Anne
Murray

HAGOOD HARDY
1976 - Composer of the Year
(*The Homecoming*)
1976 - Instrumental Artist of the Year
1977 - Instrumental Artist of the Year
(see also Peter Anastasoff)

OFRA HARNOY
1989 - Best Classical Album (Solo
or Chamber Ensemble): *Schubert:
Arpeggione Sonata*
1991 - Instrumental Artist of the Year
1993 - Instrumental Artist of the Year
1994 - Instrumental Artist of the Year
(see also The Orford String
Quartet/Ofra Harnoy)

COREY HART
1984 - Best Video: *Sunglasses At Night*
(Rob Quartly, director)
1985 - Single of the Year: *Never
Surrender*

RONNIE HAWKINS
1982 - Country Male Vocalist
of the Year

HEART
1977 - Group of the Year
(see also Mike Flicker)

DAN HILL
1976 - Best New Male Artist
1978 - Male Vocalist of the Year
1978 - Composer of the Year
(with Jeff Barry for *Sometimes
When We Touch*)
1978 - Best-Selling Album: *Longer
Fuse*
1979 - Composer of the Year
(with Jeff Barry for *Sometimes
When We Touch*)
(see also Matt McCauley and
Fred Mollin)

HOLLY COLE TRIO
1994 - Best Contemporary Jazz
Album: *Don't Smoke In Bed*

HOMETOWN BAND
1978 - Best New Group

HONEYMOON SUITE
1986 - Group of the Year

THE HUGH FRASER QUARTET
1989 - Best Jazz Album: *Looking Up*

HUGH SYME AND DEBRA SAMUELS
1982 - Best Album Design: *Moving
Pictures*, Rush
(see also Dean Motter, Jeff Jackson
and Debra Samuels)

HUGH SYME AND DIMO SAFARI
1986 - Best Album Graphics:
Power Windows, Rush
(see also Hugh Syme And Debra
Samuels)
(see also Hugh Syme)

IAN & SYLVIA
1992 - Hall of Fame Award

IDLE EYES
1985 - Most Promising Group
of the Year

I MOTHER EARTH
1994 - Hard Rock Album: *Dig*

INFIDELS
1992 - Most Promising Group
of the Year

TERRY JACKS
1974 - Canadian Male Vocalist
1974 - Canadian Contemporary
Single (Hit Parade): *Seasons In
The Sun*
1974 - Canadian Pop Music Single
(MOR): *Seasons In the Sun*
1975 - Best-Selling Single of the Year:
Seasons In The Sun

MICHAEL JACKSON
1984 - International Single
of the Year: *Billie Jean*

COLIN JAMES
1989 - Most Promising Male Vocalist
1991 - Male Vocalist of the Year
1991 - Single of the Year: *Just Came
Back*

JAMES CAMPBELL AND ERIC ROBERTSON
1986 - Best Classical Album (Solo or
Chamber Ensemble): *Stolen Gems*

JAMIE BENNETT AND SHARI SPIER
1987 - Best Album Design: *Small
Victories*, The Parachute Club

PAUL JANZ
1985 - Most Promising Male Vocalist

JAYSON & FRIENDS
1985 - Best Reggae/Calypso
Recording: *Soldiers We Are All*

THE JEFF HEALEY BAND
1990 - Canadian Entertainer
of the Year

JEFF WOLPERT AND JOHN WHYNOT
1993 - Recording Engineer of the
Year: *The Lady Of Shallot* from
The Visit, Loreena McKennitt

JIM HILLMAN & THE MERLIN FACTOR
1995 - Best Contemporary Jazz
Album: *The Merlin Factor*

JIVE BUNNY & THE MASTERMIXERS
1990 - International Single
of the Year: *Swing The Mood*

JOE AND GINO VANNELLI
1986 - Recording Engineer of the
Year: *Black Cars*, Gino Vannelli
1987 - Recording Engineer of the
Year: *Wild Horses* and *Young Lover*,
Gino Vannelli
(see also Gino Vannelli, Joe Vannelli
And Ross Vannelli)

ELTON JOHN
1976 - International Album:
Greatest Hits

JOHN TRAVOLTA/ OLIVIA NEWTON-JOHN
1979 - Best Selling Single (Foreign or
Domestic): *You're The One That I
Want*

FRANCE JOLI
1980 - Most Promising Female
Vocalist

JON BALLANTYNE TRIO FEATURING JOE HENDERSON
1990 - Best Jazz Album: *Skydance*

MIKE JONES
1980 - Recording Engineer
of the Year: *Factory* and *We're OK*,
Instructions

1982 - Single of the Year: *Turn Me Loose*
1983 - Group of the Year
1983 - Album of the Year: *Get Lucky*
1984 - Group of the Year
(see also Mike Reno And Paul Dean)
(see also Paul Dean And Bruce Fairbairn)
(see also Keith Stein And Bob Rock)

LUBA
1985 - Female Vocalist of the Year
1986 - Female Vocalist of the Year
1986 - Best Video: *How Many Rivers* (Greg Masuak, director)
1987 - Female Vocalist of the Year

STEVE MACKINNON
(see Steve MacKinnon and Marc Jordan)

GENE MACLELLAN
1971 - Special Award: Canadian Composer

RITA MACNEIL
1987 - Most Promising Female Vocalist
1990 - Female Vocalist of the Year
1991 - Country Female Vocalist of the Year

MADCATS
(see Alan Gee and Greg Lawson)

MADONNA
1987 - Best-Selling International Album: *True Blue*
1991 - Best-Selling International Single: *Vogue*

MAESTRO FRESH WES
1991 - Rap Recording of the Year: *Symphony In Effect*
1991 - Best Video: *Drop the Needle* (Joel Goldberg, director)

CHARLIE MAJOR
1994 - Country Male Vocalist of the Year
1995 - Country Male Vocalist of the Year

EVAL MANIGAT
1995 - Best Global Recording: *Africa +*

MANTECA
1990 - Instrumental Artist of the Year

M.A.R.R.S.
1989 - Best-Selling International Single: *Pump Up The Volume*

CARLA MARSHALL
1995 - Best Reggae Recording: *Class and Credential*

MARTHA & THE MUFFINS
1981 - Single of the Year: *Echo Beach* (tie with Anne Murray)

LAWRENCE MARTIN
1994 - Best Music Of Aboriginal Canada Recording:*Wapistan*

GENE MARTYNEC
1973 - Best Produced Single of the Year: *Last Song,* Edward Bear
1981 - Producer of the Year: *Tokyo,* Bruce Cockburn and *High School Confidential*, Rough Trade

JULIE MASSE
1993 - Most Promising Female Vocalist

GREG MASUAK
1986 - Best Video: *How Many Rivers*, Luba

BOB MCBRIDE (LIGHTHOUSE)
1973 - Outstanding Performance of the Year, Male

MATT MCCAULEY AND FRED MOLLIN
1978 - Producer(s) of the Year (Single): *Sometimes When We Touch,* Dan Hill
1978 - Producer(s) of the Year (Album): *Longer Fuse,* Dan Hill

PAUL MCCARTNEY
1975 - Best-Selling International Album: *Band On the Run*

LOREENA MCKENNITT
1992 - Best Roots/Traditional Album:*The Visit* (tie with Various Artists, *Saturday Night Blues*)
1995 - Best Roots/Traditional Album: *The Mask and the Mirror*
(see also Jeff Wolpert and John Whynot)

BOB & DOUG MCKENZIE
1982 - Comedy Album of the Year: *The Great White North*

1984 - Best Comedy Album: *Strange Brew*

SARAH MCLACHLAN
1992 - Best Video: *Into The Fire* (Philip Kates, director)

MURRAY MCLAUCHLAN
1974 - Canadian Composer of the Year: *Farmer's Song*
1974 - Canadian Country Single of the Year, *The Farmer's Song*
1974 - Canadian Folk Single of the Year, *The Farmer's Song*
1975 - Folksinger of the Year
1976 - Country Male Artist of the Year
1977 - Country Male Vocalist of the Year
1979 - Folk Artist of the Year
1980 - Country Male Vocalist of the Year
1984 - Country Male Vocalist of the Year
1985 - Country Male Vocalist of the Year
1986 - Country Male Vocalist of the Year
1989 - Country Male Vocalist of the Year

SUE MEDLEY
1991 - Most Promising Female Vocalist
(see also Robert LeBeuf)

MEN AT WORK
1983 - International Album: *Business As Usual*

THE MERCEY BROTHERS
1971 - Top Country Instrumental Group
1972 - Country Group of the Year
1973 - Country Group of the Year
1974 - Canadian Country Group
1976 - Country Group of the Year

MIKE RENO AND PAUL DEAN
1982 - Composer(s) of the Year: *Turn Me Loose*, Loverboy
(see also Loverboy)

MILLI VANILLI
1990 - International Album: *Girl You Know It's True* (Later withdrawn)

FRANK MILLS
1980 - Composer of the Year:
Peter Piper
1980 - Instrumental Artist of the Year
1981 - Instrumental Artist of the Year

JOHN V. MILLS, O.C., Q.C.
1994 - Walt Grealis Special
Achievement Award (Industry
Builder)

JONI MITCHELL
1976 - Female Vocalist of the Year
1981 - Hall Of Fame Award

KIM MITCHELL
1983 - Most Promising Male Vocalist
1987 - Album of the Year: *Shakin' Like
A Human Being*
1990 - Male Vocalist of the Year

MOIST
1995 - Best New Group

MONSTER VOODOO MACHINE
1995 - Best Hard Rock Album:
Suffersystem

THE MONTREAL JUBILATION GOSPEL CHOIR
1995 - Best Blues/Gospel Album:
Joy To the World Jubilation V

WM. HAROLD MOON
1992 - Walt Grealis Special
Achievement Award
(Industry Builder)

OSKAR MORAWETZ
1990 - Best Classical Composition:
*Concerto For Harp and Chambre
Orchestra/Morawetz Harp Concerto*

DEAN MOTTER
1983 - Best Album Graphics: *Metal
On Metal*, Anvil and Various Artists

ROBERT MUNSCH
1985 - Best Children's Album:
Murmel Murmel Munsch

MIKE MURLEY
1991 - Best Jazz Album: *Two Sides*

ANNE MURRAY
1971 - Top Female Vocalist
1972 - Female Vocalist of the Year
1973 - Female Vocalist of the Year
1974 - Canadian Female Vocalist

1974 - Canadian Pop Music Album
(MOR): *Danny's Song*
1975 - Female Artist of the Year
1975 - Country Female Artist
of the Year
1976 - Country Female Artist
of the Year
1979 - Female Vocalist of the Year
1979 - Children's Album: *There's
A Hippo In My Tub*
1980 - Female Vocalist of the Year
1980 - Country Female Vocalist
of the Year
1980 - Album of the Year: *New Kind
Of Feeling*
1980 - Single of the Year: *I Just Fall In
Love Again*
1981 - Female Vocalist of the Year
1981 - Country Female Vocalist
of the Year
1981 - Album of the Year:
Greatest Hits
1981 - Single of the Year: *Could I Have
This Dance* (tie with Martha and the
Muffins)
1982 - Female Vocalist of the Year
1982 - Country Female Vocalist
of the Year
1983 - Country Female Vocalist
of the Year
1984 - Country Female Vocalist
of the Year
1985 - Country Female Vocalist
of the Year
1986 - Country Female Vocalist
of the Year
1993 - Hall of Fame Award
(see also Ken Friesen)
(see also Kevin Doyle)
(see also Brian Ahern)

ALANNAH MYLES
1990 - Most Promising Female Vocalist
1990 - Album of the Year:
Alannah Myles
1990 - Single of the Year: *Black Velvet*

MYLES & LENNY
1975 - Best New Group

JOHN NASLEN
1984 - Recording Engineer of the
Year: *Stealing Fire*, Bruce Cockburn

BILLY NEWTON-DAVIS
1986 - Most Promising Male Vocalist
1986 - Best R&B/Soul Recording:

Love Is A Contact Sport
1990 - Best R&B/Soul Recording:
Spellbound

OLIVIA NEWTON-JOHN
(see John Travolta/
Olivia Newton-John)

DAVE NICOL
1974 - Canada's Most Promising
Folk Singer

PHIL NIMMONS
1977 - Best Jazz Album: *Nimmons
'N Nine Plus Six*

THE NYLONS
(see Dean Motter, Jeff Jackson
and Debra Samuels)

OPUS
1986 - Best Selling International
Single: *Live Is Life*

ORCHESTRE SYMPHONIQUE DE MONTREAL, CHARLES DUTOIT
1982 - Best Classical Album: *Ravel:
Daphnis et Chloe (Complete Ballet)*
1985 - Best Classical Album (Large
Ensemble): *Ravel: Ma Mère
L'oye/Pavane Pour Une Infante
Defunte/Valses Nobles et
Sentimentales*
1986 - Best Classical Album (Large
Ensemble or Soloist(s) with Large
Ensemble Accompaniment): *Holst:
The Planets*
1989 - Best Classical Album (Large
Ensemble or Soloist(s) with Large
Ensemble): *Bartok: Concerto For
Orchestra, Music For Strings,
Percussion and Celesta*
1991 - Best Classical Album (Large
Ensemble or Soloist(s) with Large
Ensemble Accompaniment): *Debussy:
Images Pour Orchestre/Trois
Nocturnes*
1992 - Best Classical Album (Large
Ensemble or Soloist(s) with Large
Ensemble Accompaniment): *Debussy:
Pelleas et Melisande*
(See also Choeur et Orchestre
symphonique de Montréal)

THE ORFORD STRING QUARTET
1985 - Best Classical Album (Solo Or
Chamber Ensemble): *W.A. Mozart -
The String Quartets*

1991 - Best Classical Album (Solo Or Chamber Ensemble): *Schafer: Five String Quartets*

THE ORFORD STRING QUARTET/OFRA HARNOY
1987 - Best Classical Album (Solo Or Chamber Ensemble): *Schubert - Quintet In C*
(see also Ofra Harnoy)

THE OSCAR PETERSON FOUR
1987 - Best Jazz Album: *If You Could See Me Now*
(see also Oscar Peterson)

ARTHUR OZOLINS
1980 - Best Classical Recording: *Stravinsky - Chopin Ballads*

PAUL PAGE
1977 - Recording Engineer of the Year: *Are You Ready For Love?* Patsy Gallant

PAPER LACE
1975 - Best Selling Single (Foreign or Domestic): *The Night Chicago Died*

PARACHUTE CLUB
1984 - Most Promising Group of the Year
1984 - Single of the Year: *Rise Up*
1985 - Group of the Year
1987 - Best Video: *Love Is the Fire*
(Ron Berti, director)
(see also Jamie Bennett and Shari Spier)

HAYWARD PARROTT
1985 - Recording Engineer of the Year: *Underworld*, The Front

PAUL DEAN AND BRUCE FAIRBAIRN
1982 - Producer of the Year: *Working For the Weekend* and *When It's Over*, Loverboy
(see also Bruce Fairbairn and Loverboy)

PAYOLA$
1983 - Most Promising Group of the Year
1983 - Single of the Year:

Eyes Of A Stranger
(see also Bob Rock And Paul Hyde)
(see also Bob Rock)

FRED PENNER
1989 - Best Children's Album: *Fred Penner's Place*

P.J. PERRY
1993 - Best Jazz Album: *My Ideal*

FRANCOIS PERUSSE
1994 - Best Selling Francophone Album: *L'Album Du Peuple, Tome 2*

COLLEEN PETERSON
1977 - Best New Female Vocalist

OSCAR PETERSON
1978 - Hall of Fame Award
(see also Oscar Peterson Four)

PINK FLOYD
1981 - International Album of the Year: *The Wall*
1981 - International Single of the Year: *Another Brick In The Wall*

POLICE
1984 - International Album of the Year: *Synchronicity*

CAROLE POPE
1981 - Most Promising Female Vocalist
1983 - Female Vocalist of the Year
1984 - Female Vocalist of the Year

J. LYMAN POTTS
1984 - Walt Grealis Special Achievement Award (Industry Builder)

POWDER BLUES
1981 - Most Promising Group of the Year

PRAIRIE OYSTER
1986 - Country Group Or Duo of the Year
1987 - Country Group Or Duo of the Year
1991 - Country Group Or Duo of the Year
1992 - Country Group Or Duo

of the Year
1995 - Country Group Or Duo of the Year

PRISM
1981 - Group of the Year
(see also Bruce Fairbairn)

RONNIE PROPHET
1978 - Country Male Vocalist of the Year
1979 - Country Male Vocalist of the Year

QUALITY RECORDS
1971: Top Canadian Content Company

ROB QUARTLY
1984 - Best Video: *Sunglasses At Night*, Corey Hart
1985 - Best Video: *A Criminal Mind*, Gowan

RAFFI
1990 - Walt Grealis Special Achievement Award (Industry Builder)
1995 - Best Children's Album, *Bananaphone*

LEONARD RAMBEAU
1995 - Global Achievement Award

THE RANKIN FAMILY
1994 - Canadian Entertainer of the Year
1994 - Group of the Year
1994 - Country Group or Duo of the Year
1994 - Single of the Year - *Fare Thee Well Love*

RCA LTD.
1973 - Promotion Record Company of the Year

REBECCA BAIRD AND KENNY BAIRD
1993 - Best Album Design: *Lost Together*, Blue Rodeo

RED LIGHT
1994 - Best Dance Recording: *Thankful (Raw Club Mix)*

SKYDIGGERS
1993 - Most Promising Group
of the Year

SLIK TOXIC
1993 - Hard Rock Album of the Year:
Doin' the Nasty

SAM SNIDERMAN
1989 - Walt Grealis Special
Achievement Award (Industry
Builder)

SNOW
1994 - Best Reggae Recording:
Informer

HANK SNOW
1979 - Hall of Fame Award

SPIRIT OF THE WEST
(see Marty Dolan)

BRUCE SPRINGSTEEN
1985 - International Album of the
Year: *Born In the USA*

THE STAMPEDERS
1972 - Vocal Instrumental Group
of the Year
(also see Mel Shaw)

STANDARD BROADCASTING
1971: Broadcaster of the Year

ERROLL STARR
1989 - Best R&B/Soul Recording:
Angel

**STEVE MACKINNON
AND MARC JORDAN**
1994 - Producer of the Year: (Greg
Penny, co-producer) *Waiting For
A Miracle* and *Reckless Valentine*,
Marc Jordan

DONALD STEVEN
1987 - Best Classical Composition:
(tie with Malcolm Forsyth) *Pages of
Solitary Delights*, Maureen Forrester
with the McGill Symphony Orchestra

SUZANNE STEVENS
1975 - Most Promising Female
Vocalist

STREETHEART
1980 - Most Promising Group
of the Year

SUPERTRAMP
1980 - International Album
of the Year: *Breakfast In America*

SURVIVOR
1983 - International Single
of the Year: *Eye Of The Tiger*

**SUSAN HAMMOND
AND BARBARA NICHOL**
1990 - Best Children's Album:
Beethoven Lives Upstairs
(see also Susan Hammond)

SWEENEY TODD
1977 - Best-Selling Single of the Year:
Roxy Roller

HUGH SYME
1989 - Best Album Design: *Levity*,
Ian Thomas
1990 - Best Album Design: *Presto*,
Rush
1992 - Best Album Design: *Roll
The Bones*, Rush
(see also Hugh Syme
And Debra Samuels)
(see also Hugh Syme
And Dimo Safari)

**TAFELMUSIK BAROQUE
ORCHESTRA**
1990 - Best Classical Album (Large
Ensemble or Soloist(s) with Large
Ensemble Accompaniment):
*Boccherini: Cello Concertos and
Symphonies*
1994 - Best Classical Album (Large
Ensemble Or Soloist(s) with Large
Ensemble Accompaniment): *Handel:
Concerti Grossi Op. 3, No. 1-6*
(Jeanne Lamon, director)
1995 - Best Classical Album (Large
Ensemble Or Soloist with Large
Ensemble Accompaniment):
Bach Brandenburg Concertos Nos. 1-6
(Jeanne Lamon, musical director)

**TAFELMUSIK
WITH ALAN CURTIS,
CATHERINE ROBBIN,
LINDA MAGUIRE,
NANCY ARGENTA,
INGRID ATTROT
AND MEL BRAUN**
1993 - Best Classical Album (Large
Ensemble or Soloist(s) with Large
Ensemble Accompaniment):
Handel: Excerpts From Floridante
(Jeanne Lamon, leader)

IAN TAMBLYN
(see Michael Bowness)

LYDIA TAYLOR
1983 - Most Promising Female
Vocalist

TBTBT
1994 - Rap Recording of the Year:
One Track Mind

IAN THOMAS
1974 - Canada's Most Promising Male
Vocalist

DON THOMPSON
1985 - Best Jazz Album: *A Beautiful
Friendship*

T.H.P. ORCHESTRA
1977 - Best New Group

**TOM COCHRANE
AND RED RIDER**
1987 - Group of the Year
(see also Tom Cochrane)
(see also Mike Fraser)

TOMMY BANKS BIG BAND
1979 - Best Jazz Recording:
Jazz Canada Montreux

**TORONTO SYMPHONY
ORCHESTRA**
1978 - Best Classical Recording:
Three Borodin Symphonies
1987 - Best Classical Album (Large
Ensemble): *Holst: The Planets*
(conducted by Andrew Davis)

**TRACEY PRESCOTT
AND LONESOME DADDY**
1993 - Country Group or Duo
of the Year

And a Special Juno To The Canadian
People for their support of the
Northern Lights For Africa initiative,
presented by David Foster to Prime
Minister Brian Mulroney, who
accepts on their behalf during the
1985 Juno Award show.

JUNO AWARD WINNERS CATEGORICALLY

The following are the past and present winners of The Juno Awards in the major categories. Though categories have gone through various name changes, the names listed are the ones in effect as of the 24th annual Juno Awards held in 1995. Certain awards, you will see, were discontinued. The years noted are the years in which the awards were presented and reflect activity for the previous year. You will note that 1988 is passed over. After the Junos were given out in November 1987, it was decided to move the awards presentation to the spring. The next Juno presentation was held in the spring of 1989 and covered 1988 releases.

ENTERTAINER OF THE YEAR

1987 - Bryan Adams; 1989 - Glass Tiger; 1990 - The Jeff Healey Band; 1991 - The Tragically Hip; 1992 - Bryan Adams. 1993 - The Tragically Hip; 1994 - The Rankin Family; 1995 - The Tragically Hip.

INTERNATIONAL ENTERTAINER OF THE YEAR

1989 - U2; 1990 - Melissa Etheridge; 1991 - The Rolling Stones; 1992 - Garth Brooks; 1993 - U2.

BEST-SELLING ALBUM (FOREIGN OR DOMESTIC)

1975 - *Band On the Run*, Paul McCartney; 1976 - *Greatest Hits*, Elton John; 1977 - *Frampton Comes Alive*, Peter Frampton; 1978 - *Rumours*, Fleetwood Mac; 1979 - *Saturday Night Fever*, The Bee Gees; 1980 - *Breakfast In America*, Supertramp; 1981 - *The Wall*, Pink Floyd; 1982 - *Double Fantasy*, John Lennon; 1983 - *Business As Usual*, Men At Work; 1984 - *Synchronicity*, The Police; 1985 - *Born In the USA*, Bruce Springsteen; 1986 - *Brothers In Arms*, Dire Straits; 1987 - *True Blue*, Madonna; 1989 - *Dirty Dancing Soundtrack*, Various Artists; 1990 - *Girl You Know It's True*, Milli Vanilli (Withdrawn); 1991 - *Please Hammer Don't Hurt 'Em*, MC Hammer; 1992 - *To the Extreme*, Vanilla Ice; 1993 - *Waking Up the Neighbours*, Bryan Adams; 1994 - *The Bodyguard*, Various Artists featuring Whitney Houston; 1995 - *Colour Of My Love*, Celine Dion.

BEST SELLING SINGLE (FOREIGN OR DOMESTIC)

1975 - *The Night Chicago Died*, Paper Lace; 1976 - *Love Will Keep Us Together*, The Captain & Tennille; 1977 - *I Love To Love*, Tina Charles; 1978 - *When I Need You*, Leo Sayer; 1979 - *You're the One That I Want*, John Travolta/Olivia Newton-John; 1980 - *Heart Of Glass*, Blondie; 1981 - *Another Brick In the Wall*, Pink Floyd; 1982 - *Bette Davis Eyes*, Kim Carnes; 1983 - *Eye of the Tiger*, Survivor; 1984 - *Billie Jean*, Michael Jackson; 1985 - *I Want To Know What Love Is*, Foreigner; 1986 - *Live Is Life*, Opus; 1987 - *Venus*, Bananarama; 1989 - *Pump Up the Volume*, M.A.R.R.S.; 1990 - *Swing the Mood*, Jive Bunny & the Mastermixers; 1991 - *Vogue*, Madonna; 1992 - *More Than Words*, Extreme; 1993 - *Achy Breaky Heart*, Billy Ray Cyrus.

BEST SELLING FRANCOPHONE ALBUM

1992 - *Sauvez Mon Ame*, Luc De Larochellière; 1993 - *Dion Chante Plamondon*, Celine Dion; 1994 - *L'Album Du Peuple, Tome 2*, Françoise Perusse; 1995 - *Coup de Tete*, Roch Voisine.

ALBUM OF THE YEAR

1975 - *Not Fragile*, Bachman-Turner Overdrive; 1976 - *Four Wheel Drive*, Bachman-Turner Overdrive; 1977 - *Neiges*, Andre Gagnon; 1978 - *Longer Fuse*, Dan Hill; 1979 - *Dream Of A Child*, Burton Cummings; 1980 - *New Kind Of Feeling*, Anne Murray; 1981 - *Greatest Hits*, Anne Murray; 1982 - *Loverboy*, Loverboy; 1983 - *Get Lucky*, Loverboy; 1984 - *Cuts Like A Knife*, Bryan Adams; 1985 - *Reckless*, Bryan Adams; 1986 - *The Thin Red Line*, Glass Tiger; 1987 - *Shakin' Like A Human Being*, Kim Mitchell; 1989 - *Robbie Robertson*, Robbie Robertson; 1990 - *Alannah Myles*, Alannah Myles; 1991 - *Unison*, Celine Dion; 1992 - *Mad Mad World*, Tom Cochrane; 1993 - *Ingenue*, k.d. lang; 1994 - *Harvest Moon*, Neil Young; 1995 - *Colour Of My Love*, Celine Dion.

SINGLE OF THE YEAR

1975 - *Seasons In the Sun*, Terry Jacks;

1982 - Good Brothers; 1983 - Good Brothers; 1984 - Good Brothers; 1985 - The Family Brown; 1986 - Prairie Oyster; 1987 - Prairie Oyster; 1989 - The Family Brown; 1990 - The Family Brown; 1991 - Prairie Oyster; 1992 - Prairie Oyster; 1993 - Tracey Prescott and Lonesome Daddy; 1994 - The Rankin Family; 1995 - Prairie Oyster.

SONGWRITER OF THE YEAR

1971 - Gene MacLellan; 1972 - Rich Dodson; 1973 - Gordon Lightfoot; 1974 - Murray McLauchlan; 1975 - Paul Anka; 1976 - Hagood Hardy; 1977 - Gordon Lightfoot; 1978 - Dan Hill; 1979 - Dan Hill; 1980 - Frank Mills; 1981 - Eddie Schwartz; 1982 - Mike Reno and Paul Dean; 1983 - Bob Rock and Paul Hyde; 1984 - Bryan Adams and Jim Vallance; 1985 - Bryan Adams and Jim Vallance; 1986 - Jim Vallance; 1987 - Jim Vallance; 1989 - Tom Cochrane; 1990 - David Tyson and Christopher Ward; 1991 - David Tyson; 1992 - Tom Cochrane; 1993 - k.d. lang and Ben Mink; 1994 - Leonard Cohen; 1995 - Jann Arden.

INSTRUMENTAL ARTIST(S) OF THE YEAR

1976 - Hagood Hardy; 1977 - Hagood Hardy; 1978 - André Gagnon; 1979 - Liona Boyd; 1980 - Frank Mills; 1981 - Frank Mills; 1982 - Liona Boyd; 1983 - Liona Boyd; 1984 - Liona Boyd; 1985 - The Canadian Brass; 1986 - David Foster; 1987 - David Foster; 1989 - David Foster; 1990 - Manteca; 1991 - Ofra Harnoy; 1992 - Shadowy Men On A Shadowy Planet; 1993 - Ofra Harnoy; 1994 - Ofra Harnoy; 1995 - André Gagnon.

BEST ROOTS/ TRADITIONAL ALBUM

1989 - *The Return of the Formerly Brothers*, The Amos Garrett-Doug Sahm-Gene Taylor Band; 1990 - *Je Voudrais Changer D'Chapeau*, La Bottine Souriante; 1991 - *Dance & Celebrate*, Bill Bourne & Allan MacLeod; 1992 - TIE: *The Visit*, Loreena McKennitt; *Saturday Night Blues: The Great Canadian Blues Project*, Various Artists; 1993 - *Jusqu'aux P'tites Heures*, La Bottine

Souriante; 1994 - *My Skies*, James Keelaghan; 1995 - *The Mask and Mirror*, Loreena McKennitt.

BEST CHILDREN'S ALBUM

1979 - *There's A Hippo In My Tub*, Anne Murray; 1980 - *Smorgasbord*, Sharon, Lois & Bram; 1981 - *Singing 'n' Swinging*, Sharon, Lois & Bram; 1982 - *Inch By Inch*, Sandra Beech; 1983 - *When You Dream A Dream*, Bob Schneider; 1984 - *Rugrat Rock*, The Rugrats; 1985 - *Murmel Murmel Munsch*, Robert Munsch; 1986 - *Ten Carrot Diamond*, Charlotte Diamond; 1987 - *Drums*, Bill Usher; 1989 - *Fred Penner's Place*, Fred Penner/and *Lullaby Berceuse*, Connie Kaldor and Carmen Campagne; 1990 - *Beethoven Lives Upstairs*, Susan Hammond and Barbara Nichol; 1991 - *Mozart's Magic Fantasy*, Susan Hammond; 1992 - *Vivaldi's Ring Of Mystery, A Tale Of Venice and Violins*, Classical Kids, Susan Hammond, Producer; 1993 - *Waves Of Wonder*, Jack Grunsky; 1994 - *Tchaikovsky Discovers America*, Susan Hammond/Classical Kids; 1995 - *Bananaphone*, Raffi.

BEST CLASSICAL ALBUM (SOLO OR CHAMBER ENSEMBLE)

1977 - *Beethoven - Volumes 1, 2 & 3*, Anton Kuerti; 1978 - *Three Borodin Symphonies*, Toronto Symphony Orchestra; 1979 - *Hindesmith: Das Marienleben*, Glenn Gould and Roxolana Roslak; 1980 - *The Crown of Ariadne* (R. Murray Shafer, Composer), Judy Loman; 1981 - *Stravinsky - Chopin Ballads*, Arthur Ozolins; 1982 - *Ravel: Daphnis et Chloe*, L'Orchestre Symphonique de Montréal conducted by Charles Dutoit; 1983 - *Bach - The Goldberg Variations*, Glenn Gould; 1984 - *A. Brahms - Ballades op. 10, Rhapsodies op. 79*, Glenn Gould; 1985 - *W.A. Mozart - The String Quartets*, The Orford String Quartet; 1986 - *Stolen Gems*, James Campbell and Eric Robertson; 1987 - *Schubert - Quintet In C*, The Orford String Quartet/Ofra Harnoy; 1989 - *Schubert: Arpeggione Sonata*, Ofra Harnoy; 1990 - *20th Century Piano Transcriptions*, Louis Lortie; 1991 - *Schafer: Five String

Quartets*, The Orford String Quartet; 1992 - *Franz Liszt: Annees De Pelerinage: Italie*, Louis Lortie, piano; 1993 - *Beethoven Piano Sonatas*, Louis Lortie; 1994 - *Beethoven: The Piano Sonatas, Op. 10, No. 1-3*, Louis Lortie; 1995 - *Erica Goodman Plays Canadian Harp Music*, Erica Goodman, harp.

BEST CLASSICAL ALBUM (LARGE ENSEMBLE OR SOLOIST(S) WITH LARGE ENSEMBLE ACCOMPANIMENT)

1985 - *Ravel - Ma Mère L'oye/Pavane Pour Une Infante Defunte/Valses Nobles et Sentimentales*, L'Orchestre Symphonique de Montréal; 1986 - *Holst: The Planets*, Toronto Symphony conducted by Andrew Davis; 1987 - *Holst: The Planets*, L'Orchestre Symphonique de Montréal; 1989 - *Bartok: Concerto For Orchestra, Music For Strings, Percussion and Celesta*, L'Orchestre Symphonique de Montréal conducted by Charles Dutoit; 1990 - *Boccherini: Cello Concertos and Symphonies*, Tafelmusik Baroque Orchestra; 1991 - *Debussy: Images Pour Orchestre/Trois Nocturnes*, Montréal Symphony Orchestra, Charles Dutoit, conductor; 1992 - *Debussy: Pelleas et Melisande*, L'Orchestre Symphonique de Montréal, conducted by Charles Dutoit; 1993 - *Handel: Excerpts From Floridante*, Tafelmusik with Alan Curtis, Catherine Robbin, Linda Maguire, Nancy Argenta, Ingrid Attrot and Mel Braun; Jeanne Lamon, leader; 1994 - *Handel: Concerti Grossi Op. 3, No. 1-6*, Tafelmusik; Jeanne Lamon, director; 1995 - *Bach: Brandenburg Concertos Nos. 1-6*, Tafelmusik, Jeanne Lamon, musical director.

BEST CLASSICAL ALBUM: VOCAL OR CHORAL PERFORMANCE

1994 - *Debussy Songs*, Claudete Leblanc, soprano; Valerie Tryon, piano; 1995 - *Berlioz: Les Troyens*, Choeur et Orchestre symphonique de Montréal, Charles Dutoit, conductor.

BEST CLASSICAL COMPOSITION

1989 - *Songs Of Paradise*, Alexina Louie; 1990 - *Concerto For Harp and Chambre Orchestra/Morawetz Harp

Concerto, Oskar Morawetz; 1991 - *String Quartet No. 5 "Rosalind"*, R. Murray Schafer: *Five String Quartets* ; 1992 - *Concerto For Piano & Chamber Orchestra*, Michael Conway Baker - Music Of Michael Conway Baker, Robert Silverman, piano - CBC Vancouver Orchestra, Kazuyoshi Akiyama, conductor; 1993 - *Concertos for Flute and Orchestra*, R. Murray Schafer; 1994 - *Among Friends*, Chan Ka Nin: AMICI, Joaquin Valdepenas, clarinet; David Hetherington, cello; Patricia Parr, piano; 1995 - *Sketches From Natal*, Malcolm Forsyth; Milhaud, Maurice, Forsyth & Sowande - CBC Vancouver Orchestra.

BEST JAZZ ALBUM

1977 - *Nimmons 'N Nine Plus Six*, Phil Nimmons; 1978 - *Big Band Jazz*, Rob McConnell and the Boss Brass; 1979 - *Jazz Canada Montreux*, Tommy Banks Big Band; 1980 - *Sackville 4005*, Ed Bickert/Don Thompson; 1981 - *Present Perfect*, Rob McConnell and the Boss Brass; 1982 - *The Brass Connection*, The Brass Connection; 1983 - *I Didn't Know About You*, Fraser MacPherson/Oliver Gannon; 1984 - *All In Good Time*, Rob McConnell and the Boss Brass; 1985 - *A Beautiful Friendship*, Don Thompson; 1986 - *Lights Of Burgundy*, Oliver Jones; 1987 - *If You Could See Me Now*, The Oscar Peterson Four; 1989 - *Looking Up*, The Hugh Fraser Quartet; 1990 - *Skydance*, Jon Ballantyne Trio featuring Joe Henderson; 1991 - *Two Sides*, Mike Murley; 1992 - TIE: *In Transition*, Brian Dickinson; *The Brass Is Back*, Rob McConnell and the Boss Brass; *For the Moment*, Renee Rosnes; 1993 - *My Ideal*, P.J. Perry.

BEST CONTEMPORARY JAZZ ALBUM

1994 - *Don't Smoke In Bed*, Holly Cole Trio; 1995 - *The Merlin Factor*, Jim Hillman & The Merlin Factor.

BEST MAINSTREAM JAZZ ALBUM

1994 - *Fables And Dreams*, Dave Young/Phil Dwyer Quartet; 1995 - *Free Trade*, Free Trade.

BEST R&B/SOUL RECORDING

1985 - *Lost Somewhere Inside Your Love*, Liberty Silver; 1986 - *Love Is A Contact Sport*, Billy Newton-Davis; 1987 - *Peek-A-Boo*, Kim Richardson; 1989 - *Angel*, Erroll Starr; 1990 - *Spellbound*, Billy Newton-Davis; 1991 - *Dance To the Music (Work Your Body)*, Simply Majestic featuring B. Kool; 1992 - *Call My Name*, Love & Sas; 1993 - *Once In A Lifetime*, Love & Sas; 1994 - *I'll Be There For You: The Time Is Right*, Rupert Gayle; 1995 - *First Impressions For the Bottom Jigglers*, Bass Is Base.

BEST DANCE RECORDING

1990 - *I Beg Your Pardon (I Never Promised You A Rose Garden)*, Kon Kan; 1991 - *Don't Wanna Fall In Love (Knife Feels Good Mix)*, Jane Child;1992 - *Everyone's A Winner (The Chocolate Movement Mix)*, Bootsauce; 1993 - *Love Can Move Mountains (Club Mix)*, Céline Dion; 1994 - *Thankful (Raw Club Mix)*, Red Light; 1995 - *Higher Love (Club Mix)*, Capital Sound.

BEST WORLD BEAT RECORDING

1985 - *Heaven Must Have Sent You*, Liberty Silver and Otis Gayle; 1986 - *Revolutionary Tea Party*, Lillian Allen; 1987 - *Mean While*, Leroy Sibbles; 1989 - *Conditions Critical*, Lillian Allen; 1990 - *Too Late To Turn Back Now*, The Sattalites; 1991 - *Soldiers We Are All*, Jayson & Friends; 1992 - *The Gathering*, Various Artists; 1993 - *Spirits of Havana*, Jane Bunnett.

BEST GLOBAL RECORDING

1994 - *El Camino Real*, Ancient Cultures; 1995 - *Africa +*, Eval Manigat.

BEST REGGAE RECORDING

1994 - *Informer*, Snow; 1995 - *Class and Credential*, Carla Marshall.

BEST MUSIC OF ABORIGINAL CANADA RECORDING

1994 - *Wapistan*, Lawrence Martin; 1995 - *Arctic Rose*, Susan Aglukark.

BEST BLUES/ GOSPEL RECORDING

1994 - *South At Eight, North At Nine*, Colin Linden; 1995 - *Joy To The World, Jubilation V*, The Montreal Jubilation Gospel Choir .

PRODUCER OF THE YEAR

1975 - Randy Bachman; 1976 - Peter Anastasoff, *The Homecoming* (Hagood Hardy); 1977 - Mike Flicker, *Dreamboat Annie* (Heart); 1978 - Matt McCauley and Fred Mollin, *Sometimes When We Touch* (Dan Hill), single, Matt McCauley and Fred Mollin, *Longer Fuse* (Dan Hill) album; 1979 - Gino Vannelli, Joe Vannelli and Ross Vannelli, *Brother To Brother* (Gino Vannelli); 1980 - Bruce Fairbairn, *Armageddon* (Prism); 1981 - Gene Martynec, *Tokyo* (Bruce Cockburn) and *High School Confidential* (Rough Trade); 1982 - Paul Dean and Bruce Fairbairn, *Working For the Weekend* and *It's Over* (Loverboy); 1983 - Bill Henderson and Brian MacLeod, *Watcha Gonna Do* and *Secret Information* (Chilliwack); 1984 - Bryan Adams, *Cuts Like A Knife* (Bryan Adams); 1985 - David Foster, *Chicago 17* (Chicago); 1986 - David Foster, *St. Elmo's Fire* (John Parr); 1987 - Daniel Lanois, *So* (Peter Gabriel) and *The Joshua Tree* (U2); 1989 - Daniel Lanois and Robbie Robertson, *Robbie Robertson* ; 1990 - Bruce Fairbairn, *Pump* (Aerosmith); 1991 - David Tyson, *Don't Hold Back Your Love* (Hall & Oates) and *Baby It's Tonight* (Jude Cole); 1992 - Bryan Adams (John 'Mutt' Lange, co-producer): *(Everything I Do) I Do It For You*; *Can't Stop This Thing We Started - Waking Up the Neighbours*, Bryan Adams; 1993 - k.d. lang and Ben Mink (Greg Penny, co-producer) *Constant Craving, The Mind Of Love* and *Ingenue* by k.d. lang; 1994 - Steven MacKinnon, Marc Jordan (Greg Penny, co-producer): *Waiting For A Miracle*: *Reckless Valentine*, Marc Jordan; 1995 - Robbie Robertson for *Skin Walker, It Is A Good Day To Die* (*Music For the Native Americans*), Robbie Robertson & the Red Road Ensemble.

RECORDING ENGINEER OF THE YEAR

1976 - Michel Ethier, *Dompierre* (Dompierre); 1977 - Paul Pagé, *Are You Ready For Love?* (Patsy Gallant); 1978 - Terry Brown, *Hope* (Klaatu) and

David Greene, *Big Band Jazz* (Rob McConnell and the Boss Brass); 1979 - Ken Friesen, *Let's Keep It That Way* (Anne Murray); 1980 - David Greene, *Hoffert: Concerto For Contemporary Violin* (Paul Hoffert); 1981 - Mike Jones, *Factory, We're OK* (Instructions); 1982 - Gary Gray, *Attitude* and *For Those Who Think Young* (Rough Trade) and Keith Stein and Bob Rock, *When It's Over* and *It's Your Life* (Loverboy); 1983 - Bob Rock, *No Stranger To Danger* (Payola$); 1984 - John Naslen, *Stealing Fire* (Bruce Cockburn); 1985 - Hayward Parrott, *Underworld* (The Front); 1986 - Joe & Gino Vannelli, *Black Cars* (Gino Vannelli); 1987 - Joe & Gino Vannelli, *Wild Horses* (Gino Vannelli); 1989 - Mike Fraser; 1990 - Kevin Doyle, *Alannah Myles* (Alannah Myles); 1991 - Gino & Joe Vannelli, *The Time Of Day/Sunset On LA* (Gino Vannelli); 1992 - Mike Fraser, *Thunderstruck*; *Moneytalks - The Razor's Edge*, AC/DC; 1993 - Jeff Wolpert and John Whynot for *The Lady Of Shallot* and *The Visit* by Loreena McKennitt; 1994 - Kevin Doyle: *Old Cape Cod* and *Cry Me A River. Croonin'*, Anne Murray; 1995 - Lenny DeRose for *Lay My Body Down*, *Charms* (The Philosopher Kings), The Philosopher Kings.

BEST ALBUM DESIGN

1975 - Bart Schoales, *Night Vision* (Bruce Cockburn); 1976 - Bart Schoales, *Joy Will Find A Way* (Bruce Cockburn); 1977 - Michael Bowness, *Ian Tamblyn* (Ian Tamblyn); 1978 - Dave Anderson, *Short Turn* (Short Turn); 1979 - Alan Gee and Greg Lawson, *Madcats* (Madcats); 1980 - Rodney Bowes, *Cigarettes* (The Wives); 1981 - Jeanette Hanna, *We Deliver* (Downchild Blues Band); 1982 - Hugh Syme and Debra Samuels, *Moving Pictures* (Rush); 1983 - Dean Motter, *Metal On Metal*; 1984 - Dean Motter, Jeff Jackson and Debra Samuels, *Seamless* (The Nylons); 1985 - Rob MacIntyre and Dimo Safari, *Strange Animal* (Gowan); 1986 - Hugh Syme and Dimo Safari, *Power Windows* (Rush); 1987 - Jamie Bennett and Shari Spier, *Small Victories* (The Parachute Club); 1989 - Hugh Syme, *Levity* (Ian Thomas); 1990 - Hugh

Syme, *Presto* (Rush); 1991 - Robert LeBeuf, *Sue Medley* (Sue Medley); 1992 - Hugh Syme, *Roll The Bones*, Rush; 1993 - Rebecca Baird and Kenny Baird, co-art directors, *Lost Together*, Blue Rodeo; 1994 - Marty Dolan, *Faithlift*, Spirit of the West; 1995 - Andrew MacNaughton/Our Lady Peace for *Naveed*, Our Lady Peace.

BEST VIDEO
(Presented to
director and artist)

1984 - Rob Quartly, *Sunglasses At Night* (Corey Hart); 1985 - Rob Quartly, *A Criminal Mind* (Gowan); 1986 - Greg Masuak, *How Many Rivers* (Luba); 1987 - Ron Berti, *Love Is the Fire* (The Parachute Club); 1989 - Blue Rodeo and Mike Buckley, *Try* (Blue Rodeo); 1990 - Cosimo Cavallaro, *Boomtown* (Andrew Cash); 1991 - Joel Goldberg, *Drop the Needle* (Maestro Fresh Wes); 1992 - Philip Kates, *Into the Fire* - Sarah McLachlan; 1993 - Curtis Wehrfritz, *Closing Time*, Leonard Cohen; 1994 - Jeff Weinrich, *I Would Die For You*, Jann Arden; 1995 - *Tunnel Of Trees*, Gogh Van Go; director, Lyne Charlebois.

BEST HARD ROCK ALBUM

1991 - *Presto*, Rush; 1992 - *Roll The Bones*, Rush; 1993 - *Doin' the Nasty*, Slik Toxik; 1994 - *Dig*, I Mother Earth; 1995 - *Suffersystem*, Monster Voodoo Machine.

BEST RAP RECORDING

1991 - *Symphony In Effect*, Maestro Fresh Wes; 1992 - *My Definition Of A Boombastic Jazz Style*, Dream Warriors; 1993 - *Keep It Slammin'*, Devon; 1994 - *One Track Mind*, TBTBT; 1995 - *Certified*, Ghetto Concept.

BEST ALTERNATIVE ALBUM

1995 - *Shiver*, Rose Chronicles.

FOLKSINGER OF THE YEAR

1971 - Bruce Cockburn; 1972 - Bruce Cockburn; 1973 - Bruce Cockburn; 1974 - Valdy; 1975 - Murray McLauchlan; 1976 - Gordon Lightfoot; 1977 - Gordon Lightfoot; 1978 - Gordon Lightfoot; 1979 - Murray McLauchlan; 1980 - Bruce Cockburn; 1981 - Bruce Cockburn; 1982 - Bruce Cockburn.

COMEDY ALBUM
OF THE YEAR

1979 - *The Air Farce Comedy Album*, The Royal Canadian Air Farce; 1980 - *A Christmas Carol*, Rich Little; 1982 - *The Great White North*, Bob & Doug McKenzie; 1984 - *Strange Brew*, Bob & Doug McKenzie.

HALL OF FAME AWARD

1978 - Guy Lombardo and Oscar Peterson; 1979 - Hank Snow; 1980 - Paul Anka; 1981 - Joni Mitchell; 1982 - Neil Young; 1983 - Glenn Gould; 1984 - The Crew Cuts, The Diamonds and The Four Lads; 1985 - Wilf Carter; 1986 - Gordon Lightfoot; 1987 - The Guess Who; 1989 - The Band; 1990 - Maureen Forester; 1991 - Leonard Cohen; 1992 - Ian & Sylvia; 1993 - Anne Murray; 1994 - Rush; 1995 - Buffy Sainte-Marie.

WALT GREALIS SPECIAL
ACHIEVEMENT AWARD
(Industry Builder Award)

1984 - J. Lyman Potts; 1985 - A. Hugh Joseph; 1986 - Jack Richardson; 1987 - Bruce Allen; 1989 - Sam Sniderman; 1990 - Raffi; 1991 - Mel Shaw; 1992 - Wm. Harold Moon; 1993 - Brian Robertson; 1994 - John V. Mills, O.C., Q.C.; 1995 - Louis Applebaum.

GLOBAL
ACHIEVEMENT AWARD

1992 - Bryan Adams.
1995 - Leonard T. Rambeau.

LIFETIME
ACHIEVEMENT AWARD

1989 - Pierre Juneau.

SPECIAL JUNO FOR THE
SUPPORT OF THE NORTHERN
LIGHTS FOR AFRICA
INITIATIVE

1985 - The Canadian People.

DEDICATION

This book is dedicated to Leonard T. Rambeau, a former president of CARAS and manager of Canadian artists Anne Murray, Rita MacNeil, and George Fox. We miss you Leonard but rejoice in the example you set for those who will come after, many of whom will take their first steps into the music business through a scholarship established in your name at Saint Mary's University in Halifax.

COPYRIGHT © CANADIAN ACADEMY OF RECORDING ARTS & SCIENCES 1996

All rights reserved.

The publisher wishes to thank Lee Silversides and Martin Melhuish for their prescience, diligence, vigilance, and good will.

Canadian Cataloguing in Publication Data

Melhuish, Martin, 1950 –
   Oh what a feeling :
a vital history of Canadian music

(Quarry music books)
ISBN 1-55082-164-4

   1. Popular music – Canada – History and criticism.
I. Title. II. Series.

ML 3484.M44 1996   781.64'0971
C96-900124-X

Design by Susan Hannah.

Film and separations by The LINOshop, Belleville, Ontario. Printed and bound in Canada by Love Printing, Ottawa, Ontario.

Published by Quarry Press, Inc., P.O. Box 1061, Kingston, Ontario.

ACKNOWLEDGEMENTS

The author would like to thank the endlessly-enthusiastic Lee Silversides, President of CARAS, who tackled the planning of the Juno Awards silver anniversary celebrations with a gleam in his eye and a determination, on behalf of the Canadian music industry, to do justice to this milestone occasion; CARAS executive director Daisy Falle, who is the constant in the ever-changing world of the Junos; Lesley Wakefield, Carol-Lee Matthews, and, of course, Casey at the CARAS office; CHUM Limited, and specifically Ross Davies and Bob Laine at Toronto's CHUM-FM, who were unwaveringly supportive from the beginning and whose syndicated seven-hour radio feature *Oh What A Feeling* took this extraordinary story of Canada's music and recording heritage across Canada the week prior to the 25th anniversary Juno Awards; network radio production guru Doug Thompson; Bob Hilderley and Susan Hannah at Quarry Press, who examined the original finished manuscript of this book as Weight Watchers regard a bloated newcomer, accepting it with the reassuring (sort of), "There's some editing needed, but don't worry, it's what we do!"; Kathy Hahn in CBC Communications, who worked tirelessly with technical whiz Steve "Sava" Radonic on 'capturing' the selected images from the 20 years of televised Juno shows that you'll find throughout this book; and also at the CBC, Phyllis Platt, George Anthony, Ed Robinson, Diane Kenyon, Catherine Sproule, and John Rahme.

PHOTO CREDITS

While the majority of the photographs and illustrations in this book were supplied by the author from his own collection, supplemented by the publisher's files, many other individuals and corporations generously provided materials, including Alert Music Inc. (Julie Rich); Mercury / Polydor (Gerry Vogel); Radioland Enterprises (Greg Sutherland); Stony Plain (Linda Nichols); Polytel (Pamela Nalewajek); Don Grashey Management (Don Grashey); EMI Music Canada (Sam McClure); CARAS (Lesley Wakefield and Carol-Lee Matthews); Attic Records Limited (Kevin Shea); True North Records (Elizabeth Blomme); Backstage Productions (Steve Thomson); Anthem Records; BMG Music Canada; Warner Music Canada; MCA Records Canada; A&M Records; Sony Music Entertainment; Canada Wide Features Ltd; *The Record*; *Billboard*; National Archives of Canada; Brian's Record Option.

Photographers of the images supplied include Robert C. Ragsdale; Joel Berstein; John Rowlands; Henry Diltz; Ritchie Yorke; Hines; Horst Ehricht; Richard Creamer; Michael Tighe; Andrew MacNaughton; Joseph Ciancio; Denise Grant; Moshe Brakha; Matthew Wiley; John Phillips; Elisabeth Feryn; Andrew Caitlin; Stephen Danelian; George Whiteside; Equus; Frank Griffin; Patrick Harbron; Bernie Dobbin.